C000179143

A REGIONAL HISTORY OF
THE RAILWAYS OF GREAT BRITAIN

General Editors: DAVID ST JOHN THOMAS
J. ALLAN PATMORE

VOLUME XIV

THE LAKE COUNTIES

Volume 1 THE WEST COUNTRY
David St John Thomas

Volume 2 SOUTHERN ENGLAND
H. P. White

Volume 3 GREATER LONDON
H. P. White

Volume 4 NORTH EAST ENGLAND
K. Hoole

Volume 5 THE EASTERN COUNTIES
D. I. Gordon

Volume 6 SCOTLAND
(The Lowlands & The Borders)
John Thomas

Volume 7 THE WEST MIDLANDS
Rex Christiansen

Volume 8 SOUTH & WEST YORKSHIRE
David Joy

Volume 9 THE EAST MIDLANDS
Robin Leleux

Volume 10 THE NORTH WEST
G. O. Holt

Volume 11 NORTH & MID WALES
Peter E. Baughan

Volume 12 SOUTH WALES
D. S. M. Barrie

Volume 13 THAMES & SEVERN
Rex Christiansen

Volume 14 THE LAKE COUNTIES
David Joy

Volume 15 THE NORTH OF SCOTLAND
John Thomas and David Turnock

A REGIONAL HISTORY OF
THE RAILWAYS OF GREAT BRITAIN

Volume XIV

THE LAKE COUNTIES

by
David Joy

WITH 45 PLATES
21 ILLUSTRATIONS IN THE TEXT
AND LARGE FOLDING MAP

DAVID ST JOHN THOMAS
DAVID & CHARLES
Newton Abbot   London   North Pomfret (Vt)

British Library Cataloguing in Publiction Data

Joy, David
  The Lake Counties. – (A Regional history of the railways of
  Great Britain)
  1. Railroads – England – Cumbria – History
  I. Title   II. Series
  385'.09427'8   HE3019.C/

  ISBN 0–946537–56–9

Published by David St John Thomas
and distributed by David & Charles Limited

Printed in Great Britain
by Redwood Press Limited, Melksham
for David St John Thomas
and distributed by David & Charles Brunel House Newton Abbot Devon
Distributed in the United States of America
by David & Charles Inc
North Pomfret, Vermont, 05053, USA

Frontispiece Steam in the Westmorland fells. A striking study of Royal Scot No 6168 pounding over Dillicar troughs on the approach to Shap. (*Author's collection*)

Contents

NOTE ON THE MAPS

The majority of the maps, including the folding map inside the back cover, depict the network at its maximum extent rather than at any specific date. Exceptions are maps 1 and 4, the chronological diagrams of Carlisle and Barrow giving opening and (in brackets) closing dates, which should in both cases be used in conjunction with the detailed map on the facing page. Significant changes in station names are shown with the original name in brackets.

CHAPTER I

Introduction

The signals were permanently at danger now. Rails were rusting, sleepers rotting; the passengers had gone. Weeds, shooting up between the tracks, had won a hundred years' war with ashes, oil and soot, and their growth had become the fastest form of movement on the line. Cars no longer waited at closed level-crossing gates while their drivers fumed, cursed and nibbled their finger nails as a goods train shuffled across the road; they too had won a hollow victory. Decay was removing the paintwork from stations and adding cobwebs; deliberate damage and destruction seeing window panes and roofing slates shattered or stolen. The bells in the signal-boxes that used to beat out important, decisive messages were silent, and already the telegraph wires had been taken down. Nothing remained for the station staff to do, and so they had moved on or simply retired. Forlorn-looking buffer stops now meant the end of the line in another, more poignant sense.

It was 1966. The single-track railway from Keswick through Cockermouth to Workington had just been closed with surprisingly little protest. For precisely a century its trains had skirted the shores of Bassenthwaite Lake, crossed the oft-turbulent waters of the River Derwent and nudged against the foothills of Skiddaw. They ran close to grassy banks which in spring were tinted yellow with newly unfurled daffodils. Around them the foliage on the trees lost its light pastel shades and slowly took on the sombre green of late summer. Bracken and ferns sprung up and died down, and their rotting fronds were finally lost from view as the snows came sweeping across from the Solway Firth. The railway, like the pattern of the seasons, had remained basically unchanged as decade had succeeded decade, and had become very much taken for granted.

Complacency was ruffled if not shattered when the first closure proposals were were put forward in 1959. Indignant protests came from all quarters: hoteliers and shopkeepers expressed alarm for the future of the tourist industry; workpeople living in Keswick claimed they would find it difficult to get to their places of employment; Cockermouth feared that Wordsworth's birthplace would cease to be on the list of places to be 'done' by visiting Americans. And so it went on – there were doubts about supplies of coal, rural depopulation, excursions for children, the status of communities along the line. But protests are one thing and practicalities another. The seven local authorities which would be affected by the closure held a conference at Keswick, and an embarrassing moment came when a delegate asked how many of the representatives had travelled by rail. Only one in seven had done so.

This time there was a reprieve. The line faded out of the public eye and the decline in the number of folk using it continued, thus dissipating opposition to what proved to be the final axe in 1966. Cockermouth was left in the cold but Keswick managed to cling on to its rail link from Penrith for another six years until that too went the same way. It was the end of both the only railway to run through Britain's largest National Park and to any hope that there might be an alternative to the all-pervading motor vehicle in such sensitive surroundings. The Lake District is the one area in this country that might have supported a network of inter-valley and mountain railways similar to those which today flourish in parts of Austria and Switzerland. Such a system, had it been tolerated by preservationists and properly developed, could have done much to pre-empt road-traffic problems which have plagued the region in recent years. As it is, Lakeland has turned its back on the railway and has chosen to change whole tracts of its unique landscape by building massive modern highways.

The Lake District is only a small part of the area covered in this volume. Yet in the space of a few hundred square miles it contains England's highest mountains, largest concentration of natural lakes and most dramatic scenery. It undoubtedly forms the dominant influence on the Lake Counties as a whole, a clearly defined region embracing Cumberland, Westmorland and the detached portion of Lancashire north of Morecambe Bay, since 1974 administratively united in a single county which adopted the ancient Celtic name of Cumbria.

The Lakeland fells are contiguous with those of Westmorland and the Pennines, creating a natural barrier which along with the deep estuaries of the Furness coast severely retarded the region's progress. Defoe in 1724 described Westmorland as 'a country eminent only for being the wildest, most barren and frightful of any that I have passed over in England'. The next hundred years saw little change and at the dawn of the railway age in the 1830s Cumberland and Westmorland were the two most sparsely populated counties in England. Nevertheless, many Cumbrian towns experienced their most rapid period of growth in the pre-railway period of the nineteenth century when the Lake District tourist trade also became established. Thus, railways were slow in coming to the area in comparison with the more industrialised parts of northern England and also initially acted as accelerator rather than innovator of social and economic change.

The first line to penetrate the region, the Newcastle & Carlisle, was the culmination of a long campaign, originally involving canal schemes, to bring Northumberland and Durham coal to the Irish Sea across the narrowest part of England. It was opened throughout in 1838, but it took another seven years for a locally promoted extension westwards across easy terrain to Maryport to be completed. A much more important outside influence on the Lake Counties was the northward extension of the West Coast route from Lancaster to Carlisle. Initial progress was delayed by disputes as to whether it should detour round the Cumbrian coast, tunnel under the Lakeland passes or climb over the Westmorland fells, but once these had been resolved in favour of the last option the line was speedily completed in a race against time to gain supremacy over the embryo East Coast route. Opened in 1846, it was backed by powerful railway investors and represented by far and away the largest sum of money then poured into any Cumbrian enterprise.

Completion of the Lancaster & Carlisle brought a noticeable change to much of the Lake Counties, breaking down the area's traditional isolation from the rest of England and acting as a catalyst to agricultural and commercial expansion. Similarly, its offshoot, the Kendal and Windermere Railway, an early example of a line built primarily to stimulate tourist traffic, triumphed over opposition from Wordsworth and transformed the area around its terminus into both an inland resort for trippers from industrial Lancashire and a haven for *nouveau riche* settlers.

The growth of a railway-orientated tourist industry in Lakeland arcadia was coincidental with development beyond the mountains that was to turn the region into two quite different worlds. It was the major landowners on the seaboard who made the first modest moves towards industrialisation by building purely local lines to convey minerals to the coastal ports. These eventually extended right round the Cumbrian coast from the southern end of the Maryport & Carlisle to Carnforth, the somewhat ramshackle chain being revitalised by discovery in the late 1850s that the rich haematite ores of Furness and West Cumberland were uniquely suited for Bessemer's new process of steel-making. The railways in this remote north-western corner of England found themselves easily the most prosperous in the country as for a few brief years they provided the arteries for the emergence of a whole host of new industrial centres and the development of a regional iron and steel enterprise into an institution of world importance.

. Lord Lonsdale put up the capital for a group of lines centred on the ancient tobacco port of Whitehaven, but his efforts were completely eclipsed by the mushroom growth of Barrow. Here the Earl of Burlington (later 7th Duke of Devonshire), although largely an absentee landlord, had the foresight to invest in steel and shipbuilding interests as well as acting as a founding father of the Furness Railway. The result of what today would probably be regarded as benevolent dictatorship was the rapid rise of the leading railway company in the Lake Counties, exercising paternal control over the fortunes of Barrow which witnessed almost uncontrollable expansion from coastal hamlet to boom steel town with the then third largest docks in Britain. Yet despite assuming the mantle of greatness, the Furness – in common with contemporary West Cumberland lines – by no means entirely lost its feudal nature and at one time had the unique distinction of having on its board two dukes and a lord! The Duke of Devonshire had his own private carriage and was treated in virtually the same vein as royalty.

The meteoric rise of the local haematite and steel industry, representing Cumbria's equivalent of the gold rush, brought in its wake some remarkable lines. These included the South Durham & Lancashire Union, a bold concept which brought hard-structured Durham coke some 130 miles over the Stainmore gap to coal-barren Furness and thus turned the area into a centre of pig-iron and steel manufacture as opposed to an exporter of raw haematite. A similarly motivated extension westwards from Kirkby Stephen to West Cumberland in the form of the Eden Valley and the Cockermouth, Keswick & Penrith lines created one of the most difficult cross-country routes in England. Even more imbued with the spirit of the age was the improbable Solway Junction, crossing the firth from Bowness to Annan by a viaduct that at the time of completion was the longest in Europe and forming a brave scheme to carry ore to Lanarkshire ironworks without detouring through Carlisle. Significant in a different way was the Cleator & Workington Junction, promoted by industrialists in the mid-1870s specifically to counter what was seen as monopolistic 'outside' control following a series of take-overs of hitherto local lines. The last major railway undertaking in the Lake Counties to be completed, it almost entirely duplicated existing routes.

By this date other lines remote from the roar of furnaces had materialised, among the most intriguing being the Port Carlisle, a conversion from a canal, and its associated Carlisle & Silloth Bay. Initially representing a corporation-backed attempt to improve Carlisle's links with sea-going trade, they rapidly assumed a dual function following the dubious use of railway funds to develop a resort among hitherto desolate sand dunes along the Silloth shore. Finally, in 1862 they provided an English foothold for the North British Railway, one of the most expansionist of Scottish companies, which against all opposition forced a way south from Hawick through thinly populated Border country by means of its 'Waverley Route'.

A decade later the Lake Counties gained a second Anglo-Scottish main line when the Midland in a supreme gesture of defiance made a determined move northwards and flung its Settle to Carlisle route over the harsh tops of the Pennines. A *tour de force* of Victorian railway engineering, there is perhaps nowhere else in the world where a potentially high-speed line has been driven across such difficult country. At Carlisle, by now assuming its role as one of Britain's great railway centres, the Midland met its allies, the North British and Glasgow & South Western, forming a partnership that was for ever at odds with the deeply entrenched West Coast alliance of the London & North Western and Caledonian. They all shared common platforms at Citadel, the finest piece of railway architecture in the North West and the nearest this country has come to a European-style frontier station.

Completion of the Settle & Carlisle in 1876 coincided with the onset of a period of change that was to alter the whole character of the area's railways. The introduction of alternative methods of steel-making, coupled with increasing world competition as a result of the steamship revolution, caused the Cumbrian iron industry to enter a phase of gradual but irreversible decline. The haematite ore was becoming difficult to extract and the region's remoteness from the main industrial centres now proved a major handicap. All the local railways, which a decade earlier had been paying huge dividends, found that they could no longer be almost totally dependent on mineral traffic and had to look elsewhere for revenue. The proximity of some outstanding coastal and lakeland scenery and the early success of the Windermere line pointed to fostering of the tourist trade as one way out of the difficulties. The Furness assumed this new role with great verve, developing its branches to Coniston and Lake Side as well as the recently acquired Windermere steamer services, encouraging the growth of select resorts at Grange and Seascale and later inaugurating a host of combined road/rail tours in conjunction with boat sailings across Morecambe Bay from Fleetwood to Barrow. Numerous other attempts were made to climb on the bandwagon and open up the interior of the region to rail transport, but without exception these were rebuffed by Wordsworth's successors who pioneered England's conservation movement and fought an increasingly well-orchestrated campaign to prevent what they saw as intrusion of the worst kind.

Not all parts of the region offered scenic exploitation as an alternative to economic downfall. West Cumberland found itself in a particularly unfortunate position, struggling on through the early years of the twentieth century only to plunge into a catastrophic slump in the 1920s and '30s which eliminated passenger services on its predominantly mineral-orientated lines virtually at a stroke. One result of this early contraction in the network is that closures since nationalisation have not seemed as drastic as in many other parts of the country. However, these have included the Coniston and Lake Side branches, as well as the Penrith–Keswick–Workington route, all lines running into the Lake District which has as its only surviving rail link the ailing Windermere branch.

Yet despite all that has gone, much of interest remains. Cumbria boasts one of the most scenically inspiring stretches of the West Coast main line, although this cannot remotely compare with the neighbouring Settle & Carlisle, highspot of the Midland route to Scotland which in the 1980s arguably became Britain's most publicised railway as it triumphantly survived attempts at closure. Inter-City and local services continue to converge on the imposing Carlisle Citadel station, approaching on the tracks of six different pre-Grouping companies under the guidance of one of the most sophisticated of power-signalling systems. Those not in a hurry can use some of the slowest trains in Britain to make the great journey round the coast from Carnforth to Carlisle via Barrow and White-haven, enjoying magnificent vistas out to sea, watching waders skimming the tide-line or shelduck waddling over the wet sands and pausing at such architecturally splendid stations as Grange and Ulverston. There are the preserved lines – Lakeside & Haverthwaite, Ravenglass & Eskdale and Steamtown at Carnforth, the latter providing motive power for the steam specials of recent years which have done so much to put the area in the forefront of enthusiast activity. And there are other places less obvious. Barrow's broad streets, the new town of

Millom, forlorn viaducts between Ingleton and Low Gill, the slolid-looking Keswick Hotel, West Cumberland's maze of abandoned track-beds, and graceful Silloth staring out over the Solway to distant Criffel, are just as much products of the railway age in the Lake Counties and reminders of its extraordinary diversity.

CHAPTER II

The West Coast Route

RIVAL ROUTES

The main line which was to form both the backbone of the Lake Counties' railways and the dominant link between the region and the rest of England had its origins in 1835, in the period which witnessed England's first major flurry of railway speculation and saw the early trunk lines making their bold strides out of London. A chain of railways was under construction for some 220 miles from the capital as far north as Preston by the London & Birmingham, Grand Junction and North Union companies. In addition, the Preston & Wyre had been formed to link this chain with what would become the new port of Fleetwood, creating a steamship route to Scotland, though thoughts of taking railways further north still belonged to the realm of pipe-dreams. In the many miles of sparsely populated country between Preston and Glasgow, only Carlisle was physically aware of the pending transport revolution. Here the western end of the Newcastle & Carlisle Railway was approaching completion, and it was perhaps this activity which inspired the *Carlisle Journal* in a far-sighted editorial of 22 August 1835 to put forward the first known detailed proposals for completing a West Coast trunk railway route from London to Glasgow. John Steel, the editor and a discerning investor in railways, carefully compared and contrasted East and West Coast routes before coming down in favour of the latter on the grounds that it already existed in embryo form as far as Preston, whereas no railway between London and York had even been authorised. He also contended that the West Coast would have the easier gradients in Scotland, and suggested the matter was of sufficient importance to merit a government survey.

This editorial no doubt came to the attention of the Grand Junction Railway, for on 21 October the board instructed its chief engineer 'to make an early opportunity to inspect the country north of Preston to see if there was a practicability of a line to Carlisle'. Two weeks later a more sweeping directive 'to report on the practicability of making a railway communication between Preston and Glasgow' was issued. The company's chief engineer was Joseph Locke, soon to be nationally famous as one of 'the great triumvirate' but at this time a young man of only thirty years of age who had held his appointment for just a few weeks. His report, published on 27 January 1836 under the title *London & Glasgow Railway through Lancashire*, was astonishing not only for the speed of its completion but also for the way it revealed Locke's ability to grasp the broad essentials of railway route planning through hitherto unfamiliar country. George Measom, a pioneer compiler of railway guide books, later succinctly commented:

> The genius of Joseph Locke showed itself. He grappled with the mountain region of Westmorland, and looked steadily at the summits and valleys which had deterred others. Whether to bend round by Kirkby Lonsdale and Appleby, or to keep more westward by Kendal and Penrith; whether to tunnel under the bleak Shap Fell, or to ascend the passes between its summit by

---

COASTAL TRILOGY

Top: London & North Western passenger and goods trains in charge of 0–6–2Ts passing beside the shore at Parton, north of Whitehaven. *(Cumbrian Railways Association–Pattinson Collection)* *Middle:* The delightfully simple Piel terminus on Roa Island which was approached by a causeway from the mainland. For many years it was popular for Sunday outings from Barrow, such as those brought by this 2–4–0 No 75. *(K. J. Norman collection) Bottom:* Maryport station, headquarters of the Maryport & Carlisle Railway, with one of the company's 2–4–0s No R1 on a train of four and six-wheeled stock. Note the pair of chaldron wagons at the end of the platform. *(Locomotive Publishing Company)*

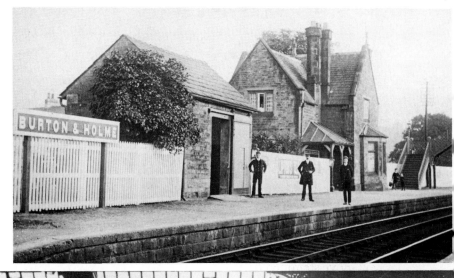

steep inclines, or to avoid it altogether by a detour; whether to make tunnels and viaducts and embankments . or steep gradients?

Locke rejected routes northwards from Kendal via both Dunmail Raise and Longsleddale, and favoured a main line running east of Lancaster and up the Lune Valley through Kirkby Lonsdale before piercing the ridge of Shap Fell by a summit tunnel some $1\frac{1}{4}$ miles in length and then descending by way of Bampton, Askham and Penrith to Carlisle. At no point would the gradients exceed 1 in 100. Not surprisingly, Locke's report was well received by the Grand Junction board which thought it 'highly satisfactory', but in practical terms there was little further that could be done at this stage.

The next move stemmed from West Cumberland when on 6 June 1837 the committee of the proposed Whitehaven, Workington & Maryport Railway asked George Stephenson to report on the possibility of taking a main line round the Cumbrian coast from Lancaster to Carlisle via Ulverston and Whitehaven, and at the same time compare this with Locke's direct route over Shap. Stephenson boldly surveyed a route cutting across Morecambe Bay on a curving embankment from Poulton-le-Sands (later Morecambe) to Humphrey Head, crossing the mouth of the Leven estuary to Ulverston, tunnelling under the Furness peninsula before spanning the Duddon estuary, and then closely following the Cumbrian coast to link up with the already proposed lines at Whitehaven. At no point would the height above sea-level exceed 40 ft, a point which 'the Father of Railways' emphasised in his comments on the disadvantages of the Shap route (see Appendix I).

LANCASTER & CARLISLE STATIONS

Top: Burton & Holme, closed to passengers in 1950. *(Cumbrian Railways Association) Middle:* Carnforth in LNWR days. *(L&GRP) Bottom:* Penrith, an attempt to harmonise with the nearby castle. Note the model 'T' Ford and the charabanc on a connecting service to Ullswater. *(Real Photographs)*

Just as Locke's report had delighted the Grand Junction interests, so the West Cumbrians seized on Stephenson's comments and made maximum capital from them to support their case. Their next practical move was to keep interest alive by forming another committee, this time for a grandly named Caledonian, West Cumberland & Furness Railway, and in 1838 asking two further engineers to make more detailed surveys. John Hague specifically looked at the crossing of Morecambe Bay and proposed an even longer embankment running in a straight line for 10½ miles from Poulton to Leonard's Point, about midway between Ulverston and Barrow. John Rastrick, engineer to the London & Brighton Railway, surveyed the route from Lancaster to Maryport, crossing Hague's projected embankment and then going straight across to Hodbarrow Point but otherwise closely following Stephenson's proposals. His report prophetically concluded: 'If you do not bring forward this line of railway and support it with all your might, West Cumberland will for ever remain in the back settlements.'

The scene of major activity had by now switched to Kendal, then a town of some 9,000 inhabitants and the largest settlement between Lancaster and Carlisle to be bypassed by Locke in his 1835 survey. This was not at all to the liking of several civic dignitaries who refused to accept Locke's comment that 'although there is no difficulty in reaching Kendal there are very great ones in leaving it'. It was Cornelius Nicholson, later the town's mayor, who rallied to the cause and in 1837 wrote a now rare pamphlet, *The London and Glasgow Railway: The Interests of Kendal considered.* This led to the formation of a Kendal provisional committee which instructed Job Bintley, a local surveyor, to report on a line through the town from Lancaster to Penrith. He recommended a route passing through Carnforth, Milnthorpe and then just to the east of Kendal before climbing up to the head of Longsleddale. Here there would be a 2¼ mile tunnel under Gatescarth with two of the three working shafts over 700 ft deep, after which the line would dramatically bridge Mardale and descend alongside the western shores of Haweswater to Bampton and Penrith. Locke also had a look at this route without any great enthusiasm, and at the same time emphasised his dislike of tunnels by advocating a possible deviation to his 1835 survey between Tebay and Penrith. This went to the east with a shorter tunnel under Orton Scar prior to curving gradually westwards through Crosby Ravensworth, Morland and Clifton.

By this time not only were there three rival proposals for extending the West Coast route, but an embryo East Coast route had been authorised as far north as Gateshead and was already benefiting from the powerful influence of George Hudson, just beginning his tempestuous reign as the 'railway king'. It was still widely accepted that there was insufficient traffic potential to support more than one route into Scotland, and therefore in November 1839 the government of Sir Robert Peel attempted to bring some order into the situation and took the then unprecedented step of appointing two commissioners to report on the various proposals. The initial mandate of Lt Col Sir Frederic Smith and Peter Barlow, Professor of Mathematics in the Royal Military Academy at Woolwich, was 'to enquire and report upon the relative merits, and the preference which might be given, to the respective already-surveyed and projected railways between London and the cities of Edinburgh and Glasgow following, namely via York, Newcastle-upon-Tyne and Berwick; via York, Newcastle-upon-Tyne and Hexham; via Lancaster, Whitehaven and Carlisle; and via Lancaster, Penrith and Carlisle...'

In their first report relevant to routes through the Lake Counties, the commissioners considered evidence submitted by Messrs Hague and Rastrick for the coastal route, and by Bintley for a line through Kendal, but not by Locke who apparently chose to play a background role and delegate the work to George Larmer, previously resident engineer for the western end of the Newcastle & Carlisle Railway. Published in May 1840 this report had an immense influence on the future economic development and communications of the North West. The commissioners rejected the coastal line on the grounds that it was almost 30 miles longer than either of the inland routes and would pose considerable constructional problems because of the long embankment across Morecambe Bay. In a few carefully worded sentences they dashed the hopes of West Cumberland and effectively laid the pattern for the region's future railway development: a trunk route skirting the eastern edge of the Lake mountains, leaving the area to the west to be served by lines of purely local significance. Although Smith and Barlow had grave reservations about both the length and depth of Bintley's proposed tunnel under Gatescarth, they did not come out wholly in favour of the Lune Valley route. They realised that 'the advantages of railway communication to the population of the lower part of the valley of the Kent, and to the thriving town of Kendal in particular' were much to be desired, and with remarkable prescience suggested it might be possible to join the southern portion of Bintley's line from Lancaster to Kendal with the northern half of Larmer's extending from Borrow Bridge in the Lune Gorge to Carlisle via Orton. Larmer swiftly surveyed the intervening ground, and by July was able to recommend a route leaving Bintley's survey some 2 miles south of Kendal so as to make a dog's-leg curve through Oxenholme and Grayrigg on acceptable gradients. It thus just missed Kendal itself, but nevertheless was an acceptable compromise both for the various inland-route parties and for the commissioners who in November completed a separate report recommending this line in preference to all others between Lancaster and Carlisle. Blessed by officialdom, one of the most critical portions of the West Coast route had in essence assumed its final form.

RAILS TO SCOTLAND

As in so many official enquiries, the government commissioners carefully avoided coming to a definite conclusion on the main point at issue. Rather than come out decisively in favour of either an East or West Coast route, they simply commented:

> ... the amount of traffic which in the present state of the commercial and other relations of England and Scotland may be expected between Edinburgh and Glasgow and the South is not such as would be likely to afford an adequate return for the outlay of capital required for the construction of two distinct lines of railway.

Yet, it was now becoming clear that the commissioners had been overtaken by events, and that despite their remarks two separate main lines must inevitably extend northwards into Scotland. By the first half of 1841 the East Coast route was open as far as Darlington, while the West Coast route had reached Lancaster with the successful promotion and completion of the Lancaster & Preston Junction Railway. From this ancient county town passengers could travel north by a connecting coach service through Penrith and Carlisle to arrive in Glasgow in about twenty-five hours from London. A rival and more novel Anglo-Scottish service commenced in May 1841, and involved travelling to Fleetwood by rail, taking an overnight steamer to Ardrossan and then completing the journey into Glasgow by a connecting boat train. Again, the overall time was about twenty-five hours.

Two years later the East Coast route was under construction to the south bank of the Tyne at Gateshead and had announced its intention to press on to Berwick. Hudson's efforts had galvanised the various partners into action and had more than made up for the head start achieved by the West Coast route. Here matters were temporarily in the doldrums owing to the great difficulty of raising railway finance in the depressed early 1840s. Not until November 1843 did a meeting of subscribers in Kendal learn that sufficient money had been raised locally to match amounts already promised by the established companies to the south, and that it would therefore at last be possible to promote a railway from Lancaster to Carlisle. From this moment the East and West Coast partners were effectively engaged in a race to Scotland. Locke was asked to be engineer-in-chief and made several last-minute route changes in order to cut construction costs and time. The line would follow the course recommended by the government commissioners from Lancaster to Tebay via Oxenholme and Grayrigg, but instead of tunnelling through Orton Scar on gradients no steeper than 1 in 140 would go straight over Shap without any tunnel at all. Thus in haste were created the 4 infamous miles of 1 in 75 which were to be such a notorious handicap to West Coast route operation for more than a century. North of Shap, Lord Lonsdale had taken exception to Locke's original survey through Bampton and Askham and so the route was deviated by way of Thrimby Grange and Clifton.

Work now went ahead on preparing the Lancaster & Carlisle Railway Bill so that the company could be incorporated in the session of 1844. With opposition largely confined to the Lancaster Canal the royal assent was duly given on 6 June, the Act providing for capital of £900,000 to be raised and confirming that subscriptions from the southern partners in the West Coast route would be: London & Birmingham Railway, £100,000; Grand Junction Railway, £250,000; North Union Railway, £65,000; Lancaster & Preston Junction Railway, £65,000. There were to be sixteen directors, seven appointed by the ordinary shareholders and eight by the contributing railways. Interestingly, the total was made up by a director appointed by Lord Lonsdale, to be a member of the Lowther family or one of the MPs for Cumberland or Westmorland, 'as long as the Lord Lonsdale for the time being holds £1,000 in shares'.

In their eagerness to commence construction, the directors had placed orders for rails six months before the passing of the Act and in March had conditionally accepted the joint tender of £591,605 by Messrs Brassey & Mackenzie and John Stephenson for building the 69 miles of main line. This was then by far the largest single railway contract ever placed, but it did not deter the contractors from undertaking completion within two years of gaining possession of all necessary land. Later they specifically promised to have the line ready for 1 July 1846, a staggering undertaking when one considers the nature of the country to be crossed and the almost total lack of mechanical aids. That they ultimately overshot this date by almost six months was due entirely to delays in obtaining land, labour difficulties and bad weather.

John Stephenson played the most direct role in construction, working in close collaboration with Locke, who was confirmed as engineer-in-chief; J. E. Errington, the engineer; and Larmer and S. B. Worthington, the resident engineers. The first sod of the line was cut exactly six weeks after the passing of the Act, apparently at a location near Shap Wells. In November the decision was taken to build a double rather than a single line of rails as had originally been proposed, and

Shap cutting (*W. H. Nutter*)

in the same month the first permanent rail was laid on Shap
Fell. By January 1845 the ground had been broken at seventy-
five places and close on 4,000 navvies and 400 horses were at
work on the line. Construction continued to gather momentum, particularly at the site of the major engineering works
such as the summit cutting at Shap. Here rock had to be
removed to a depth of 60 ft for ¼ mile, the work being
accomplished by 23 tons of gunpowder and 500 men who were
accommodated in a shanty town comprising three rows of
huts, a school and a church. The number of navvies on the line
as a whole rose to a peak figure of almost 10,000, and from the
outset the mixture of English, Irish and Scots caused trouble.
After several relatively minor skirmishes, matters came to a
head in February 1846 with the Penrith riots when 500
Irishmen symbolically armed with shovels and picks marched
against the English, who promptly fled. Two thousand
Englishmen then gathered in the town intent on thrashing the
Irish once and for all, the ensuing disturbances only being
quelled by calling out the Westmorland Yeomanry and
arresting several of the ringleaders who were later tried at the
Carlisle Assizes. A major problem for the contractors was that
navvy wages increased by some 50 per cent during the
building of the line, mainly due to the sudden labour demand
created by the Railway Mania. At one stage men were in such
short supply that look-outs were posted on the main roads

between Lancaster and Carlisle, their aim being to intercept potential labourers and take them to the nearest beer shop where they could be primed into accepting a job. The navvies, aware of this shortage and conscious of the fixed completion date for the line, made the most of the situation by going on strike for more money and reduced working hours.

Despite all these difficulties, much of the line was complete by the summer of 1846, and on 22 September public traffic commenced over a single line of rails from Lancaster to Kendal, the last 2 miles forming part of the Kendal & Windermere Railway (see Chapter VII). On the formal opening the previous day the special train of fourteen coaches would not hold all the passengers and 'the surplus were allowed to ride on the tops'. Connecting coach services for Glasgow now departed from Kendal instead of Lancaster. By December double track extended all the way from Lancaster to Carlisle (except for a short stretch at Wreay cutting where the second line of rails was brought into use in mid-January 1847). Capt Coddington, the government inspector, passed the line north of its junction with the Kendal & Windermere and commented that he had never seen handsomer or more substantial masonry on any other railway. Jubilation and junketings marked the formal opening through to Carlisle on 15 December, and according to some contemporary accounts Locke himself rode on the footplate of the tiny 2-2-2 locomotive hauling the inaugural train. Public traffic commenced two days later, when the connecting coach services moved north to Carlisle and rail travellers between the 'Border City' and London ceased to use the indirect route via Gateshead which had existed since 1844. Freight services began early in January 1847, by which time the Caledonian Railway was under construction north from Carlisle, it being opened through to Glasgow on 15 February 1848. The dream of the West Coast partners had triumphantly been realised, more than two years ahead of the East Coast route which did not have a continuous chain of rails from London to Edinburgh until the Tweed was bridged in August 1850.

The completed West Coast route was a trunk main line which happened to pass through the Lake Counties on its way from London to Scotland. Like the Roman roads before it and the latter-day M6 motorway, it revolutionised travelling but otherwise seemed curiously remote from the region itself. As if to emphasise the national rather than local nature of the route, it was agreed as early as 1845 that the Lancaster & Carlisle would not work its own line but would delegate this task to its largest subscriber, the Grand Junction Railway. Before any portion of the route was opened, one of the most important amalgamations in British railway history saw the Grand Junction become part of the new London & North Western Railway on 16 July 1846. Thus it was the so-called 'Premier Line' which, apart from two locomotives for coal trains, supplied all the rolling stock until, in 1856, it gave notice to terminate the agreement. The Lancaster & Carlisle then arranged to work the line from 1 August 1857, purchasing forty locomotives from the London & North Western, ordering twenty-five new engines and erecting repair shops at Carlisle. It was a short-lived burst of independence for at the half-yearly meeting in September 1859 it was agreed that the Lancaster company should be leased to the 'Premier Line' at a minimum dividend of 8 per cent per annum. The formal indenture of 22 December effectively marked the passing of one of the most efficient and prosperous of early railway companies, but it lingered on as a legally separate entity until full amalgamation took place under an Act of 21 July 1879.

A related casualty a few years later was the Lancaster Canal, which at one stage had an extraordinary relationship with the Lancaster & Carlisle. As is more fully described in Volume 10 (The North West) in this series, the two companies became involved from 1844 to 1849 in a legal tussle over leasing the Lancaster & Preston Junction Railway. The opening of the first portion of the West Coast main line north from Lancaster caused the canal company to withdraw its fast Preston–Kendal packet boats which had been competing with the road coach services, but otherwise relations between the two concerns remained surprisingly cordial. In 1850 they came to a sensible traffic-sharing agreement under which the railway conveyed passengers and merchandise to Kendal leaving the canal to handle coal and heavy goods. The agreement was abruptly terminated in 1858, possibly at the behest of the London & North Western which leased the canal north of Preston in 1864 and absorbed it in 1885.

THE LINE AND ITS JUNCTIONS

Although the Lancaster & Carlisle's independent working life was only thirteen years, the route it created has become a classic of main-line railway construction and has never waned in interest. Soon after leaving Lancaster the West Coast route reaches its closest point to the sea at Hest Bank, the line running across low-lying land and at Bolton-le-Sands crossing a 20 ft deep peat bog which posed severe filling problems. Climbing begins in earnest at Milnthorpe, the next 13 miles being on a continuous uphill gradient. Features on this stretch include the $\frac{1}{4}$ mile long and 50 ft high Sedgwick embankment north of the Lancaster Canal and the substantial cuttings and embankments near Oxenholme. These are followed by an abrupt curve to the east, the line coming out into the open on the shoulder of Hay Fell and offering superb views over Longsleddale towards the Lakeland Fells. The exceptionally attractive six-arch Docker Garths viaduct marks the start of the steepest part of the climb to Grayrigg, 2 miles at 1 in 106, after which the tracks curve back to the north to enter the most impressive stretch of mountain country on the English portion of the West Coast route. This is the Lune Gorge, taking the railway between the Borrowdale Fells and the many peaks of the Howgills on a shelf at first as much as 150 ft above river level. The line crosses a tributary valley by the three-arched Borrow Beck viaduct, once immediately followed by Dillicar water troughs which for sheer spectacle had an unrivalled setting. Trains thundering down Shap hit the troughs like an arrow in full flight, while northbound expresses made the most of the preceding favourable gradient to build up speed, and picked up water in a tremendous cacophony of smoke, steam and spray. The 4 miles of 'Shap' are scenically an anticlimax, although the cutting on the south side of the 916 ft summit forms one of the most substantial engineering works on the entire route. The descent to Penrith includes 7 miles at 1 in 125 and a few short stretches of 1 in 106, the main features being the Lowther and Eamont viaducts respectively of six and five

Lowther Viaduct (*W. H. Nutter*)

arches. The last 18 miles into Carlisle are relatively gently graded, although the final 3¾ miles of 1 in 131 could prove particularly trying for up trains in steam days.

The original intermediate stations on the line, all designed by the noted Victorian architect, William Tite, were Hest Bank, Carnforth-Yealand, Burton & Holme, Milnthorpe, Lambrigg, Shap, Clifton, Penrith, Plumpton, Southwaite and Brisco. All were quite small structures except for Penrith and, more surprisingly, Milnthorpe. This was the proposed junction for lines from Kirkby Lonsdale and Ulverston which did not materialise, and also formed the connecting point for the Furness coaches prior to opening of the Ulverstone & Lancaster Railway in 1857. This same event brought enormous changes to Carnforth-Yealand, for as described in Chapter V it changed from a small wayside station to a major railway junction and, indicative of its new-found status, dropped the 'Yealand' suffix in February 1864. Brisco closed as early as December 1852, a replacement station at Wreay being opened the following year. Other openings about this time included Bolton (1850; renamed Bolton-le-Sands by

September 1861) and Calthwaite (about 1855). Grayrigg was opened in November 1861, although Lambrigg some 1¾ miles to the west was closed on 1 November 1849.

Several other junction stations apart from Carnforth were gradually to develop on the line. Working northwards from this point, the first and also the earliest chronologically was at the divergence of the Kendal & Windermere Railway from the Lancaster & Carlisle at Oxenholme. Initially there were only exchange facilities here, but a rudimentary station was opened in July 1847 and had acquired permanent buildings by 1852. It was for many years known as Kendal Junction, the name of Oxenholme first coming into use in the early 1860s and being generally adopted in all timetables from May 1873. The frontier nature of the station was greatly reduced when the two companies using it effectively became part of the London & North Western in 1859, but more variety appeared in 1876 when opening of the Arnside–Hincaster Junction line (see Chapter V) led to the introduction of a Grange–Kendal service worked throughout by the Furness. On 1 July 1897 the North Eastern commenced to operate a daily service to Kendal, reversing at Oxenholme. The junction continued to develop as the point where many freights stopped to receive banking assistance up to Grayrigg. A shed for banking engines had been erected prior to the station itself, and over the years growth in traffic led to establishment of an adjoining railway village. Activity increased from 1908 when, as an alternative to being banked up Shap, heavy passenger trains took on a pilot at Oxenholme which would work through to Shap Summit or Carlisle.

Low Gill was originally just a small wayside station near Beck Foot crossroads, although it did have connecting omnibus services to and from Sedbergh. On 16 September 1861 it was replaced by a new station ½ mile north to serve the Ingleton branch (opened concurrently) which had an unusual arrangement of separate platforms for the main line and the branch a short distance from the actual junction. (Railway life here had its compensations, a favourite leisure-time occupation being poaching, which was regarded as a way of replenishing empty larders rather than an illegal sport. Jackets were turned inside out so that railway buttons could not be seen and 20 lb salmon were frequently hauled out of the nearby River Lune.) In other respects Low Gill was totally eclipsed by a railway community just 4 miles to the north which in its way was among the most famous in Britain. Its origins lay in the need to bank trains up Shap, the banking engine at first being housed in a shed 'tastefully roofed with zinc' and situated at the foot of Loups Fell, on which a reservoir was built to supply a water crane. In 1862 the primitive loco-motive depot was moved to new sheds on the down side of the main line a mile to the south at Tebay, where a station had been opened ten years earlier.

The number of banking engines increased over the years as traffic developed, helping to augment Tebay's other source of railway activity. This was provided by the South Durham & Lancashire Union Railway, covered in Volume 4 (The North East) of this series but nevertheless of special relevance to the Lake Counties. A grandiose concept to get Durham coke over to the rich haematite ores of the Barrow area, the line was supported by several Furness capitalists and also by the Lancaster & Carlisle Railway which undertook to subscribe £10,000. Incorporated on 13 July 1857, its epic route extended from West Auckland via Barnard Castle, the 1,370 feet Stainmore Summit and Kirkby Stephen to Tebay, from where traffic was to reach Furness by travelling over the West Coast main line as far as Carnforth (see Chapter V). Mineral traffic commenced on 4 July 1861 and passenger services on 8 August, the company being absorbed on 1 January 1863 by the Stockton & Darlington Railway which in turn became part of the North Eastern Railway later the same year. Prior to the opening it had been mutually agreed that Tebay station should be enlarged on a shared basis to accommodate the additional traffic, and it thus became London & North Western and North Eastern Joint. Locomotive facilities were not shared, the North Eastern having its own turntable and until 1902 its own shed. Prior to the railway age Tebay was a tiny village of a dozen houses, but by the turn of the century it had mushroomed into a small town with a population of about 700. Some eighty houses were built for railway employees and their families, three of these being reserved for the refreshment-room staff and as drivers' lodgings. The village had its own railwaymen's brass band which used to practise in a warehouse near the goods yard. The station itself was extremely lively, especially at weekends, when special refreshment stalls were laid out to cater for the extra demand, and during the staging of the annual horse fairs at Brough Hill and Kendal, when local farmers rounded up the fell ponies and dispatched them by rail.

In total contrast to Tebay was Clifton, an active junction station for little more than a year. The incoming line was the Eden Valley Railway (also covered in Volume 4 of this series), diverging from the South Durham & Lancashire Union at Kirkby Stephen. Incorporated on 21 May 1858, it was opened for minerals on 8 April 1862 and for passengers on 7 June. Exchange sidings, a turntable and a small engine shed were provided at Clifton, where the connection with the main line faced south at the insistence of the Lancaster & Carlisle, nervous that the seemingly innocuous nature of the Eden Valley line might conceal grand designs for a new trunk route seeking to reach Scotland. The position changed with the successful promotion of the Cockermouth, Keswick & Penrith Railway in 1861 (see chapter VII), for this meant that the branch through the Eden Valley would now become part of a cross-country route connecting the mineral-rich areas of County Durham and West Cumberland. The need to reverse at Clifton would be an obvious drawback, and so on 7 July 1862 an Act was obtained for a spur from the existing line at Weatherriggs Junction to a north-facing connection with the West Coast route at Clifton North Junction (later Eden Valley Junction), $3\frac{1}{4}$ miles south of Penrith. The original proposal had been to continue into Penrith parallel to the main line, but this was dropped when the London & North Western agreed to grant running powers. Virtually all traffic was diverted on to the new spur on its opening on 1 August 1863, by which time the Eden Valley had ceased to exist as an independent company. Like the South Durham & Lancashire Union, it was absorbed by the Stockton & Darlington on 1 January 1863 and became part of the North Eastern in the same year. It was not until 1874 that sanction was obtained to abandon the original route into Clifton, which was finally removed in August 1875. The station here reverted to a state of rural quietude, being renamed Clifton & Lowther on 1 February 1877 and closed to passengers as early as 4 July 1938. It was for many years associated with the ostentatious comings and goings of the Earls of Lonsdale, who had their seat at nearby Lowther Castle and had the right to have any train stopped at any time. The 'Yellow Earl', so nicknamed because of the livery he adopted for his servants, carriages and cars, acceded to the title in 1882 and in the halcyon years before World War I entertained kings, queens, emperors and crown princes on a lavish scale. When he moved to Lowther from one of his other seats, a special train was hired for his personal entourage which would number well over a hundred. Along the route station-masters paraded on their platforms, at whatever the hour, to see the Lonsdale train safely through and to be rewarded with a £5 note, handed out by the Earl's valet, who was required to stay up all night for the purpose. One first-class sleeper was reserved for his lordship and another for his dogs! A second Clifton station was provided on the North Eastern's new spur and was renamed Clifton Moor on 1 September 1927; it had a large waiting room on the up platform for the private use of the Lowther household.

Penrith, the last of the junction stations working northwards, came into its own following the opening of the Eden Valley Railway and then the Cockermouth, Keswick & Penrith in 1865. Railways had initially made a questionable

Penrith station (*W. H. Nutter*)

contribution to the civic amenities of the town by using part of the historic castle site for the station, although the surviving ruins did inspire the adoption of a Tudor style of architecture with the waiting hall boasting a fine eight-light mullioned and latticed window. Rail traffic soon brought such development that a mini-suburb known as Castletown was laid out alongside the main line. A major factor in the local economy was that Penrith was the point where many tourists forsook the train to travel to Ullswater, and down the years numerous connecting services were provided by wagonettes, charabancs or – most recently – buses.

A CENTURY OF PROGRESS

The many junctions between Lancaster and Carlisle brought much additional activity to this section of the West Coast route, and also a number of noteworthy 'foreign' workings (see Chapters III and V), but did not greatly increase the amount of originating traffic. This was always relatively small, examples being limestone from Burton & Holme, granite and limestone from private sidings near Shap, farm produce from Tebay and – more unusually – gunpowder, which was manufactured at Gatebeck Powder Mills near Endmoor and transported to Milnthorpe station on a narrow-gauge tramway (on which there were several fatal explosions!) This same station also handled large quantities of milk from the adjoining dairy.

As with most trunk lines, major changes to the portion of the West Coast route within the Lake Counties were not locally

---

SCENES ON SHAP

Top: One of Tebay's begrimed 2–6–4Ts banking a freight train up the four miles of 1 in 75. *(Peter W. Robinson) Middle:* Birmingham–Glasgow express, LNWR 2–4–0 No 2155 *Liver* piloting 4–4–0 No 1908 *Royal George. (L&GRP) Bottom:* Overhead wiring in progress prior to electrification of the West Coast main line through the Lake Counties in 1974. *(British Rail)*

orientated but stemmed from national developments in the form of changes in motive power and the pattern of train services. The line itself remained remarkably unaltered until well into LMS days, although minor deviations at Low Gill and Wreay were authorised in 1888 and from Eamont Junction to Penrith in the following year, this last being opened on 27 June 1892. In 1898 the London & North Western chairman, Lord Stalbridge, announced that 'steps were being taken to do away with the one blot on their perfect route, the intention being to avoid the Shap incline by making a deviation which would improve the gradient from 1 in 75 to 1 in 135'. The 8½ mile deviation including a tunnel over a mile in length was authorised on 12 August 1898, although apart from some preliminary work construction was never put in hand. The LMS renewed the powers in the 1930s but they were again allowed to lapse.

Not until 1952 did change begin to come to the Lancaster–Carlisle line with the first of what was to be a string of closures affecting the junction stations. On 1 December passenger services were withdrawn between Kirkby Stephen and Tebay, although on a predominantly mineral route this was not the catastrophe it might seem. The real blow came eight years later on 4 July 1960 when through mineral traffic over the Stainmore line was diverted via Çarlisle. This abruptly ended Tebay's junction status and undermined its solidarity as a railway community. More than 150 families moved away, leaving houses which remained permanently empty, further decline coming in 1968 with the closure of the locomotive sheds on 1 January and the station itself on 1 July. The demise of steam in the same year meant there was no longer any call for a permanent fleet of Shap banking engines. Virtually all

---

ENGINE SHEDS GREAT AND SMALL

Top: Oxenholme (c 1906) which provided the motive power for assisting trains up Grayrigg bank. *(L&GRP) Middle:* A fine array of motive power outside the Midland sheds at Durran Hill in 1900. *(L&GRP) Bottom:* Ingleton's one-engine shack in terminal decay in 1951. *(L&GRP)*

remaining traffic on the Stainmore route ceased on 22 January 1962, although the extreme western end of the Penrith line from Eden Valley Junction to Clifton Moor remained open to goods until 15 May 1966. Penrith lost its other feeder with closure of the truncated portion of the Cockermouth line to Keswick in 1972. Low Gill also ceased to be a junction with the withdrawal of passenger trains on the Ingleton branch in 1954 and freight traffic eleven years later. North of Carnforth, only Oxenholme manages to cling on to a feeder line in the form of the Windermere branch. As with Tebay, banking work which provided the other source of activity here virtually ceased with the end of steam haulage. Since 1970, Oxenholme and Penrith have been the only stations between Lancaster and Carlisle served by main-line trains.

Change also came with completion in 1970 of the M6 motorway from Forton to Penrith, a project which had involved similar problems of route selection to that of the railway some 130 years earlier. Once again, pressure from West Cumberland was discounted in favour of a route which paralleled the main line remarkably closely and, sadly, ended its virtual isolation in the scenically splendid Lune Gorge. By this time the railway itself was on the verge of transformation. The most important trunk route through the Lake Counties had almost missed the diesel age, for when steam was still occasionally to be seen on Grayrigg and Shap banks in 1968 plans for extending electrification from Weaver Junction, north of Crewe, through to Glasgow were already awaiting government approval. It took almost two years for this to be received, although in the meantime preliminary work was done on track improvements and desperately needed modernisation of a signalling system which was getting decidedly archaic.

Once the £75 million electrification scheme had received the go-ahead, several innovations were employed to speed up construction. These included preparing foundations for the overhead structures by means of hydraulically operated grabs and a system of coring using solid blocks of polystyrene. A concrete train, carrying its own sand, aggregate and cement, was brought into service. A simplified support was designed for the overhead which had the additional environmental advantage of being much less conspicuous than that adopted south of Crewe, and further costs were saved by the use of steel-reinforced aluminium instead of copper for the catenary and stainless-steel wire as opposed to bronze-strand for the droppers. A new form of circuit breaker was installed in trackside-switching stations with a less complex mechanism and reduced maintenance liabilities.

Apart from electrification work itself, other visible signs of transformation were the realignment of curves, removal of surplus track and installation of colour light signals. This last work was completed in the first half of 1973, the entire Lancaster–Carlisle section being controlled from just two power boxes at Preston and Carlisle. The overhead wires on this stretch were energised in February 1974, electric haulage throughout from London to Glasgow being inaugurated on 6 May. After more than a century, Shap ceased to be an obstacle and drivers found themselves in the extraordinary position of topping the summit at anything up to 95 mph and then having to brake for the ensuing speed restriction!

CHAPTER III

The Midland Challenge

THE MIDLAND MOVES NORTH

The second of the spectacular main lines through the Lake Counties stemmed from the expansionist policy pursued by the Midland Railway, one of the most successful of provincial-based pre-Grouping companies. Created in 1844, when George Hudson master-minded the first large-scale railway amalgamation, it was based on Derby and had as one of its three constituents the North Midland Railway extending as far as Leeds. During the same year Hudson promoted the Leeds & Bradford Railway, which was opened in July 1846 and by the late summer of 1847 had been continued up the Aire Valley to Skipton. Its immediate leasing by the Midland brought the company within 40 miles of the West Coast route.

A number of schemes were proposed during the Railway Mania of 1844–6 to connect the Leeds & Bradford with the Lancaster & Carlisle, and thus complete a reasonably direct route from the West Riding to Scotland. The only successful contestant was the North Western Railway, incorporated on 26 June 1846 with powers to build a main line from Skipton to Low Gill via Settle, Ingleton and Kirkby Lonsdale and a branch from Clapham to Lancaster. It was always unofficially known as the 'little' North Western to avoid confusion with the London & North Western Railway, formed less than three weeks later. Its development is more fully described in Volume 10 (The North West) in this series, but it is important to note that the economic slump following the collapse of the Railway Mania forced a change of priorities. The company called in Robert Stephenson, who advised that work on the Clapham–Low Gill section with its heavy engineering operations should be abandoned and preference given to completing the

Lancaster line which, although forming a less direct route to the north, would be cheaper to build. Construction between Clapham and Ingleton was however already so far advanced that it was decided to complete this stretch as a single-line branch. On 30 July 1849 opening took place from Skipton to a temporary wooden terminus at Ingleton, beyond which the completed foundations and rail-level staging of an eleven-arch viaduct over the River Greta pointed optimistically towards the north. Connecting coach services took passengers on to Milnthorpe on the Lancaster & Carlisle until 1 June 1850 when the Clapham–Lancaster line was completed throughout, through trains then being introduced from Leeds and Bradford to Lancaster as well as through carriages to Kendal. The 4¼ mile Ingleton branch was closed to passengers on the same date, although it appears to have continued to carry some unofficial horse-worked traffic.

Occupying a strategic position between larger neighbours, the 'little' North Western was from the outset embroiled in national railway politics. At the time of its completion the Midland was forced to respect the wishes of the London & North Western in order to gain access to the capital, and had become part of the 'Euston Square Confederacy' in an effort to stifle the upstart Great Northern Railway and prevent it becoming an established trunk route to the north. The Great Northern, which had by this time gained access to Leeds, now attempted to absorb the 'little' North Western, which it saw as a potentially independent outlet to Scotland. Although unsuccessful, this move sufficiently alarmed the Midland for it to reach agreement to work all the latter company's traffic from 1 June 1852, it having already purchased the Leeds & Bradford Railway the previous year.

The 'little' North Western was in a frustrating position as at either end it connected with lines under the influence of the London & North Western, which was anxious to stop a rival route being formed from London to Carlisle and effectively prevented the development of through traffic. After several years of wrangling the company in desperation decided to go it alone. In 1856, probably encouraged by the Great Northern, it deposited a Bill which sought running powers to Leeds in one direction and Gretna in the other and thus, once the Ingleton–

Low Gill link had been completed, would have created a direct route from Leeds to Glasgow via the Glasgow & South Western Railway. Despite opposition from the Midland, London & North Western and Lancaster & Carlisle, this Bill not only got as far as a third reading before being thrown out, but the Commons committee agreed that it would create the shortest route from many parts of England to Scotland and was therefore desirable. During the evidence an illegal 'common purse' arrangement which the London & North Western and Midland had been operating was exposed, the result being the break up of the 'Euston Square Confederacy' and a shift of allegiance by the Midland, which began to lean more towards the Great Northern.

Freed from the shackles of Euston, the Midland now cast its covetous eyes firmly towards Scotland. The Lancaster & Carlisle, at this time becoming increasingly independent and about to have its working agreement with the London & North Western terminated, feared imminent invasion of its territory and in self-defence promoted its own Bill in 1857 for a Low Gill–Ingleton line. This was considered at the same time as a 'little' North Western Bill, broadly on the same lines as that of the previous session, the Commons committee giving preference to the Lancaster & Carlisle scheme providing that the new link was used as a through route. Agreement was reached for land and already commenced works – including the Ingleton viaduct – to be purchased, construction of the $18\frac{3}{4}$ mile line being authorised by an Act of 25 August 1857. The Midland now made the next and obvious move by leasing the 'little' North Western with effect from 1 January 1859 (full amalgamation took place from 1 July 1871), thus gaining a northern outpost at Ingleton in close proximity to the West Coast route. No doubt it had high hopes of entering into working arrangements or even outright amalgamation with the Lancaster & Carlisle, but these were dashed when that company – perhaps fearing an interminable round of parliamentary battles – agreed to be leased by the London & North Western. Ingleton now began its role as a frontier between two great rival railways, and the Midland was forced to evolve a more ambitious strategy in order to gain independent access to Scotland.

THE INGLETON BRANCH

Under the new regime no effort was made to hasten construction of the Ingleton–Low Gill line, and progress was retarded by the unlucky Ingleton viaduct which lost its scaffolding during a violent gale early in 1859 and partially collapsed in the winter of 1860–1. Opening for goods traffic finally took place on 24 August 1861 and for passengers on 16 September. The Midland doubled its Clapham–Ingleton branch and reopened it for passenger services on 1 October, but hopes of a conciliatory spirit and a new joint station at Ingleton were quickly dashed. A few weeks after the reopening the Midland replaced its 'temporary' station of 1849 with a new structure, but at the opposite end of the viaduct the London & North Western had built its own Ingleton station, always known locally as Thornton. Beyond here the line soon left the West Riding of Yorkshire and cut across country to Kirkby Lonsdale, where the station was in Lancashire and $1\frac{3}{4}$ miles from the Westmorland town it purported to serve, before running through parkland and the sylvan surroundings of the Lune Valley. With the route continuing to straddle county boundaries, there were further intermediate stations at Barbon (once busily employed handling cans of Irish cream for the local dairy) and Middleton in Westmorland and at Sedbergh in Yorkshire. Major engineering works were the single-span iron skew bridge across the River Rawthey, the Lune viaduct of one iron and six brick arches some $1\frac{1}{2}$ miles north of Sedbergh and the spectacularly sited eleven-arch Low Gill viaduct on its gentle curve.

The desire of Parliament that the new line should be used as a through route was never fully realised and from the outset it was officially referred to as 'The Ingleton Branch', a description which well summarised the prevalent attitudes. At first the two rival companies scarcely recognised each other's presence as they ran into their respective stations at Ingleton, and many pen pictures have been painted of passengers for the north staggering through the town with voluminous amounts of luggage only to arrive at Thornton station just in time to see the 'connecting' train for Tebay disappearing into the distance. Such descriptions can be misleading, for by 1862 arrangements had been improved and London & North Western passenger trains were running over the viaduct at Ingleton into the Midland station. Better connections and through carriages were also introduced, so that journeys from King's Cross (the Midland's London terminus until the opening of St Pancras in 1868) to Glasgow via Leeds, Ingleton and Tebay took a little over twelve hours and in some cases offered overall times only marginally slower than corresponding services from Euston.

The Midland however remained far from satisfied and by 1865 was committed to seeking an independent outlet to Scotland. When this move finally culminated in the opening of the Settle & Carlisle line in 1876, the Ingleton–Low Gill route became a branch in fact as well as in name and settled down to a long period of relatively uneventful existence. The basic service normally consisted of four stopping trains each way, all running to or from Tebay because of the absence of locomotive facilities at Low Gill. In 1881 additional semi-fast trains were introduced to improve connections between Leeds and Penrith, and a major development followed the 1909 agreement of the London & North Western, Midland and Lancashire & Yorkshire companies to work co-operatively. This was the inauguration on 1 July 1910 of the Lake District Express which left Leeds at 10am and officially ran non-stop via the Ingleton branch to Penrith, where it detached through carriages for Keswick, before continuing to Carlisle and Glasgow. It appears the service was worked throughout by Midland locomotives, although there is contrary evidence that an unadvertised stop was made at Clapham for a London & North Western engine to take over the train. The express lasted in this form only until 1912, but was replaced in 1913–14 by a similar Leeds–Keswick working which was reintroduced in 1923. An unusual service between the wars was a through train from Kendal to Ingleton, mainly intended for the benefit of Lune Valley folk returning from market, which in its 35 mile journey reversed at both Oxenholme and Low Gill.

The London & North Western station at Ingleton was closed to passengers on 1 January 1917 and all trains then used the Midland station. A further improvement came when the

Grouping of 1923 finally ended the frontier nature of Ingleton and enabled the whole line from Clapham to Low Gill to be worked as a single unit. Middleton station was renamed Middleton-on-Lune on 19 July 1926 and lost its passenger services on 13 April 1931, but otherwise there were few changes until 1 February 1954 when regular passenger traffic was withdrawn. The branch continued to be fully maintained, for it had already proved its value as a diversionary route for both West Coast and Midland traffic and had been extensively used in the winter of 1947 when the Settle & Carlisle was blocked by snow. It also continued to be used by beginning- and end-of-term special trains serving the boarding schools on either side of the line. These at various times conveyed through carriages to or from Euston, Leeds and Carlisle, and called at Sedbergh, Barbon (for Casterton school) and Kirkby Lonsdale (for Cressbrook and the local grammar schools). They continued running until the early 1960s, by which time the only other scheduled traffic over the branch comprised a thrice-weekly return freight working from Tebay to Clapham. This was withdrawn following the closure of the goods depots at Sedbergh and Kirkby Lonsdale on 1 October 1964, although a service continued to operate from Clapham to both the ex Midland and London & North Western depots at Ingleton until these too were closed on 1 March 1965. The line then lapsed into a state of suspended animation, for it was still theoretically a diversionary route and had been used as such as recently as the winter of 1963 when the Settle & Carlisle was again blocked by snow. It was however soon decided that maintenance of the track for such infrequent traffic was unjustified, and accordingly the branch was officially closed on 26 July 1966 and had been lifted by the end of the following year.

MAIN LINE OVER THE PENNINES

The Ingleton branch ended its days in 1966 largely because of determination shown by the Midland Railway just a century earlier. The first move in the chessboard-like confrontation which existed at Ingleton from 1861 was made when the Midland let it be known that it was not content with the existing situation and proposed to build a rival route to Scotland. This sufficiently worried the London & North Western for it to announce in 1864 that it was to introduce a Bill to enable the Midland to become joint lessee of the Lancaster & Carlisle and to have equal rights over the line for through traffic. The two rival companies then began serious discussions which lasted until February 1865 when they abruptly broke down. The point of disagreement was the insistence of Euston on including Carlisle in the category of an intermediate Lancaster & Carlisle station at which the Midland would not be free to fix its own charges.

Frustrated by what it regarded as unnecessary obstinacy, the Midland promptly decided to take advantage of the cheap money supply of 1865 and the resulting rash of railway promotion. It resolved to gain its own route to Carlisle, and saw an ideal springboard in the shape of the North of England Union Railway which the previous autumn had deposited a Bill for a line from the 'little' North Western at Settle to Kirkby Stephen (the scheme was quickly contracted so as to extend only to Hawes). Within two months of ceasing negotiations with the London & North Western, the Midland had taken over the new company. Agreement was reached that its Bill should be withdrawn to be replaced in the session of 1866 by a Midland scheme for a line running on an improved route and extending all the way to Carlisle. This ambitious proposal duly came before Parliament where it was steadfastly supported by the Lancashire & Yorkshire, Glasgow & South Western and North British companies, all seeking a new Anglo-Scottish route. Their torrent of complaints about existing facilities had the desired effect, an Act of 16 July 1866 authorising construction of the 72 mile line and permitting the Midland to raise additional share capital of £1,650,000 plus loans of £550,000. It was a milestone in the company's history, although the Act was not the first to sanction a railway over these wild Pennine uplands. In the Railway Mania of 1846 the Northern Counties Union received powers to build a main line from Thirsk to Penrith via Hawes and Kirkby Stephen; it came close to being constructed in 1851–2 by the Great Northern and Glasgow & South Western as part of a new trunk route, but it seems that London & North Western pressure caused the Scottish company to back out at the last moment.

By a strange touch of irony it was to the Glasgow & South Western that the Midland now turned as soon as it had obtained its Settle & Carlisle Act, proposing a merger of the two companies to form a unified route from London to Glasgow. The resulting Bill was thrown out in 1867 by a Parliament suspicious of large-scale amalgamation, but not before it had sparked off a revolt among a section of Midland shareholders who, in the slump following the monetary boom of 1865, went on to oppose construction between Settle and Carlisle. Their campaign achieved such success that on the last day of 1867 a worried Midland board instructed the contractors not to commence work on the line and decided that land purchases should be halted. By this time Euston was regretting its previous intractability and offered to reopen negotiations for joint use of the Lancaster & Carlisle. Agreement was finally reached in the autumn of 1868, the Midland promoting a Bill in the following session for abandonment of its Carlisle line. Unfortunately, two of the companies which had so strongly supported the case for the original Act were now equally vociferous in opposing the new Bill. The Lancashire & Yorkshire stated that the Midland would provide the shortest link between Manchester and Glasgow and would end the company's dependence on the London & North Western at Preston. The North British argued just as forcefully that it had incurred massive expenditure on its 'Waverley Route' from Edinburgh and was desperate to overcome the situation where its traffic was regarded as second best once it reached Carlisle. The petitions against the Bill were successful and it was thrown out. The Midland found itself in the extraordinary position of having to build a main line it no longer wanted.

More words have probably been penned about the construction and scenic splendours of the Settle & Carlisle than any comparable length of railway in England, and yet another superlative-seeking eulogy would be out of place. Nevertheless, the supreme confidence, panache and style which were displayed by the Midland in driving the line across the tops of the Pennines must not be underestimated. From a junction with the 'little' North Western near Settle the route climbed up Ribblesdale between the high mountains of Ingleborough and Penyghent. It then kept above the 1,000 ft contour for more than 15 miles, tunnelling through an outlier of the 2,414 ft peak of Whernside before running along the high slopes of Dentdale and again tunnelling so as to enter the upper reaches of Garsdale. Here one of the great watersheds of northern England, where the rivers Ure and Eden rise within yards of one another, provided a natural pass into the Eden Valley and hence a gradual descent all the way to Carlisle. To its credit, the Midland did not take pique and build its 'unwanted' route to the poorest and cheapest standards possible. Instead, it constructed a main line which, with its striking visual unity and magnificent masonry work, represented a superb example of Victorian railway engineering.

The Settle & Carlisle was the last of the great trunk routes to be almost wholly dependent on the traditional navvy for its creation. At the peak of construction in the summer of 1871 the work-force numbered almost 7,000 navvies, although it should be stressed this was somewhat of a generic term covering many different skills and degrees of muscle power. Mechanical aids included tramways with attendant locomotives, tip-wagons, fixed steam engines at the heads of tunnel shafts and mobile cranes for erecting the viaducts. Dynamite, then a novelty, was brought by road from Newcastle and Carlisle. Over 500 horses were also employed by the various contractors, but there was none of the wholesale dependence on the steam excavator which was to characterise construction of the Great Central Railway two decades later.

On the windswept and treeless upper section of the route, which had hitherto remained almost immune from the influence of human settlement, a major problem was the provision of accommodation for the navvies. Shanty towns appeared at many places between Settle and Appleby, the largest and most famous being that at Batty Green, Ribblehead, which in its often overcrowded and rat-infested wooden huts housed a maximum of 2,000 men, women and children, and a vast assortment of domestic animals. Reminiscent of something out of the American Mid-West, this was a complete community which boasted shops, an abundance of pubs, a hospital, post office, bakery, slaughterhouse, library, mission house and day and Sunday schools, as well as stables, stores, workshops, a brickworks and a sawmill. The contractors had to offer high wages and short-time working in order to tempt men to wrestle with the bog and boulder clay of the Pennines, but even so many navvies drifted away in search of an easier livelihood and by 1871 the turnover had reached 73 per cent annually. In a two-pronged approach to maintaining harmony, both

Smardale viaduct under construction

scripture readers and policemen were appointed to watch over the work-force. Fortunately, there were no disturbances on the scale of those seen during the building of the Lancaster & Carlisle three decades earlier, even though there was the same potentially explosive mixture of English, Irish and Scots. There were however numerous isolated incidents such as the 'dreadful commotion' at Armathwaite one pay-day which culminated in an Irishman being beaten to death and a muster of a hundred English navvies coming into confrontation with the armed constabulary. Many deaths resulted from inebriation and wild living, as well as from outbreaks of smallpox, and the tiny graveyards at Chapel-le-Dale church, west of Batty Green, and at Cowgill in Dentdale had to be extended.

In the autumn of 1871 the contractor responsible for the southern section of the line from Settle to Dent Head got into financial difficulties. The Midland took over the work itself, and now became directly aware of the almost superhuman problems involved in building a railway through such challenging countryside. The extremes of the local climate, with its howling gales, 'horizontal' blizzards, persistent mists and seemingly incessant rainfall, proved too much on top of the delays already caused by a fickle labour force. By 1873, when the line should have been completed, only $3\frac{3}{4}$ miles were open for mineral traffic between Settle Junction and the Craven Lime Company's siding at Stainforth. A further frustrating two years elapsed before through freight services commenced on 2 August 1875 (one contemporary source gives the date as 3 August), and even then part of the line was still single track. Only when the earthworks had fully consolidated did the passenger opening take place without official ceremony on 1 May 1876. Rejoicing was undoubtedly tempered by the fact that the new line had cost £3,800,000 compared with the initial estimate of £2,200,000, but the Midland had at long last realised its ambition of having an independent Anglo-Scottish route and could look forward to the future with confidence.

FEATURES OF THE ROUTE

Many travellers from England to Scotland, preferring to sample the scenic wonders of the high Pennines at the expense of a slightly slower journey, have found the experience memorable. From Settle Junction the line immediately begins its almost unbroken 15 mile climb at 1 in 100 to Blea Moor, a stretch of railway nicknamed the 'Long Drag' by generations of perspiring enginemen. Settle itself, a market town and the largest community served by the route, is reached after 2 miles. As at all other stations on the line, its buildings are of a standard 'Midland Gothic' design notable for its distinctive weatherboarding and massive proportions. There was at first considerable confusion for passengers as Settle already had a station of that name a mile south-west of the town on the 'little' North Western. Without overstretching the imagination, this became Settle (Old) in contrast to Settle (New) on the Carlisle route. However, the situation became even more fraught when an exchange station between the two lines was built at Settle Junction, the Board of Trade giving approval for its opening on 10 November 1876. Perhaps fortunately, this had an extremely short life, closing on 1 November 1877, and to remove all vestiges of doubt Settle (Old) was renamed Giggleswick on the same date.

Immediately north of Settle station, which finally dropped its 'New' suffix in August 1879, the line is carried above the town on two minor viaducts and a long embankment containing more than a million cubic yards of earth. The climb up Ribblesdale continues with a short tunnel at Stainforth preceding the difficult limestone gorge of Sheriff or Sherwood Brow, which necessitated the construction of two skew viaducts and the diversion of the river so that the railway could occupy its former course. Three miles north comes Horton (renamed Horton-in-Ribblesdale on 26 September 1927), at the opening of the line the only intermediate station between Settle and Kirkby Stephen. Still climbing, the tracks pass the hamlet of Selside and the superbly positioned Salt Lake Cottages, like others on the route very much Midland in style and making no attempt to harmonise with the local vernacular architecture. At 1,025 ft above sea-level the extremely isolated station at Ribblehead, opened on 4 December 1876, is notable for the fact that Sunday evensong was held in the booking hall until as recently as 1956. From 1938 it was an official meteorological reporting point, the station-master or his wife being responsible for the dispatch of hourly weather reports. Just beyond the station is the line's outstanding feature, the 440 yd long and majestically curved Ribblehead viaduct with its twenty-four arches reaching a maximum height of 104 ft above the boggy moorland. At a focal point among Yorkshire's famous Three Peaks, Ingleborough, Whernside and Peny-ghent, Ribblehead pays the price for its magnificent setting by being subject to climatic extremes. Rainfall can be over 100 in per annum, and gale-force winds of up to 100 mph have blown heavy trains to a halt on the viaduct. The line continues to curve round to the even more remote Blea Moor, with its passing loops and at one time a cluster of lonely cottages, and finally ends its long climb by entering the 1 mile 869 yd Blea Moor tunnel predominantly on a downgrade of 1 in 440.

Emerging from the tunnel, which at its maximum depth is 500 ft below ground level, the tracks run on a ledge high above green and winding Dentdale. There are magnificent views, particularly from the viaducts of Dent Head, ten arches and 199 yd long, and Arten Gill with its marginally more impressive statistics of eleven arches and a length of 220 yd. Snow fences herald the approach to Dent station, at 1,145 ft the highest on an English main line when it was opened on 6 August 1877. Features of note are the station-master's house, a pioneer in the employment of double-glazing, and the huts used as a canteen by snow-clearing crews. One of the most extraordinarily sited of stations, the access is a corkscrew road from the valley bottom which climbs 450 ft in little more than $\frac{1}{2}$ mile on a gradient of 1 in 5. The village of Dent, or 'Dent Town' as it is known locally, is a full 4 miles away; it suffered hard times when the industrial revolution caused the collapse of its knitting industry, and the railway provided some welcome employment. Some $\frac{3}{4}$ mile beyond the station is the second of the two major tunnels on the route, the 1,213 yd Rise Hill taking the line on to another ledge, this time above the straight and not-so-green Garsdale. It is at first a remote and rather secretive stretch of railway, a fitting location for the highest water troughs in the world installed here in 1907 at a cost of £4,396. For many years steam-heated against frost, they were fed by a 43,000 gallon storage tank which collected the abundant rainwater descending on the surrounding moorland.

Hawes Junction station, opened on 1 August 1876, has undergone a series of name changes, the most important occurring on 1 September 1932 when it became Garsdale. It is the Settle & Carlisle's equivalent of Tebay, although it never achieved quite the same fame. Similarities between the two were that here also the North Eastern worked in from the east (see the Hawes branch below), considerable traffic was generated through heavy trains requiring assistance up steep gradients, and as a result a railway community grew up in a hitherto rural location. The main difference was that at Hawes Junction the planned locomotive shed – for twenty-four engines – never materialised, largely because the station was at the top rather than the foot of the gradients. It was thus found practicable for trains to be assisted up the banks from either Hellifield or Carlisle by pilot engines which were detached and then worked back light to their respective depots. They were turned on what was probably the most famous turntable in Britain with its unique stockade of upright sleepers, apparently erected following an incident in December 1900 when an engine was caught by a freak wind and sent whirling round like a spinning top, although a more mundane explanation is that they were to stop snow drifting into the pit. In the event Hawes Junction had only a quarter of the railwaymen's cottages that Tebay possessed, although it made up for its smaller scale with some delightful idiosyncrasies. These included the social centre, complete with stage, under the commodious water tank, and the solemn ceremony each Sunday when a portable organ was wheeled into the down waiting room for divine service.

The 9¾ miles from Garsdale to Kirkby Stephen was until closures the longest distance between intermediate stations on the line. The first feature is the twelve-arch Dandry Mire or Moorcock viaduct, a structure only built after ¼ million tons of earth had been tipped in an unsuccessful attempt to form an embankment. Up to this point the railway has been running on relatively gentle undulating gradients all the way from Blea Moor, but it now begins its final climb through the short Moorcock and Shotlock Hill tunnels to the highest summit on an English main line at Ais Gill, a lonely spot 1,169 ft above sea-level where pilot engines were once detached prior to being turned at Hawes Junction. The next 15 miles as far as Ormside are on a virtually continuous descent, largely at 1 in 100, and commence with the four-arch Ais Gill viaduct. The tracks then run along a ledge above evocatively named Mallerstang and below the rugged slopes of 2,342 ft Wild Boar Fell before disappearing into Birkett tunnel, only 424 yd long but passing through shale, limestone, grit, slate, iron, coal and lead!

The tunnel marks the beginning of kinder terrain with the bleak Pennine wastes left behind and the fertile Eden Valley stretching away to the north. Kirkby Stephen station, way out in the country, is a mile from the one-time junction station on the Barnard Castle to Tebay and Penrith lines and 2 miles from the town centre. From 1 October 1900 to 1 January 1935 it boasted the suffix '& Ravenstonedale', although the village which inspired this addition was 3½ miles distant. From this point the duplicate nature of the route is clearly evident in that, although Carlisle is still over 40 miles away, the Lancaster & Carlisle is never more than 10 miles to the west. Somewhat surprisingly, it is on the less spectacular stretch of line north of Kirkby Stephen that the highest viaduct on the Midland Railway is found, at Smardale, striding 131 ft above Scandal Beck. Built of 60,000 tons of grey limestone, it had the Barnard Castle–Tebay line passing under one of its twelve arches. It is the last of the really major engineering works on the route, although northwards there are still numerous tunnels, viaducts, embankments and cuttings which on any other line would be considered outstanding features. Scenically the most attractive stretch is between Lazonby and Cotehill with the tracks running through the thickly wooded Eden Gorge above the winding river. All the intermediate stations north of Kirkby Stephen were completed for the opening of the line, with the exception of Culgaith which was not brought into use until 1 April 1880 and is architecturally in a completely different style. The most significant of these stations is Appleby, situated directly opposite the station on

In the Eden gorge near Armathwaite

the Kirkby Stephen–Penrith line and serving the ancient county town of Westmorland. In medieval times this was one of the largest settlements of northern England, but by the late nineteenth century its importance had greatly declined and was about on a par with that of Settle at the beginning of the route. Indeed, the two communities must have had much in common to those Victorians who gazed in awe at the line's 'wild scenery', for they both marked a point where 'civilisation' ended and a forbidding and desolate region began.

CHANGING FORTUNES

From the outset the Midland, at a disadvantage with the London & North Western in terms of both distance and gradients, was determined that its new main line would strive to compete by offering superior standards of comfort and punctuality. How well it fared in the latter ambition is debatable, but there is no doubt that the transformation in Midland rolling stock immediately before the opening of the Settle & Carlisle put it way ahead of its rivals. The most revolutionary development was the introduction of both parlour and sleeping Pullman cars, the first to be seen in Britain when they were shipped over from the USA and reassembled at Derby in 1874. With their all-American outline, they must have seemed strange and futuristic to many Dales farmers living out an isolated existence alongside the more remote sections of the new route.

The Settle & Carlisle, even more than the Shap route, was built primarily as a main line to Scotland and local traffic was never more than minimal. Indeed, it is quite remarkable that in over 70 miles the route did not provide a single town with its first rail facilities, for as noted above Settle, Kirkby Stephen and Appleby – the only communities larger than villages – were already served by existing lines. Even in the peak years there were only six local trains each way, while originating freight traffic has never been of really major importance. At various periods this has included slate from Helwith Bridge, limestone from Stainforth, Horton and Ribblehead, 'marble' (blue limestone) from Dent, milk from the 'Express Dairy' at Appleby, gypsum from Newbiggin, anhydrite from Long Meg, near Lazonby, and cement from Cotehill. Considerable livestock traffic was at one time carried, particularly from Settle, Appleby and Lazonby. The Midland endeavoured to take advantage of the fact that Langwathby station was only 5 miles from Penrith and had the connecting road improved not only for the carting of goods but also for the operation of horse buses and charabancs, which in the summer months ran as far as the shores of Ullswater.

The formation of the London Midland & Scottish Railway in 1923 brought to an end the traditional rivalry between the Midland and the London & North Western which had been responsible for the creation of the Settle & Carlisle. It inevitably led to a gradual decline, but at least the company did show some enterprise in promoting scenic excursions from Leeds and Bradford 'along the Backbone of England' to Carlisle, returning via Shap and Ingleton for an overall fare of 2s 11d (14½p)! In the last year of the LMS the line suffered closure, not due to a deliberate policy decision but as a result of the snows of February and March 1947 which blocked the route for no less than eight weeks. Snow ploughs, the Army, German prisoners of war and even a flame-thrower had no effect on drifts up to 12 ft thick and ½ mile long which had turned to ice. Engines which had frozen on to Garsdale troughs were eventually removed, and when one track was reopened the railway became a lifeline for remote farms in upper Ribblesdale and Dentdale by transporting foodstuffs and hay. It was early April before normal services were fully restored. The line was again blocked in 1963 when the Edinburgh–London sleeper became stranded in a drift south of Rise Hill tunnel and a heroic rescue operation was necessary to get the passengers back to Carlisle. Another factor which brought the route into prominence during these years was its use as a locomotive testing ground. Soon after Grouping the LMS undertook trials to compare the Midland Compound with ex London & North Western Prince of Wales and Claughton 4–6–0s and ex-Caledonian 4–4–0s, and solo tests with a dynamometer car continued into the early 1960s with remarkable performances by such locomotives as Stanier 4–6–2 No 46225 *Duchess of Gloucester* and the prototype Deltic diesel.

By this time a distinct question mark was hanging over the future of the Settle & Carlisle, and to realists there was perhaps some surprise that it had not been abandoned in favour of the much shorter Ingleton route with its lower maintenance costs. Policy statements of the 1960s proposed that all passenger services be withdrawn and the line reduced to two 'sidings' to serve the mineral workings at either end, through traffic being diverted on to an electrified West Coast route at either Preston or Carnforth. As a result maintenance was cut to a minimum, speed restrictions enforced and the whole line began to take on an air of neglect. The stations at Crosby Garrett, Ormside, Cotehill, Cumwhinton and Scotby had already been closed, while annual ticket sales along the route had shrunk from a peak of 150,000 at the turn of the century to 35,000. A proposal to withdraw local services and close all remaining stations apart from Settle and Appleby was refused by the Minister of Transport in 1964 on the grounds of hardship, and matters seemed to be taking a turn for the better when diesel multiple-unit 'paytrains' were introduced in April 1966. It proved a short-lived reprieve, the closure proposals being implemented on 4 May 1970 even though the North Western Area of the Transport Users' Consultative Committee had stated that 'severe or very severe hardship' would be caused to local people, as well as considerable inconvenience to travellers from other areas who used the stations for access to the Yorkshire Dales National Park. Goods facilites had been withdrawn from all stations by 1971.

Ironically, during what were feared to be the terminal years of the line, a sudden upsurge of traffic was created by the diversion of West Coast route services during electrification operations. It was the difficulty of interlacing slow freight trains with 100 mph electric-hauled expresses on this route which influenced a change of policy and led to a decision that at existing traffic levels the Settle & Carlisle would have to be retained for freight and diversionary purposes. Massive arrears of maintenance were tackled, track relaid, colour light signalling installed at selected locations and speed restrictions eased.

Symptomatic of the new era was the success of 'Dales Rail', a collaboration between British Rail and the Yorkshire Dales

National Park Committee with the support of the Countryside Commission, Cumbria County Council and the National Bus Company, which in the summer of 1975 saw the reopening of Horton-in-Ribblesdale, Ribblehead, Dent, Garsdale and Kirkby Stephen stations for weekend 'charter' trains between Leeds and Appleby. The fare structure was designed to encourage visitors to travel into the National Park by rail instead of road and, as additional attractions, guided walks were provided from several of the stations and connecting bus services put on from Garsdale to the Sedbergh and Hawes areas. A return working enabled local residents deprived of public transport facilities five years earlier to have a day out in Leeds. A total of more than 10,000 passenger journeys were made during the twelve days of the service, which had an operating surplus. During 1976 'Dales Rail' trains also ran from Manchester, Preston and Colne, and the Saturday service was extended to Carlisle with additional stations being reopened at Langwathby, Lazonby and Armathwaite. This pattern has basically been maintained with the connecting buses from Garsdale gradually being extended to such destinations as Dent, Cautley Spout, Ingleton and Richmond. Three other associated bus services have also been introduced – Teeslink from Kirkby Stephen to Bowes Museum and Langdon Beck in Teesdale; Tynelink from Appleby or Langwathby to Alston and Hadrian's Wall; and Lakeslink from Lazonby to Borrowdale or Ullswater (a throwback to Midland days).

Contrary to gloomy predictions of only a few years earlier, England's highest and most spectacular main line had achieved its centenary. On 1 May 1976 – a day which perhaps appropriately was extremely cold, wet and windy – special trains, steam locomotives and vintage rolling stock converged on Settle for celebrations culminating in a grand banquet. The mood of optimism was heightened in 1978 when BR agreed to a limited return of steam specials over the line, this development leading to the introduction in 1980 of the Cumbrian Mountain Express (later the Cumbrian Mountain Pullman). Steam-worked from Carlisle to Skipton and Skipton to Carnforth, with electric haulage over Shap completing the third leg of the triangle, it complemented the already well-established

Cumbrian Coast Express (see Chapter V) and proved an enormous success.

The euphoria was perhaps too good to last. Early in 1981 the bombshell broke that Ribblehead viaduct was deteriorating to such an extent that within as little as five years it would either have to be replaced at a cost variously put at between £4½ and £6 million or the line closed. Coincidentally – although the chorus of opposition to any closure insisted the two events were linked – it was announced that from May 1982 the existing Nottingham–Glasgow passenger services were to be rerouted from Sheffield via the Hope Valley, Manchester and Preston because of the greater traffic potential and shorter journey time. A replacement Leeds–Glasgow timetable via connections at Lancaster, leaving just two locomotive-hauled trains between Leeds and Carlisle to cater for Settle and Appleby traffic, added to fears that this was at last the beginning of the end for a railway which has become a legend in its own lifetime. The fears became a step nearer to reality in August 1983 with publication of formal closure proposals, but as is more fully related in the postscript these merely precipitated a quite unparalleled campaign of opposition. After almost six years of move and countermove the Settle & Carlisle was finally reprieved in April 1989. There is still a feeling of unreality which brings more and more people to revel in the glories of the line – Mallerstang on a summer morn as trains disturb the dawn echoes; Dentdale in mid-afternoon as a steam special sweeps past like a toy train perched on the ledge far above the valley floor; or Ribblehead at evening time as the rays of the dying sun highlight a locomotive trundling across the vastness of moor and landscape.

CONNECTING LINES

As the Settle & Carlisle was a latecomer in the railway age and passed through such thinly populated countryside, it is hardly surprising that only two connecting lines were ever completed. The most important of these was the 5¾ mile branch descending from Hawes Junction to the Wensleydale market town of Hawes, to which point the North Eastern extended its existing Northallerton–Leyburn line. Although authorised at the same time as the main line, completion of the Midland branch was delayed by disagreements regarding the joint station at Hawes. Goods services into Hawes were eventually commenced by the North Eastern on 1 June 1878 and by the Midland in August, passenger traffic over both companies' lines being inaugurated on 1 October. Engineering features on the Midland branch included the 245 yd Moss Dale Head tunnel, Moss Dale Gill viaduct and Appersett viaduct. The two companies enjoyed reciprocal running powers to Leyburn and Settle Junction, although these were only exercised on a regular basis by passenger trains between Northallerton and Hawes Junction which were worked throughout by the North Eastern. The Midland local services into Hawes, some of which were through trains from Hellifield, were augmented by occasional excursions to Aysgarth, for the falls, and Leyburn. There was considerable milk traffic from Hawes, and in the 1900s the afternoon Midland goods was instructed 'to wait till butter is ready on Tuesdays'! Until 1939 the North Eastern and later the LNER rented a small engine shed at Hawes Junction; it burnt down on 6 October 1917 causing considerable damage to the unlucky BTP 0–4–4T shedded there at the time. Withdrawal of passenger services between Northallerton and Hawes on 26 April 1954 left just one train each way on the former Midland branch which closed to all traffic on 16 March 1959. Hawes station itself remained open for goods trains from the Northallerton end until 27 April 1964 and has now been converted into an information centre and folk museum.

The only other connection, a short spur at Appleby North Junction on to the North Eastern's Eden Valley route, was both authorised and opened for goods traffic at the same time as the main line. From July 1880 it began to carry a passenger service between Appleby (Midland) and Penrith, worked by the North Eastern in connection with expresses from St Pancras and intended to compete with London & North Western services. These trains perhaps stimulated the 1881 improvement in Leeds–Penrith via Ingleton connections referred to earlier in this chapter, and in any event were not a permanent success, being withdrawn on 1 October 1893. On closure of the majority of the Stainmore route in 1962 the spur continued in use as an outlet for traffic from Merrygill Quarry, east of Kirkby Stephen, although this ceased on 26 June 1976 to leave only occasional workings of freight and troop specials as far as Warcop army base until complete closure took place on 31 March 1989. A corresponding south spur at Appleby was authorised by a Midland Act of 29 June 1875 and had been completed by June 1877 except for the actual connection with the North Eastern. It appears that this was never made, and the tracks were eventually lifted in 1902.

CHAPTER IV

Carlisle

THE 'BORDER CITY'

Carlisle has a unique flavour. In atmosphere neither English nor Scottish, it has long been known as the 'Border City' and was fought over until comparatively recent times. An ancient walled town dating back to the era of Hadrian's Wall, it suffered greatly through protracted warfare and as late as 1759 could be described as 'a small, deserted, dirty city: poorly built and poorly inhabited'. Yet by the beginning of the nineteenth century it had recovered sufficiently to boast a population of over 8,000 and was a thriving textile centre. Carlisle might have remained relatively small had it not been for its position as the lowest bridging point of the River Eden and a superb communications centre, with natural routeways converging from the south, through the Tyne Gap immediately to the east and from over the Scottish border a few miles to the north. By the 1820s it was the departure point for stage and mail coaches to London via York, Liverpool, Manchester, Kendal, Whitehaven, Newcastle, Edinburgh, Glasgow and Portpatrick, and it was thus a natural turn of events that it later became the most important railway centre in the Lake Counties.

Norman Nicholson, the Cumberland poet, has perceptively stated, 'All the threads of the county are gathered together at Carlisle and knotted. Sometimes they appear to be in a tangle.' He could well have been referring to the city's railways, which for complexity were in a class of their own. Ultimately seven companies met here in a kaleidoscopic common station, and within or close to the city each had its own goods yard and locomotive sheds. Conflict owing to sheer weight of numbers was exacerbated by the criss-crossing of two London–Glasgow trunk routes and, more particularly, the fact that four of the companies were English and three Scottish. The railways regarded Carlisle rather than Gretna as being the border, and it was almost as if the various alliances felt obliged to feud in a city so associated with strife. Such hostile relationships created colour and character but scarcely made for efficient handling of the two-thirds of Anglo-Scottish traffic which passed through Carlisle. Only in the last few years has this rail centre ceased to be a byword for congestion and delay.

Although the 'Border City' had passed its peak growth rate by the time the railways were established – it was described by Dickens in 1857 as 'congenially and delightfully idle' – there is no doubt that the superabundance of converging lines was of great benefit to local industry which both diversified and expanded. In 1861 Carlisle had a population of just over 30,000, several cotton mills – including one described as rivalling some of the largest in Lancashire – a growing woollen trade and a famous biscuit works. There were also numerous small firms, typified by the partnership of John Cowans and Edward Pattison Sheldon who served their apprenticeships with Robert Stephenson & Co and moved to Carlisle in 1857. Two years later they made their first $2\frac{1}{2}$ ton hand-power travelling crane; today the firm of Cowans Sheldon & Co Ltd is known the world over for its speciality in cranes and all types of harbour, dockyard and railway installations. The variety of employment in Carlisle prevented disaster a century later when rationalisation greatly reduced the importance of railways in the city's economy.

LINKING THE SEAS

Although Anglo-Scottish routes came to dominate Carlisle, the first lines to serve the city ran east–west, their earlier presence laying the foundations for much of the internecine activity that was to follow. Their origins lay in proposals from the 1790s onwards to 'unite the German Ocean with the Irish Channel' by a canal running from Newcastle to Maryport via Carlisle. It was argued this would increase trade from Tyneside to Ireland and from West Cumberland to the Baltic and Holland, and would reduce economic and social isolation in the corner of north-west England centred on Carlisle. Following continued failure of these schemes, the 11¼ mile Carlisle Canal running from a basin on the north-west side of the city to join the Solway Firth at Fisher's Cross (soon renamed Port Carlisle) was locally promoted and opened in 1823. It gave the city its first direct access to the sea and for the next fifteen years formed its most important trading link with the outside world. Its success revived interest, particularly at the Newcastle end, in improving communications through the Tyne Gap, several public meetings being held to solicit support. Railways had yet to prove themselves, and the strong body of opinion still in favour of a canal included the *Carlisle Patriot* which in July 1824 thundered: 'The Railway scheme ought to be and we have no doubt will be opposed by every man of sense and spirit in the district.' Such laudable sentiments took second place to financial considerations when estimates put the cost of a railway at £252,488 and a canal at £888,000, although despite the overwhelming difference it was 22 May 1829 before the Newcastle-upon-Tyne & Carlisle Railway was incorporated (the '-upon-Tyne' was soon dropped from its title except in a legal context).

The western end of the line running from a terminus 'in the modern Gothic style' at London Road, well away from the city centre on the south-eastern outskirts, to Greenhead (Blenkinsopp Colliery), just over the Northumberland border, was opened 'with tremendous ceremony and awe' on 19 July 1836, the locomotives apparently being brought by road from Newcastle. A general holiday was declared and a crowd estimated at 40,000 assembled at London Road to witness 'a memorable event in the history of Carlisle'. Much of the eastern end of the line was already in use and further sections of the route were completed in stages, so that on 18 June 1838 the first line across England could be opened throughout to Gateshead in 'a ceremonial display unequalled perhaps in the history of railways'. W. W. Tomlinson, author of the standard work on the North Eastern Railway, has given us an evocative description of the events. Five trains left Carlisle at 6 am and, after celebrations at Newcastle, returned to the 'Border City' through rain, the last of them not arriving until 6 pm. The Newcastle contingent should have left an hour earlier after a procession through the streets, but instead there was 'a disorderly stampede for refreshments'. Owing to further delays departure was not until almost 10 pm, the luckless passengers having to travel through the night in a thunderstorm. In the open carriages were 'hundreds of ladies who, in expectation of a sunny day and an early return, had come in light thin dresses'.

In the meantime a 1½ mile freight-only branch, diverging from the main line just outside London Road and running round the west side of the city to staiths and sidings alongside the canal basin, had been opened on 9 March 1837. From the outset there was considerable traffic from the Earl of Carlisle's collieries around Naworth (see Chapter VIII – 'Industrial Lines'), some of which is believed to have been worked by gravity, and from pits at Greenhead, the coal being shipped to Ireland and Scotland. For a while steam power and water transport collaborated happily, the railway seeing the canal as a useful link with Whitehaven and beyond and the canal regarding the Newcastle & Carlisle as an important source of additional trade. Goods arriving on Tyneside from the Baltic were forwarded to Carlisle by rail and then reshipped for Liverpool, bacon was brought from Belfast to Newcastle and a substantial fish traffic developed. Passengers also came this way, notably German emigrants en route to the USA via Liverpool, reached by means of a daytime steamer service from Port Carlisle running in connection with swift packet boats along the canal.

It was a fascinating but short-lived method of travel. The West Coast route had reached Preston in 1838, and in February of the following year the *Carlisle Patriot* was advertising: 'The *North Briton* and *Invincible* coaches leave the *Bush* and *Coffee House* Hotels, Carlisle, daily for Preston, Liverpool, Manchester, London, etc, at 8pm, immediately after the arrival of the train from Newcastle, and arrive at Preston in time for the first morning trains South – N.B. the same coaches return from Preston in time for the morning train to Newcastle.' Until completion of London–York lines in 1840, this would be a favoured route between Tyneside and the capital. Only a few years later the Newcastle & Carlisle was again to play a key role in north–south communications.

By 1844 the East Coast route had been opened to Gateshead, thus giving Carlisle continuous if indirect rail access to London. From 1 September 1846 it became possible to travel between the two cities in a day, the 8 am from London Road arriving at Gateshead at 11 am to connect with the 11.15 am express for the south which reached Euston at 9 pm – a time over an hour quicker than the West Coast route offered when it reached Carlisle some four months later. These developments caused a serious fall in traffic via the Carlisle Canal, a decline that became almost total when, as described in Chapter VI, the Maryport & Carlisle Railway was completed in 1845 and rail access extended to Whitehaven two years later. The long-cherished vision of a direct link from Tyneside to the Irish Sea via Carlisle had at last been realised.

SPARRING PARTNERS

When the eastern end of the Maryport & Carlisle was opened from Wigton on 10 May 1843, it joined the Canal branch ½ mile west of London Road at a point known with northern directness as The Bog. Here a temporary station, usually referred to as Bogfield but also as Water Lane, was opened; it appears this was the normal passenger terminus, although the ceremonial train on 3 May ran through to London Road. The company announced at the time that it had purchased a 7 acre central site at Crown Street for a permanent station, 'valuable and convenient in every point of view', and commissioned John Dobson, the noted architect of Newcastle Central, to draw up plans for the terminus. The Bill for this extension was thrown out on technical grounds, and when it was resubmitted in 1844 the situation was totally different for it was considered along with the Bill for incorporation of the Lancaster & Carlisle Railway. Attempts to agree on a site for a common station were unsuccessful, but both Bills were sanctioned on 6 June 1844. Under these circumstances Dobson advised the company not to proceed with erection of permanent buildings; instead, a temporary Crown Street terminus, reached by an unauthorised trailing connection off the Canal branch, was opened on 30 December 1844 when Bogfield was closed.

A stimulus to resolve the station issue came the following

year with incorporation on 31 July 1845 of the Caledonian Railway, the final portion of the West Coast route extending north from Carlisle via Annandale to Carstairs where it forked to Glasgow and Edinburgh. The four companies now having an interest in Carlisle agreed the most suitable site was at Court Square, just north of Crown Street, but negotiations broke down on several points of detail and particularly over the amount of compensation to be paid to the Newcastle and Maryport companies for money spent on their existing termini. Eventually the Maryport & Carlisle entered into an agreement of 20 June 1846 under which it was to contribute towards the cost of the station and give up its land at Crown Street to form part of the site, but the Newcastle company refused to agree terms and opted to remain at London Road. Here it was joined for an uneasy nine months by the Lancaster & Carlisle which, because of the continued bickering, was forced to use this terminus when its line from Oxenholme was opened on 17 December 1846. Its trains reached the Canal branch at London Road Junction by means of a short south to east curve authorised on 21 June 1845, and then reversed into the station; this was not too great an inconvenience as initially there was just one through service a day in each direction between London and Carlisle.

By this time the Lancaster & Carlisle and Caledonian had obtained powers for what was henceforth known as Citadel station, an Act of 27 July 1846 sanctioning the Court Square site and approach lines, and a £37,982 tender being accepted in September. As work progressed the Maryport & Carlisle became increasingly obstructive and refused to surrender its

---

ROUTES TO SCOTLAND

Top: Staff on parade at Sedbergh on the Clapham–Low Gill line, relegated into obscurity on completion of the Settle & Carlisle. *(Cumbrian Railways Association) Middle:* Single track viaduct over the Solway Firth *(L&GRP) Bottom:* A 1905 view of pristine Ormside, intermediate station on the Midland's heroic main line over the Pennines which carried Anglo-Scottish expresses from 1876 until 1982. *(L&GRP)*

Crown Street site. The two main-line companies thus decided to go it alone with the joint arrangements, the ceaseless disputes meaning that it was an incomplete Citadel to which Lancaster & Carlisle trains were diverted in September 1847. The precise date is normally given as the first of the month although, despite the importance of the occasion, there is no contemporary evidence to support this statement. Certainly the transfer had taken place by 10 September when the southern portion of the Caledonian main line was opened as far as Beattock. It left Carlisle by running close to the cathedral, West Walls and the castle before crossing the Rivers Caldew, Eden and later the Esk to reach the border at Gretna.

For several years most through expresses made an extended refreshment stop at Carlisle, where passengers gobbling food may just have had time to ponder over the Latin motto over the refreshment room fireplace, *Faciam ut Hujus Loci Semper Memeris*, loosely translated as 'I will cause you ever to remember this place'. The whole of Citadel was in fact memorable, for the Lancaster & Carlisle's architect, Sir William Tite, had designed a station destined to remain quite unrivalled in the whole of the North West. Victorian-Tudor in style, its clock tower and lantern had on one side the nine-bay main building surmounted by a row of wooden dormers and on the other a handsome five-bay entrance arcade with elaborate buttressing and mullioned windows. Each entrance featured a plaque, three of these respectively displaying the royal coat of arms and the heraldic devices of the Lancaster & Carlisle and Caledonian Railways. The other two were left blank, and there seems little reason to doubt the local tradition that they had been intended for the defecting Newcastle and Maryport companies. Over the years the frontal effect of the façade was to be altered by a number of flanking buildings,

---

SETTLE & CARLISLE CONTRASTS

Top: Ribblehead viaduct, undergoing major repairs following the line's reprieve in 1989 (*Simon Warner*) *Bottom:* Dent in the savage winter of 1963 when the up platform buildings all but disappeared beneath the snow. (*Jack Sedgewick*)

Carlisle Citadel station façade (*Joseph L. Williams*)

including the County Hotel opened by George Head, a Carlisle banker, in 1853 and later immortalised in fiction as the place where Trollope had the Eustace diamonds stolen. Development also took place on the west side of the station, arrival of the main-line companies stimulating the building of 'a sort of New Town' between Citadel and the Caldew containing 'houses of superior character for the working classes' and various small factories. This growth expanded to create overspill development in Dentonholme, a suburb that soon ceased to be textile orientated with railwaymen providing one of the new diverse occupations. Like many stations of this period the running arrangements at Citadel initially consisted of just one long through platform, although as befitted the 'Border City' the atmosphere was unique. Prior to 1850, when duty on spirits was much lower in Scotland than in England, there was a brisk trade in smuggled whisky through Citadel. Excise officers were constantly on watch, but according to local lore engines often had more than coal in the tender!

Although the station was now legally joint Lancaster & Carlisle and Caledonian, their financial contributions were distinctly unequal. By the summer of 1847 over £60,000 had been spent on Citadel, entirely by the English company. Two years later total expenditure was well over £100,000, of which the Caledonian had contributed less than a third. Only in 1854, when the figure had risen to £178,324, had the Scottish company at last met something like its half share. The reason for this apparent parsimony was the Caledonian's financial chaos, described by *The Times* in 1850 as being 'just such a tangle as one might dream of after supping on lobster salad and champagne'. It had pursued a policy of reckless expansion in an endeavour to fortify its central position, one of these moves being an attempt in March 1848 to lease the Newcastle & Carlisle so as to gain access to the East Coast route.

An immediate response came from George Hudson who, in his capacity as chairman of the York, Newcastle & Berwick Railway, not only leased the Newcastle line from 1 August but also the Maryport & Carlisle from 1 October. This gave a brief spell of unified management to the two earliest railways in the 'Border City', but also brought to a head problems at the south side of Citadel which had been simmering for the previous two

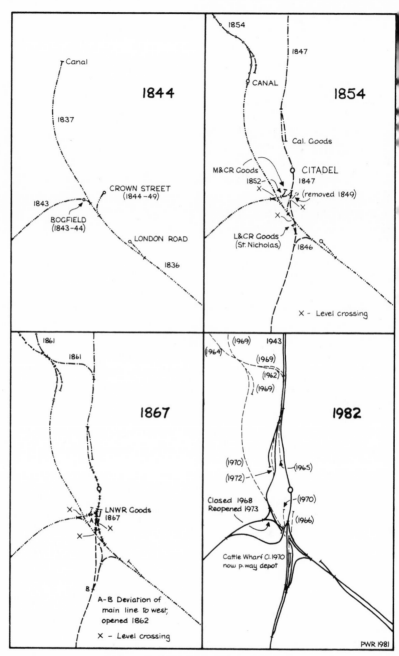

Map 1. Carlisle: Chronological diagrams

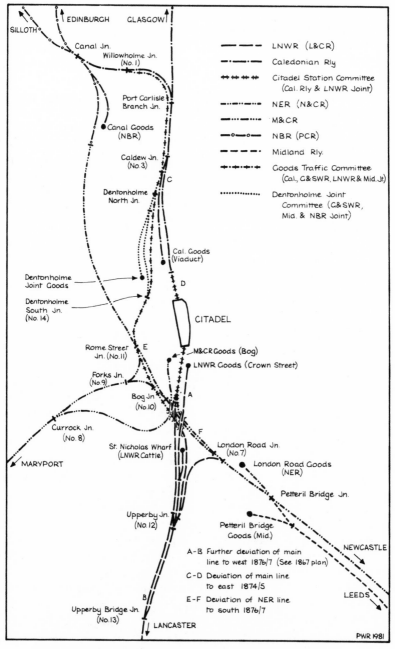

Map 2. Carlisle: Maximum development, showing pre-Grouping ownerships

years. The main-line approach of the Lancaster & Carlisle had been laid out so as to diverge northwards from the curve to London Road Junction and then cross the Canal branch on the level at St Nicholas. Immediately beyond, the Maryport & Carlisle's Crown Street branch was also crossed on the level, so that a train arriving from Maryport fouled the main line three times as it ran first forward and then back over St Nicholas crossing before making the third conflicting movement as it reversed into the terminus. Matters became even worse during 1848 when some of the Maryport trains continued to London Road after calling at Crown Street, their engines returning light and thus bringing the total crossings of the main line to five!

The reason for this extraordinary arrangement of lines was that the Lancaster & Carlisle considered the Crown Street connection both 'temporary' and contrary to a legal agreement, and also still hoped to settle terms for surrender of the terminus site which covered an area vital for the development of Citadel. A sum of £7,005 was on the point of being accepted by the Maryport company when Hudson came on the scene and demanded £100,000. The Lancaster & Carlisle decided to take swift action when it learnt that the 'railway king' was considering seeking powers for a separate joint station for the Newcastle and Maryport lines immediately to the south of Crown Street, and so went before a special jury which assessed the value of the site at £7,171. This sum was duly paid but still Hudson refused to surrender. Thus, in an event which has no exact parallel in railway history, the under-sheriff of the county arrived at Crown Street on the morning of 17 March 1849 and gave formal possession to a Lancaster & Carlisle solicitor. A gang of over a hundred men, carrying picks, shovels and crowbars, converged on the terminus and swiftly tore up the rails and platform, dismantled the coal depot and 'carried away' the station building. Crown Street and its approach line had ceased to exist, and the Maryport & Carlisle had to make immediate arrangements for all its services to terminate at London Road.

By this time Hudson's fortunes were in abrupt decline. His fall from power meant the leases of the Newcastle and Maryport lines were not sanctioned by Parliament and control reverted to their respective managements from 1 January 1850. In these changed circumstances the Maryport & Carlisle reached agreement with the two main-line companies on 2 April 1851 to become a permanent tenant of Citadel, which it began to use from 1 June. Remarkably, this was the fourth Carlisle station the company had used within seven years and the third its trains had entered in reverse, this time by means of an east to north connection from St Nicholas on the course of the 1844 approach to Crown Street. Fortunately an Act of 3 July confirming the new arrangements also authorised a direct curve from Forks Junction, just west of Bogfield, to the joint station. This crossed the Canal branch on the level, the company appointing a person 'to make signals at the passage of trains', and was brought into use on 8 August 1852. It also gave access to a new goods depot, positioned on the west side of the Lancaster & Carlisle so as to minimise conflicting movements and sited on land leased from the station owners for a peppercorn rental. Maryport & Carlisle freight traffic continued to be handled at London Road until 1 January 1852 when it was diverted to a temporary warehouse at Bogfield pending completion, in about September, of the new depot, commonly referred to as Crown Street and not to be confused with either the earlier passenger terminus or the later London & North Western depot. It was officially named Carlisle (Bog) on 2 June 1924.

BRIEF INTERLUDE

After the dramatic events of the 1840s the following decade saw a period of consolidation, although nevertheless two more railway companies began to operate into the city. The Glasgow, Dumfries & Carlisle Railway was promoted by many interests opposed to the Annandale route of the Caledonian main line which bypassed several important towns in south-west Scotland. Incorporated on 16 July 1846, the detached portion extending from Dumfries via Annan to a junction with the Caledonian at Gretna, 8¾ miles north of Carlisle, was opened on 23 August 1848. At this stage there were no workings through to Citadel, the company's engines being turned at Gretna Junction. This alternative route from

Clydeside to the south was completed on 28 October 1850 when amalgamation took place with the earlier Glasgow, Paisley, Kilmarnock & Ayr Railway to form the Glasgow & South Western Railway, thus giving birth to a company destined to be in almost ceaseless conflict with the Caledonian and to have an important bearing on the continuing feuds at Carlisle. Under an agreement of 1 March 1851 it was admitted to Citadel as a 999 year tenant, uneasily sharing both locomotive and goods facilities with the Caledonian at West Walls. The following year the South Western strove to gain an independent outlet to the south by promoting a line from Gretna to the Newcastle & Carlisle at Brampton, but this failed and in 1853 it came to a traffic arrangement with the Caledonian for the use of Citadel, paying an annual rent of between £825 and £900. The company wisely made no attempt to compete for through Glasgow–Carlisle traffic, its best time in 1852 being 4 hr 40 min compared with 3 hr 13 min by the Caledonian.

The other newcomer was the Port Carlisle Railway, a lightning conversion in 1854 from the Carlisle Canal, now rendered redundant by the rail links to Maryport and Whitehaven (see Chapter VI). At the Carlisle end the former canal basin was readily adapted as a goods yard, retaining many indications of its unusual origins. These included a three-storey red brick warehouse dated 1823, with a two-storey office building at one end which had presumably been the canal company's headquarters, as well as the alignment of the quays and bollards marked by ships' ropes. The company's passenger terminus, prosaically known as Canal station, was situated close to the end-on connection which the new line made with the Newcastle & Carlisle's Canal branch. With the opening of the Carlisle & Silloth Bay Railway in 1856, passenger services originated from Silloth rather than Port Carlisle, but still continued to terminate at Canal, more than a mile by road from Citadel and almost 2 miles from London Road. This was very much a railway backwater, and a surprising springboard by which a third Scottish company was to establish itself in the 'Border City' in a series of manoeuvres dominating local railway politics in the period from 1857 to 1864.

THE NORTH BRITISH

As related in the previous chapter, the Midland Railway was by the late 1850s committed to becoming the English partner in a third Anglo-Scottish route. It had its eyes firmly on Carlisle, prompting the Edinburgh-based North British Railway to make determined efforts to extend south from its existing railhead at Hawick, but many frustrating years were to pass before the two companies were able to exchange traffic in Citadel station. Rival schemes for lines across the 43 miles of thinly populated countryside between Hawick and Carlisle were unsuccessfully put forward by the Caledonian and North British in 1857 and 1858, the latter company finally being rewarded with authorisation on 21 July 1859 of its Border Union scheme. Forming part of the North British undertaking but having its own share capital, this involved a main line heading south via Liddesdale and entering England at Kershope Foot, 21 miles north of Carlisle, before running across the Solway Plain. It crossed over the Caledonian main line at Kingmoor and then joined the Port Carlisle Railway $\frac{1}{2}$ mile north of Canal goods station which it was empowered to use. The North British thus gained access to Carlisle independently of the Caledonian and a potential outlet to both Ireland and Liverpool via Silloth, as well as a link with the Glasgow & South Western via a $3\frac{1}{4}$ mile single-track branch from Longtown to Gretna. The Act stated that the new route 'should not be used for the Purposes of undue Competition with the Caledonian Railway in respect of traffic between Edinburgh and Carlisle', but the company was at least given powers to run into Citadel station. This was to be approached by a sharply curved branch connecting the West Coast route with the Port Carlisle line $\frac{3}{4}$ mile north of Citadel, for which the Caledonian had obtained sanction on 28 June 1858 following overtures it had made the previous year to absorb the Port Carlisle and Silloth companies. The single-track branch was sufficiently complete for a Caledonian engine to be authorised to make a trial trip over it on to the Port Carlisle on 30 June 1860, regular freight workings taking place thereafter.

The snag was that for running over $1\frac{1}{4}$ miles of Caledonian metals the North British was to be charged tolls for the equivalent of 4 miles and could only use Citadel on terms to be agreed with the owning companies. After considerable legal wrangling, during which time the North British vigorously campaigned for its own access to the station, the issue was put before an arbitrator who eventually determined that the company should pay the substantial annual sums of £600 for use of the Caledonian's 'Port Carlisle branch', £1,800 for the contiguous portion of its main line, and £1,750 for Citadel, plus £1,000 for working expenses and maintenance. In order to cater for the extra traffic, powers for the enlargement of Citadel and the provision of goods relief lines on its west side were obtained in an important Act of 22 July 1861 which put control of the station on a proper footing. By an agreement of 10 May 1857 the joint owners had created a Citadel Station Committee, having in effect the autonomy of a separate railway, to co-ordinate its management and 'for the Prevention of Accidents and Inconveniences'. The Act continued the committee, the English partner now becoming the London & North Western Railway as a result of its 1859 lease of the Lancaster & Carlisle, and confirmed agreements for use of the station by the Maryport & Carlisle and Glasgow & South Western as well as the North British.

The southern end of the Border Union from Carlisle to Scotch Dyke, 2¼ miles north of Longtown, was ready for opening in early October 1861. Only at this late stage did the North British learn to its chagrin that the Board of Trade would not sanction use of the Caledonian's connecting spur for passenger traffic until that company gave an undertaking to double the line within a specified period. Opening of the Border Union therefore had to be postponed, goods services from Canal commencing on 15 October at the same time as the Longtown–Gretna branch was opened for traffic. Use of the connecting spur by passenger trains began on 29 October when a Citadel–Scotch Dyke service was inaugurated. Through passenger traffic between Edinburgh and Carlisle commenced on 1 July 1862, the completed line soon being termed the 'Waverley Route' after the novels of Sir Walter Scott. In order to connect with Silloth services from Canal, an exchange station known as Port Carlisle Junction was opened at the convergence of the two routes (it first appeared in

Bradshaw in July 1863) and was also used by North British pass-holders who were barred from Caledonian metals. It closed on 1 July 1864 when Silloth trains began to run into Citadel and Canal henceforth became purely a goods depot.

A complex story lay behind this transfer of Silloth services. Expansion southwards by the North British had greatly concerned its neighbouring partner in the East Coast alliance, the North Eastern Railway, which decided to protect its interests by a joint working arrangement with the line separating the two concerns, the Newcastle & Carlisle. Terms were agreed in 1859 but contested at the initiation of the Edinburgh company. Other vociferous objectors included the Port Carlisle and Carlisle & Silloth Bay, at this stage being worked by a joint committee, which expressed concern at loss of traffic outlets, contended their lines had been intended to form part of a through route from Silloth to Newcastle, and to safeguard their position obtained running powers over the Canal branch to London Road under an Act of 3 July 1860. The North Eastern argument that the Port Carlisle and Silloth companies were by now merely pawns in the hands of the North British, and hence their objections were spurious, was not accepted and the proposed working arrangement was quashed. Yet only two years later the North British leased the two Cumbrian lines under Acts of 3 June 1862, and full amalgamation of the Newcastle & Carlisle with the North Eastern was sanctioned on 17 July, powers also being given to use Citadel on payment of an annual rental of £1,000 plus a share of working expenses.

Access to the joint station from the Newcastle direction was complicated by the decision of the London & North Western to straighten its main-line approach from the south, a deviation to the west from Upperby Junction northwards being built under powers of 13 August 1859 and opened on 24 January 1862. This necessitated replacement of the existing east to north connection at St Nicholas, little used since the 1852 opening of the Forks Junction–Citadel spur, except as one arm of a triangle for turning Maryport & Carlisle engines. A new single-line connection on the east side of the main line was sanctioned for goods traffic on 30 April 1862, doubling of this spur being approved by the Citadel Station

Committee on 13 June 1864. North Eastern passenger services were transferred on 1 January 1863 from London Road to Citadel, enlargement of which had by this time been completed at a cost of some £39,000.

Surprisingly, the deviated West Coast main line still crossed the North Eastern Canal branch on the level, despite an unfortunate incident in 1859 when a driver was fined 5s (25p) after he had run into another train at the old St Nicholas crossing and 'damaged two ladies'. Matters were made worse by the opening on 25 November 1867 of a new London & North Western goods depot on the site of the Maryport & Carlisle's infamous passenger terminus at Crown Street (by which name it was officially known from 2 June 1924). It was approached by a short branch which left the main line immediately north of the new St Nicholas crossing and then also crossed the North Eastern's Citadel spur on the level. Following deviation of the main line, the original goods depot on the south side of St Nicholas was served from the Upperby Junction–London Road Junction curve. It was closed on completion of the new depot, reopening in about 1871 as a cattle station.

MIDLAND RENAISSANCE

By the early 1860s it was clear that the strangle-hold on traffic through Carlisle exercised by the London & North Western and Caledonian could not last much longer. The North British was in determined mood having spent some £5 million on its 'Waverley Route' only to find that the blockade mounted by the West Coast partners meant it was little more than an expensive branch line. Conflict ran deep, with Caledonian staff reputedly changing labels on Anglo-Scottish wagons so that freight consigned via the North British travelled instead over Beattock. The Glasgow & South Western was also becoming increasingly frustrated by the lack of an effective traffic outlet to the south, both companies airing their grievances to the full when the Midland finally made its bid for Scotland and brought its Settle & Carlisle Bill before Parliament in 1866. North British complaints concerned cattle arriving from the south for Dalkeith being kept waiting for hours in the train; 'Waverley Route' passenger trains not being allowed to leave Citadel until after departure of the corresponding Caledonian service; and reluctance by the London & North Western to forward northbound goods wagons. Similar criticism by the 'Sou'-West' helped the Midland secure its Act, which at the Carlisle end authorised the new route to join the North Eastern's Newcastle line ¼ mile east of London Road Junction from where running powers were granted into Citadel. It also contained a key clause that the station owners should apply to an arbitrator to determine enlargements necessary for the additional traffic, and should then promote a Bill for these works.

There was now a brief lull while the Midland attempted to abandon its main line over the Pennines, but as soon as this had proved abortive the North British made a valiant attempt to improve facilities for the impending exchange of traffic. Although only a tenant of Citadel, it took the extraordinary step of itself promoting a Bill in 1871 for enlargement of the station. Not surprisingly this was rejected, as were similar proposals by the owning companies the following year, because they had failed to abide by the Settle & Carlisle Act and go before an arbitrator. As a result the Board of Trade appointed Joseph Cubitt, the distinguished civil engineer, to perform this task, but unfortunately he died before making an award. In order to avoid further delay the Midland therefore reached an agreement with the owners on 16 December 1872 which paved the way for the Citadel Station Act of 21 July 1873. This was at last to bring some order to a railway network that had evolved piecemeal, but left the Midland to bear a totally disproportionate amount of the cost.

A prime aim of the agreed scheme was that as far as possible goods and passenger traffic should be segregated. The goods relief lines on the west side of Citadel, constructed under the 1861 Act, were to be removed to make way for extensions, and replaced by what was basically a new loop taking freight well clear of the station approaches. Extending from near Bog Junction to Willowholme Junction on the Caledonian's Port Carlisle branch, it was to be administered by the Carlisle Goods Traffic Committee, consisting of representatives of the London & North Western, Caledonian, Midland and

Glasgow & South Western (the latter company did not immediately exercise its right to become a partner and at first merely enjoyed running powers). At the same time the existing layout at either end of the loop was to be radically altered so as to minimise conflicting movements. Half of the cost of the scheme, namely £167,136, was born by the Midland and the remainder by the London & North Western and Caledonian. The first part of this complex building programme to be put in hand involved removal of the Caledonian goods yard and engine shed from the east side of the existing main line below West Walls, where constant smoke and noise had become a source of intense friction between the company's Presbyterian directors and the Dean of Carlisle Cathedral whose study overlooked the railway. The tracks leading north out of Citadel were then deviated to the east, thus clearing space for enlargement of the other portion of the Caledonian's goods depot and yard which had stood on the west side of the former main line. The rebuilt yard connected directly with the northern end of the new goods loop which in turn joined the realigned main line at Caldew Junction. The Caledonian depot now became known as Viaduct (its official name from 2 June 1924) after the nearby Victoria Road viaduct, built as an integral part of the improvements in order to link old Carlisle with rapidly expanding industrial suburbs on the west side of the city and described as 'more massive than beautiful' when opened by Princess Louise in 1877.

New engine sheds were constructed at Kingmoor, out in the country $1\frac{3}{4}$ miles north of Citadel. Provision was made for the Glasgow & South Western to use these on the same basis as at West Walls, but the company took the opportunity to end what must have been a difficult working relationship and instead turned to its new ally. The Midland was constructing its own goods depot at Petterill (officially renamed Petteril Bridge 3 September 1909), almost directly opposite the North Eastern's premises at London Road, and here it provided the 'Sou'-West' with a temporary engine house, goods warehouse and yard by 1 January 1875. Part of the premises were so temporary they blew down within a month, but a rebuilt engine shed was brought into service on 1 April, four months before the Midland began to use the yard on opening of the

Settle–Carlisle line to freight. There must have been difficulties in exchanging traffic at this location, as for several years consignments from the Midland were apparently worked across the border to Gretna Green, the first station on the Glasgow & South Western, where shunting operations on Sundays greatly distressed the local Sabbatarians.

Major alterations at the southern end of the new goods loop at last ended the arrangement whereby both the Maryport & Carlisle and London & North Western crossed the North Eastern's Canal branch on the level. The new layout involved making a second westward deviation of the West Coast main line at this point so that it could be carried over the Canal branch, which for the same reason was moved slightly to the south. Two further lines were taken over this branch, one forming an altered access to the London & North Western's Crown Street goods depot by diverging from the main line at Upperby Junction and also bridging the North Eastern spur to Citadel. The other was the new Maryport & Carlisle approach to both the passenger station and the company's goods depot, leaving the original route at Currock Junction, where sidings were provided and an engine shed opened in January 1876 to replace the previous structure at Bogfield. Diving under all three of these lines was a new link from Upperby Junction to an end-on connection with the southern end of the Goods Traffic Committee loop. A $\frac{1}{4}$ mile north this loop intersected the Canal branch at Rome Street Junction, where a Maryport & Carlisle spur from Forks Junction created a triangle used in latter years to turn sorting carriages employed on West Coast postal services. This involved arrangement of lines meant that all four companies entering Carlisle from the south could run directly on to the new loop and also the Canal branch, which at last came into its own as a direct link for freight traffic between the Midland and the North British.

The deviated West Coast main line and the Maryport & Carlisle curve from Currock Junction were brought into use on 7 July 1877. Other lines were phased into operation in the next few weeks, the work culminating in the opening of the new London & North Western and Maryport & Carlisle approaches from the south to the Goods Traffic Committee loop on 6 August. This loop was opened on the same date, its construction having involved demolition of much slum property which caused the Carlisle Sanitary Inspector to comment: 'Overcrowding is, I am afraid, rather prevalent in the poorer parts of the City, which is no doubt owing chiefly to the large number of houses acquired and pulled down by the Railway Companies, thereby unhousing a large number of families, and causing a great scarcity of suitable houses for the working classes.' The problem was accentuated by a decision of the three partners in the new Anglo-Scottish alliance to further reduce dependence on the London & North Western and Caledonian by developing a joint goods depot at Dentonholme, reached by another loop diverging from that of the Goods Traffic Committee. Its origins stretched back to 5 July 1865 when the North British obtained powers for a depot on this site as part of an otherwise abortive project for relief lines extending to the south of Citadel, and later that year concluded an agreement with the Midland for 'the Cultivation and Development and free Interchange of Traffic between their respective Systems of Railways via Carlisle'. Further North British Acts of 23 July 1866 and 13 July 1876 in turn admitted the Midland and Glasgow & South Western as partners to the Dentonholme depot, which was opened on 1

CARLISLE: RAILWAY CENTRE PAR EXCELLENCE

Top: Interior of No 5 signalbox, controlling the approaches to Citadel station from the south. In 1973 it was superseded by Carlisle power box, embracing all running lines within the city and 74 miles of the West Coast route. *(Peter W. Robinson)* *Middle:* Reconstruction in the mid-1870s. St Nicholas crossing where the LNWR main line (running from bottom left to centre right of the picture) was intersected on the level by the North Eastern's Canal branch. Various works can be seen in progress to eliminate this dangerous arrangement which had contributed to a serious accident in 1870 when a goods train sliced through a Scotch express. *(Carlisle Public Libraries & Museum)* *Bottom:* Three Coronation class Pacifics await departure from the cathedral-like confines of Citadel with up expresses in June 1956. *(Real Photographs)*

October 1883. Ironically after such a long Parliamentary involvement, the North British opted not to use the new premises and continued to concentrate all freight traffic at Canal. Dentonholme's prime user became the Glasgow & South Western, at length gaining its first real home in Carlisle. This in effect meant each of the seven companies running into the city now had its own goods depot, a situation which seemed neat and orderly at the time but gradually created growing chaos as transfer traffic mounted and the various yards in their cramped locations became increasingly outmoded.

The financial arrangements for enlargement of Citadel were on a different basis to the goods lines, involving the Midland paying an annual percentage on money spent by the owning companies. The station as rebuilt had its original main platform, a new island platform, five bays (two at the south end of the main up platform, one for the Maryport & Carlisle and two for North British stopping services to Silloth and the 'Waverley Route') and at the west side five carriage roads. Spanning this enormous width was a magnificent roof containing $6\frac{1}{4}$ acres of glass and sporting remarkable end screens with Gothic-shaped glazing bars designed to tone with Tite's original frontage. The enlarged station was opened in an incomplete state on 4 July 1880 in time to cope with vast numbers of visitors pouring into Carlisle for that year's Royal Show. Four years earlier on 1 May 1876 crowds had gathered to watch the arrival of the first Midland expresses with their massive and stately Pullman cars, an event described by the *Carlisle Express & Examiner* as 'marking a new era in the history

---

FREIGHT AT CARLISLE

Top: A train of empty mineral hoppers passes beneath a splendid signal gantry at Durranhill. The lower set of buffers on the Maryport & Carlisle Railway 0–6–0 was designed to handle chaldron wagons on the docks at Maryport. *(L&GRP)*
Bottom: 5MT No 45295 and Jubilee No 45573 *Newfoundland* enter the new Kingmoor marshalling yard with 'The Limey' goods from Skipton in June 1965. *(Derek Cross)*

of railway developments in this country'. The Midland had finally reached the gateway to Scotland, but despite the major contribution it had made to the restructured layout at Carlisle still found it tended to receive the same treatment as had previously been meted out to the North British and Glasgow & South Western. By 1882 the situation had deteriorated to a point where the company promoted its own Citadel Station Bill, seeking to become a member of the joint station committee and accusing the owning companies of rigging the arrangements and signalling so as to favour their own traffic at the expense of that worked by the new Anglo-Scottish alliance. The London & North Western and Caledonian, unable to defend their actions, had to back down and agree certain basic rights and as a result the Bill was withdrawn.

EIGHTY YEARS ON

By 1880 Carlisle was one of Britain's major railway centres, with traffic flows destined to expand greatly in the years ahead. Yet in common with a number of other centres where joint lines proliferated, the single fact which stands out in the period right up to the 1960s is that virtually nothing was done to meet changing circumstances, the various companies being content to rest on their laurels. With the arrival of the Midland, passenger services assumed a basic pattern which was also to survive until well after nationalisation. West Coast route services normally divided into Glasgow and Edinburgh portions at Carstairs rather than Carlisle, but nevertheless there was considerable activity at Citadel in changing engines and, in pre-Grouping days, altering from Westinghouse to vacuum brake. Many Midland expresses did at first divide at Carlisle, one portion being taken on by the Glasgow & South Western and the other by the North British, but as loads increased there was a gradual tendency for Glasgow and Edinburgh trains to be worked separately throughout, particularly after the opening of the Forth Bridge in 1890.

The constraint at Citadel was that through platforms were limited to three, and in the peak years it is surprising that some of the under-utilised carriage roads were not removed to create additional platform space. Traffic tended to arrive in marked directional flows, and it was at one time commonplace for a succession of down trains to be held up outside waiting platforms when no up trains were in evidence. The atmosphere of Citadel in the 1890s was well captured by Robert Thomson, a former secretary of the station committee, when he set down his recollections in a centennial brochure in 1947: 'Hiring Saturdays with crowds of country servants, hundreds of wooden boxes overflowing from the cloakrooms – the Cumberland Militia going to and from their annual training, a rough crowd – Carlisle Races with hoards of sportsmen mixed up with Sunday school trips – and the Station policemen with their silk hats. And who could forget the frequent passage of Mr Gladstone, his white head appearing from the carriage window haranguing the crowd on the platform.' Twice yearly a North British special notice would detail an entire page of alterations for the hiring fairs, with additional trains arriving from Riccarton, Newcastleton, Langholm and Port Carlisle. During the day the farm servants bargained with the masters for work – an event encapsulated in the writings of Melvyn Bragg – and that night the local station platforms would be piled high with boxes containing the newly arrived servants' worldly goods.

On the freight side, the testing time came during World War I when during the peak period of October and November 1917 over 200,000 wagons a month were being exchanged between the yards of the seven companies. To cope with the situation a Joint Control for regulating goods-traffic working was set up in 1916 and proved most successful. After Grouping it was unfortunate that the LMS and LNER were unable to construct a combined marshalling yard, but they did at least manage to reduce the number of separate locomotive depots. The Glasgow & South Western had in December 1894 moved from Petterill to a new shed at Currock, reached by running powers authorised by an Act of 6 July 1895. The Maryport & Carlisle shed here closed in 1923, the engines going across to the 'Sou'-West' shed which in turn became redundant the following year when the locomotives were transferred to Kingmoor and Upperby. Canal shed provided motive power for the Newcastle line after the shut down of London Road shed in 1933, the other change at this time involving the Midland roundhouse at Durran Hill which was closed on 16 February 1936 but reopened during the war and finally abandoned on 2 November 1959. World War II again saw major congestion, with Carlisle becoming the crucial bottleneck for Anglo-Scottish freight workings and some trains taking as long as seven hours to cover 2 miles in travelling between yards! But it also brought one important improvement, with completion in 1943 of a new double-track viaduct across the Eden to accommodate additional goods lines from Carlisle No 3 to Kingmoor where a yard for up freight had developed over the years.

MODERNISATION

A child of the late Victorian era returning to Carlisle in the 1950s would have had little difficulty in recognising the railway scene. Citadel was still a frontier, in a sense more so than in the LMS period, for it was now the point where London Midland Region engines gave way to those of the Scottish Region. A new signal box at the station's south end was opened in September 1951 and in 1957–8 the overall roof was substantially reduced in area, the Gothic end screens being removed at the same time. The engine sheds at Upperby, Kingmoor and Canal remained active, making a sizeable contribution to the total of over 4,000 men and women employed in various railway installations in the city. Freight was still passing through Carlisle at the rate of 30,000 wagons per week, almost all requiring to be remarshalled once and often twice. Some eighteen locomotives were constantly on duty for transfer trips between the various yards which had in the main continued to be used for traffic from the lines of their respective pre-Grouping owners. Most of them could only be entered by means of reversal, and all were inadequate in size and lacked the advantages of humps.

Provision of a new marshalling yard at Carlisle received high priority in the British Railways modernisation plan. Parliamentary authority to purchase a site on the west side of the main line at Kingmoor was obtained in 1956 and construction began three years later. This huge £4½ million project had almost mind-bending statistics. Concentrated in an area $2\frac{1}{2}$ miles long by $\frac{1}{4}$ mile wide, it was designed to handle over 5,600 wagons a day in 123 sidings covering 56 track miles. More unfortunately in view of what was to follow, it also involved the loss of 420 acres of mainly arable land. The basic principle of the yard was to keep up and down traffic separated into two distinct areas, each with its own reception, sorting and departure sidings, and with control towers and stabling for locomotives between the two halves. Facilities provided included push-button route-setting, automatic point operation and floodlighting from fifteen 150 ft high towers carrying a total of 267 lamps each of 1,500 watts. Preparing the site involved diverting the Carlisle–Rockcliffe road over a new bridge straddling the main line and the entry into the yard, excavating 872,000 tons of earth and bringing in 600,000 tons of slag and 240,000 tons of bottom ballast in special trains. The slag came from the abandoned ironworks at Cleator Moor, involving running two trains nightly for most of 1961.

A power signal-box was built at Kingmoor to control lines between the northern limit of Carlisle No 3 box and the southern limit of that at Gretna, including the yard approaches which were also on a lavish scale. At the Carlisle end the normal route into the yard was via the former Goods Traffic Committee loop to Carlisle No 3 (the portion from here to Willowholme Junction was removed) and thence the 1943 goods lines as far as Etterby Junction. New up and down connections were built from this point, continuing round either side of the yard to link up $\frac{1}{2}$ mile north of Rockcliffe with the existing Rockcliffe–Floriston goods lines. These accordingly were truncated at their southern end, a flyover being constructed to take the up approach to the yard clear of the passenger tracks. This up line was extended back from Floriston over a reconstructed and widened Esk viaduct to Mossband Junction, a mile south of Gretna. An alternative path from the south was provided via the Canal branch and a new double-track curve diverging from the southern end of the 'Waverley Route' at Stainton Junction. It was access to and from the former North British main line, crossing the West Coast route immediately south of the yard, which posed the greatest difficulties. The solution for down traffic was to build a single-track curve to a reversing loop near Stainton level

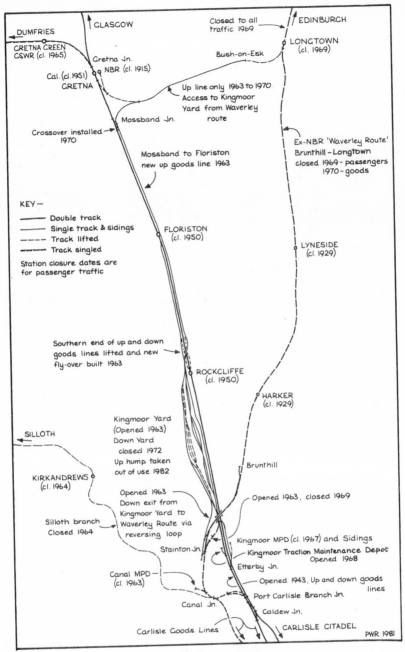

Map 3. Kingmoor and Gretna

crossing so that trains could leave facing south and the engine then run round before proceeding north, propelling out of the yard not being permitted. In the opposite direction ingenious use was made of the single-track Longtown to Gretna line, which had lost its passenger service as early as 9 August 1915 and was by this time only carrying traffic to a series of ammunition depots alongside the branch. It was now restricted to up traffic only and altered at the Gretna end so as to connect with the West Coast main line's extended up goods at Mossband Junction, thus giving a through route into the yard.

Kingmoor was completed in stages in 1963, significantly the year which also saw publication of the Beeching Report foreshadowing a switch from single wagon loads to block freight trains as well as recommending closure of the 'Waverley Route'. In 1965 the yard was handling a respectable maximum of 4,250 wagons per day and effecting economies put at over £300,000 a year, largely through savings in wagon transit times. Yet despite the promising start, Kingmoor never worked at full capacity and after only a brief life the down portion of the yard was phased out of use during 1972, further downgrading coming in January 1982 when hump shunting gave way to manual operation. Its decline had been exacerbated by closure of the 'Waverley Route' to all through traffic on 6 January 1969, an event that brought in its wake lifting of the ex-Caledonian Port Carlisle branch and the six-year-old double-track curve from Stainton Junction into the south end of the yard. Goods traffic continued as far as Longtown until 31 August 1970 when the line was cut back to an RAF depot at Brunthill, ½ mile north of the bridge over the West Coast route and reached from the yard via the reversing loop at Stainton. The Mossband Junction–Longtown branch was retained for ammunitions traffic as far as Bush-on-Esk and reverted to two-way working.

Further machinations of the Beeching era saw closure of all the city's goods depots apart from Dentonholme and London Road, coal traffic being concentrated at the latter prior to new mechanised handling facilities being opened in January 1971. Closure dates were as follows: Viaduct (ex-Caledonian), 2 August 1965; Crown Street (London & North Western), 1

February 1966 (official date – all track had been lifted by July 1965); Petteril Bridge (Midland), 1 February 1966; Canal (North British), 31 May 1969; Bog (Maryport & Carlisle), 5 October 1970; and St Nicholas (London & North Western), 7 December 1970. Withdrawal of traffic to Canal was followed by piecemeal cutting back of the Canal branch to Bog Junction, culminating in closure of the section from here to Rome Street Junction on 1 October 1972.

The most recent major change at Carlisle has stemmed from electrification and resignalling of the West Coast route, completion of this work in 1974 bringing the 'Border City' within 3 hr 45 min of London and 1 hr 20 min of Glasgow. Citadel and its approaches have been transformed by a spider's web of overhead wires, although perhaps technologically more impressive is the new power signal-box a little way south of the station on the down side. Phased into use in the first half of 1973, it controls 74 miles of main line from south of Oxenholme to Kirkpatrick in Scotland as well as the Maryport line out to Wigton, the former Glasgow & South Western to Annan, some 5 miles of both the North Eastern and Midland approaches to Carlisle and, by means of satellite interlocking, the functions of the 1963 box at Kingmoor. Track alterations in connection with resignalling included singling the former North Eastern curve into Citadel, which has thus reverted to its original state, and reinstating for through Tyne Yard–Workington steel traffic the Bog Junction–Forks Junction spur which had been closed in the first half of 1968. Modernisation has brought an end to Carlisle's long and colourful role as a railway frontier, a final break with tradition coming in April 1979 when the separate signing-on points at Citadel for Kingmoor and Upperby crews were merged. As a dyed-in-the-wool carriage & wagon examiner remarked at the time: 'They're joining up the Caley men with the Lanky men!'

Changes affecting Carlisle in the 1980s are covered in the postscript.

CHAPTER V

Furness – and Beyond

Furness, the furthest point or 'ness' of Anglian times, was prior
to the railway age one of the most remote parts of the country.
Together with the ancient deanery of Cartmel it formed
'Lancashire North of the Sands', a detached portion of the
county difficult of access owing to the deeply penetrating
estuaries of the Kent and Leven. The main route into the area
involved a treacherous 'oversands' crossing of Morecambe
Bay by coach or chaise, though virtually all goods and mineral
traffic was carried by sea. Baines' *Directory of Lancashire* noted
in 1824 that 'to men of active and enterprising minds ...
Furness is not a proper sphere of action'. Yet for at least 600
years haematite iron ore had been mined in the area, the
industry expanding rapidly in the eighteenth century. Ore
from mines around Dalton and Lindal was for a time shipped
out through the regional capital of Ulverston via John
Rennie's short and wide ship canal opened in 1796, but fickle
movements of the Leven channel soon caused the ironmasters
to turn their attentions elsewhere. They began to favour
Barrow, a small hamlet of less than twenty houses at the south-
western extremity of Furness, sheltered from the prevailing
winds by Barrow Island and the whaleback-shaped bulk of
Walney Island. Jetties were built out into the navigable
channel, trade increasing to the extent that by 1825 a mineral
tramway was proposed from the mines to the harbour.
Nothing came of this suggestion, but by the early 1840s some
40,000 tons of ore per annum were being shipped through
Barrow and exploitation of the district's mineral wealth was
receiving serious attention. Developments were spearheaded
by the two main landowners, the Duke of Buccleuch, Lord of

the Liberty of Furness, and William Cavendish, Earl of Burlington (later 7th Duke of Devonshire), owner of Furness mining royalties and Kirkby slate quarries on the eastern side of the Duddon estuary. It was Burlington who asked his friend James Walker, then president of the Institution of Civil Engineers, to report on construction of a railway to link both the iron mines at Dalton and his quarries at Kirkby with Barrow harbour. Little can he have suspected he was starting a chain of events that was to create one of the fastest growing towns in Britain and the most important railway company in the Lake Counties.

SMALL BEGINNINGS

In his report of 1 June 1843 Walker detailed proposals for lines totalling 14 miles in length, costing an estimated £100,000 and passing close to all iron ore mines in the district. Apart from Barrow, he also suggested that a line be made to Rampside a few miles to the south as both locations had 'advantages peculiar to themselves'. On the basis of this report the Furness Railway Company was formed under the patronage of Buccleuch and Burlington, although the person directly responsible for its affairs was Benjamin Currey, Clerk of the House of Lords and Agent of the Devonshire Estates. The two landowners each subscribed £15,000 and most of the remaining £45,000 was put up by their friends in London, only £1,350 coming from local sources. The prospectus, which envisaged a horse-worked line capable of future adaptation for locomotives, proposed an extension from Dalton to Ulverston, but railways were perhaps too new-fangled to appeal to this fashionable resort of the North Lonsdale gentry. The Furness directors later reported that the Ulverston extension had been cut back to Lindal, 'the undertaking not having met with sufficient encouragement from that Town to justify its adoption'.

No doubt helped by its aristocratic origins, the project went unopposed in Parliament and the Furness Railway Company was incorporated on 23 May 1844. The lines as authorised comprised a main trunk heading south-west from Lindal to Dalton before passing through a 225 yd tunnel and running close to the ruins of Furness Abbey where there was a second short tunnel. It then described a long semicircle through Roose, divergence point of the $2\frac{1}{4}$ mile Rampside branch, and crossed Salthouse Sands on an embankment to terminate at Rabbit Hill about $\frac{1}{3}$ mile south-east of Barrow village. The $6\frac{3}{4}$ mile branch from Kirkby served the slate quarries by means of exchange sidings with a 3 ft $2\frac{1}{4}$ in gauge rope-worked incline (which descended from some 460 ft above sea-level and had been in existence since at least 1809) and then ran close to the Duddon shore and past Ireleth before joining the 'main line' at Millwood, west of Dalton. The reasoning behind the Rampside branch revolved round the activities of John Abel Smith, a London banker who in 1840 had purchased Roa Island at the southern entrance to the Walney Channel. His intention was to operate a steamer service to this point from Fleetwood in connection with the Preston & Wyre Railway, in which he had a large financial interest, and in 1843 he duly obtained a quaintly worded Act, referring to tolls such as 2d for a fiddle and £1 for a corpse, to connect Roa Island with the mainland by means of a causeway. The Furness reached agreement to extend the Rampside branch along this embankment to the island, from where Smith was to construct the 810 ft long Piel Pier, having an advantage over Barrow in offering deep-water facilities at all states of the tide.

By early 1845 it had been decided for the time being to terminate the Lindal line at Crooklands, $\frac{1}{2}$ mile east of Dalton, where connections would be made with mineral tramways. A tender of £47,789 for construction of the various lines, all single with earthworks wide enough for double track, was accepted in February 1845. Work was soon well in hand, despite poetic intervention in June when Wordsworth visited Furness Abbey and was incensed to find the railway being built so close to the ruins. He penned a sonnet contrasting the respectful attitude of the navvies towards the abbey with the desecration being committed by the Furness company:

Profane Despoilers, stand ye not reproved,
While thus these simple-hearted men are moved?

One wonders if he realised that under the original proposals the line would have passed right through the abbey!

The isolation of the Furness posed great difficulties in obtaining rolling stock, which had to be brought in by sea. The first two locomotives, of the 'Bury' type with huge copper-domed fireboxes, were supplied by the Liverpool firm of Bury, Curtis & Kennedy and shipped across Morecambe Bay from Fleetwood, apparently on the decks of tug-boats. The experiences of Thomas Fisher in unloading the first engine to arrive at Barrow are entertainingly recalled in *A Popular History of Barrow-in-Furness*:

> When the tide was at a height that left the deck of the tug-boat on a level with the pier, we got to work, put a line of rails from the pier on to the boat, got the engine placed on the rails, and made fast our rope and chains on to it; and then with a long pull and a strong pull and a pull altogether, of about 100 hands, we landed it safely on the hill, in the presence of a large number of enthusiastic onlookers, who cheered most heartily as we dragged it along the pier and up the hill.

In January 1846 a step that was to have enormous consequences was taken when James Ramsden, the 'father of Barrow', was appointed locomotive superintendent. Only twenty-three years of age, he became secretary and manager of the company four years later. Ramsden was immediately impressed with the natural advantages of Barrow and guided its initial development as the railway's headquarters. The existing piers were compulsorily purchased and construction took place of a large new jetty, single platform wooden station, engine shed and workshops, and cottages and a school for the company's servants.

The whole line both to Crooklands and to Kirkby was opened for mineral traffic on 3 June 1846, followed according to some sources by inauguration of a local passenger service between Barrow and Dalton on or about 12 August. This was probably of a rudimentary nature, as later described by Ramsden:

> The rolling stock in the first instance was two four-wheeled engines and several mineral wagons ... passengers were allowed to travel in a sheep van (fitted by a carpenter with neat deal seats) on Sundays only. One engine only being needed for traffic, there was only one Driver and Fireman employed. I

observed one Sunday that the engine was running too fast, and making signals for the train to stop, I found the driver in liquor. I afterwards wrote to the Superintendent of the Liverpool and Manchester Railway and begged a man and until his arrival, which was not for some days, I worked the traffic myself.

The Board of Trade return records that the full passenger service over the complete system commenced on 24 August, although it was withdrawn at the end of the summer season owing to difficulties in working both passenger and mineral traffic over a single line.

According to the *Cumberland Pacquet*, the trains operated in connection with 'a powerful steamer' running twice daily between Fleetwood and Piel Pier. This was the *Ayrshire Lassie*, a last-minute joint arrangement with the Preston & Wyre Railway owing to Smith not having his own steamer ready for the opening of the line. Some 1,500 passengers were carried in the first week, most of them visiting Furness Abbey where their departure was apparently more welcome to the Earl of Burlington than their arrival, for he noted in his diary, 'after the train returns to Piel the mob vanishes'. The steamer also provided a quicker route to the Lake District than hitherto, 'conveyances' running from Dalton to connect at Newby Bridge with steam yachts on Windermere and also from Kirkby to Coniston. This early venture into tourism was stimulated the following year when a station was completed at Furness Abbey alongside the Manor House, which was purchased and converted into an hotel. In order to accommodate the additional traffic, doubling of the central portion of the line between Millwood and Roose Junctions was carried out during the spring of 1847.

Unfortunately, passenger traffic growth was hampered by more problems at Piel Pier. For the summer of 1847 the Furness purchased its own steamer *Helvellyn* (formerly *Windermere*) to operate a cross-bay service from Fleetwood in competition with existing sailings from that port to Bardsea. The terms demanded by Smith were unacceptable, so the boat was diverted to Barrow where the fluctuating tides caused great inconvenience. After an unsuccessful injunction had been brought by the Furness, sailings reverted to Piel from May 1848 but there was no winter service in 1848–9 and the

Rampside branch was 'discontinued for the present as not paying expenses'. By 1851 the Fleetwood sailings had been joined by steamers plying from Poulton (Morecambe) in connection with the 'little' North Western Railway, some of these being worked by the Midland Railway from 1852. In the same year Smith and some Furness ironmasters brought forward a Bill for a direct line from the pier to Lindal, but this was strenuously opposed and thrown out. Soon afterwards the Furness reached agreement with the banker to lease the whole of his Roa Island enterprise, but before arrangements were finalised a freak storm caused severe damage and the company was able to buy all his rights and property for £15,000, the purchase being confirmed by an Act of 4 August 1853.

Further difficulties had occurred in 1848, when Burlington, the company's new chairman, described the railway as being in a 'deplorable state'. An investigation found 'great fault, both with the original expenditure and with the mode of management', but after a brief period of retrenchment the position soon recovered. Additional traffic stemmed from a modest 3½ mile extension from Kirkby to Broughton in Furness, built mainly with a view to handling copper ore from the mines at Coniston. Authorised on 27 July 1846, it was opened in February 1848 (the precise date is not known but was probably directly after the Board of Trade inspection on 23 February). By 1849 Dalton haematite ore was flowing out of the district in abundance, the railway being capable of carrying between 600 and 700 tons per day for transit to the ironmasters of South Wales and Staffordshire. Such was the increase in traffic that the railway pier at Barrow had to be lengthened, the *Ulverston Advertiser* noting that 'the highway between Dalton and Barrow is becoming grass-grown for lack of use'. By February 1850 the Furness had carried 470,000 tons of minerals and 78,000 passengers, and total output of the local iron ore mines had at least trebled. Barrow had outstripped Ulverston as a port, and the quarries at Kirkby, no longer dependent on coastwise shipping, had begun a period of expansion that was to see them become the prime producers of slate in England.

THE CUMBERLAND CONNECTION

Even before the Furness opened, moves had been made which were soon to end its position of extreme isolation. By 1844, as described in the next chapter, most of the Maryport & Carlisle Railway was carrying traffic and an extension in the form of the Whitehaven Junction line had been successfully promoted by the 2nd Earl of Lonsdale with George Stephenson as consulting engineer. It was Stephenson who advised the Earl to develop the area's mineral wealth by continuing railway construction southwards. The result was the incorporation on 21 July 1845 of the Whitehaven & Furness Junction Railway, with a capital of £350,000, authorised to build a line virtually level throughout, going through St Bees and then hugging the coastline as far as Seascale, where it turned slightly inland to run parallel with the shore and under the slopes of 1,969 ft Black Combe. From a point near Borwick Rails harbour it was intended to cut straight across the Duddon estuary to join the Furness at Dunnerholme, between Ireleth and Kirkby. The following year the company promoted its Lancashire Extension Railway, commencing at Dalton and passing through Ulverston before linking up with a projected branch of the 'little' North Western Railway near Carnforth. Using only 4 miles of Furness tracks, this would have created a useful through route from West Cumberland to the West Riding of Yorkshire, but the scheme was thrown out on standing orders. In the slump following the collapse of the Railway Mania, Lonsdale was advised not to proceed with the Whitehaven & Furness Junction, but decided to go ahead on a modified route eliminating the expensive 1¼ mile viaduct across the Duddon. Authorised on 14 August 1848, this left the line as originally proposed near Kirksanton and swung north-eastwards to run along the west side of the Duddon which was crossed at a much narrower point near Foxfield. It then made an inverted 'Y' junction with the Furness's Broughton extension just under a mile from the terminus.

Work at the Whitehaven end had begun early the previous year, services over the first section south to Ravenglass commencing on 21 July 1849 in connection with a coach service to Broughton. The line was extended to Bootle on 8

July 1850 and opened throughout on 1 November, an occasion of great celebration. At the formal ceremonies three days earlier a special train conveying Lonsdale and the West Cumberland gentry was met at Broughton by another special which had on board Burlington and his entourage. A 'pretty triumphal arch of evergreens' erected in front of the station and 'a sumptuous dinner' helped to symbolise this union between Furness and Cumberland with all its advantages and imperfections. Although an important communications link had been completed, the Whitehaven & Furness Junction at 33¾ miles was a long and straggling single line encountering remarkably few settlements or sources of traffic. Further, the decision to abandon the direct route across the Duddon estuary in favour of a circuitous deviation with a reversal at remote Broughton had added some 8 miles to a Barrow–Whitehaven journey, creating what was to be a permanent legacy of inconvenience and delay.

There were no major engineering works on the line apart from timber viaducts over the Rivers Calder, Irt, Mite, Esk and Duddon, this last being a 592 yd trestle of fifty spans known locally as the 'Spile Bridge'. Intermediate stations were provided at St Bees, Nethertown, Braystones, Sellafield, Seascale, Drigg, Ravenglass, Eskmeals, Bootle, Whitbeck

Duddon viaduct (*Illustrated London News*)

Crossing, Silecroft, Kirksanton Crossing, Holborn Hill and Under Hill, with Green Road being added in 1853. Following the success of the Furness, attempts were made to cater for tourists by running coach and chaise services from Seascale and Drigg stations to Ennerdale Water and Wastwater. The Scawfell Hotel was opened alongside the station at Seascale with the same aim in mind and an hotel company formed at St Bees in 1847, but the area was just too far away from the main centres of population to attract visitors in any numbers. The line for the time being lapsed into an impoverished and poorly maintained state, paying no dividend until 1858 and carrying a few mainly mixed trains which are reputed to have made long pauses at several of the smaller stations while the staff and crew indulged in the traditional Cumbrian sport of cockfighting. *Bradshaw's Shareholders' Manual* noted in 1855 that at under £10 per mile the company was producing less than any other line in England or Scotland. It nevertheless managed to produce a rule book containing no less than 217 general and 17 specific regulations, including such gems as 'every servant must appear on duty clean' and 'guards are forbidden to pass over the tops of the carriages while the train is in motion—they must on no account allow passengers to ride on the roofs of the carriages'.

COMPLETING THE COASTAL CHAIN

A prime weakness of the Whitehaven line in terms of the Furness region was that it pointed in the wrong direction. The main need was for a direct link with the expanding markets of Yorkshire, Lancashire, the Midlands and South Wales via a connection with the southern end of the Lancaster & Carlisle. Moves towards this end had started in 1846 when an Act of 27 July authorised an extension from the existing terminus at Crooklands to Ulverston (the previously sanctioned line to Lindal being abandoned). Involving some of the heaviest engineering works on the Cumbrian coast system, the route climbed for 1¾ miles on gradients of 1 in 97 and 1 in 103 through the 439 yd Lindal tunnel to a summit level almost 250 ft above sea-level, the highest point on the Furness main line. It then curved down to Ulverston, the even more precipitous descent including a mile at 1 in 80 and a further mile at 1 in 82. After Crooklands cutting had been completed in 1847 work on the extension was stopped on 1 June 1848 as a result of the depression, compensation of over £5,000 being awarded to the contractors, Fell & Jopling. Construction as far as Lindal was resumed the following year, although progress was extremely slow and it was not until 6 May 1851 that these additional 1¼ miles of single line were brought into use.

The initial impetus had clearly been lost, but was to be regained as a result of developments further east. By this time Ulverston was one of many towns regretting its previous hostility to the coming of railways, and was acutely aware that its continued dependence on the treacherous 'oversands' journey as 'the nearest and cheapest route to Lancaster' was outmoded. Several schemes were promoted for a link with the West Coast main line, great local enthusiasm and ringing of church bells greeting the successful incorporation on 24 July 1851 of the Ulverstone & Lancaster Railway (the final 'e' on Ulverston was archaic legal spelling). These moves also persuaded the Furness directors to complete their extension to the town, the contract for a single line on double-track formation being let in June 1851. The mile of line to a temporary terminus at Halfway House, Ulverston Road (later Lindal East) was opened on 27 May 1852, completion of the remaining 2 miles into Ulverston being delayed by labour problems as well as difficulties with the contractor. Some goods traffic was being handled by April 1854, opening for passengers finally taking place on 7 June.

The Furness deliberately chose to let an independent company build the 'missing link' east from Ulverston rather than construct this line itself, although close ties were maintained with the new concern through the appointment of James Ramsden as its secretary. The reason for this cautious approach was the serious constructional problems posed by the only practicable route straight across the Leven and Kent estuaries. Many of the difficulties that lay ahead were portended by clauses in the incorporation Act, which provided for a line descending from a junction with the Furness at the west side of Ulverston, crossing the canal and spanning the Leven at a point just north of Plumpton Bight. It then ran close to the Cavendish family seat at Holker Hall, the Earl of Burlington as a director of the company obtaining special provisions protecting the amenities of his residence. After passing just north of Humphrey Head, the line continued alongside the Kent estuary through Grange-over-Sands before going across the river to Arnside and joining the Lancaster & Carlisle at Carnforth. The viaducts over the Leven and Kent were required to have a clear breadth of waterway of at least 1,400 ft for the free scour of the tides, spans with minimum dimensions of 20 ft in length and 10 ft headway, and an opening span or drawbridge of at least 36 ft. The company was responsible for providing a footpath across the Leven estuary on the landward side of the viaduct, for use on payment of ½d, and had to keep open the navigable channel to the Ulverston Canal entrance. Indicative of the coming transport revolution, it also had to make an annual payment of £20 to the 'Guide for Travellers across the Leven Estuary' in lieu of diminished fees. On the credit side the company was allowed to sell sizeable amounts of marshland which would be reclaimed during construction. The authorised capital for the 19½ mile single line was £220,000 and, apart from Burlington, the directors included the Duke of Buccleuch, Joseph Paxton – fresh from his triumphs at the Crystal Palace – and the Brogden brothers of Manchester who were the principal promoters.

The Brogdens had purchased the Ulverston Canal in 1850 and were also developing ore-mining at Stainton, near Dalton. They thus had a direct interest in creating a railway 'oversands', but at first were hampered by disappointing financial support, labour shortages and problems of land purchases, prices in one case being inflated to as much as £190 per acre. James Brunlees, then only thirty-seven, was appointed engineer in succession to McClean and Stileman who had surveyed the route. Later famous for his work on the Mont Cenis and Mersey railways and the original Channel Tunnel project, Brunlees had just carried out some reclamation on Lough Foyle for the Londonderry & Coleraine Railway and it was thought this experience would be invaluable in tackling the challenge presented by the Morecambe Bay estuaries. At first efforts were concentrated on linking the Furness with the Ulverston Canal, but by

January 1855 Brunlees was able to describe to a meeting of the Institution of Civil Engineers how he was overcoming the difficulties of the route. Embankments were being thrust out into the two major estuaries and weirs constructed at right angles to these banks and parallel with the coastline. The theory behind this operation was to force the rivers into fixed channels, thus inducing the tidal scour and current to build up sand banks on either side. The sands inland of the weirs would silt up high enough for reclaiming and those on the seaward side would provide material for building the embankments, which were faced with limestone as a protection. The theory frequently broke down in bad weather, a retreating high tide destroying in a single night the labour of many weeks.

By the end of 1855 work on the long embankments was largely complete and construction of foundations for the viaducts had begun. After Brunlees had sunk borings to a depth of up to 70 ft without finding rock, he made civil engineering history by introducing a novel form of pile using high-pressure jets of water to force the intervening sand upwards. This paved the way for Messrs W. & J. Galloway of Manchester, contractors for the viaducts, to commence work on the superstructures, that over the Leven being started on 1 April 1856 with the Kent crossing following suit on 21 October. With respective lengths of 2,400 ft and 1,300 ft, these were major undertakings which reduced the Brogdens to severe financial straits, only eased by Buccleuch and Burlington agreeing to advance £50,000 to assist completion.

Opening of the line was twice delayed by ships colliding with Leven viaduct, but ultimately goods services commenced on 10 August 1857 and passenger traffic on 26 August. There were initially three trains a day each way, the company owning some rolling stock but hiring locomotives from the Furness. Intermediate stations were at Cark-in-Cartmel (later Cark & Cartmel), Kents Bank (closed from March 1858 to May 1859), Grange and Silverdale, with a temporary structure at Arnside opening in 1858 and being replaced by permanent buildings the following year. At Ulverston the authorised terminus of the Furness extension from Crooklands was at too high a level to allow through running on to the Carnforth line. Temporary buildings were erected at this terminus and, after being blown down during a gale on 1 January 1855, were replaced by a permanent structure which apparently handled all passenger trains, those to and from Carnforth reversing in or out of the station until through platforms on the lower level were brought into use shortly after the opening of the Ulverstone & Lancaster. The 'high level' terminus then became the goods depot for the town.

Three months prior to completion of the route, twelve 'young men' had been drowned while crossing the sands. It is thus understandable that the line was seen as heralding a new era, the dry land distance from Ulverston to Lancaster being reduced from 34 miles to less than 25. Economic changes were quickly felt along its whole length, a typical development being at Cark where the first livestock market was opened in February 1858. Local agriculture benefited from the 7 miles of sea embankments which protected 20,000 acres of hitherto waste land. On the negative side, the Ulverston Canal was doomed, Sandside lost its role as a port and the Fleetwood–Piel Pier sailings were henceforth on a summer-only basis. They had been superseded by what was proudly termed 'a new and delightful route to the far-famed ruins of Furness Abbey and the Cumberland Lakes District'.

This route completed a chain of railways stretching right round the Cumbrian coast, although one involving reversal at both Furness Abbey and Broughton. To overcome this drawback two 'Expedition Curves' were opened on 1 August 1858, the more southerly being the curve north of Millwood between Dalton and Park (later Goldmire) Junctions. The second spur formed a direct connection with the Whitehaven & Furness Junction by diverging north-westwards from the Furness at Foxfield, where a new station built by the two companies was opened on the same date. Broughton was thus bypassed, the original terminus being closed on 1 June 1859 and replaced by a through station in readiness for the opening of the Coniston Railway (see Chapter VII). It was for a brief period the meeting point of three companies, an agreement of 1 January 1862 formalising the basis on which it was used by the Whitehaven & Furness Junction. The same agreement covered Foxfield, and the connecting line between the two stations, thus suggesting the original approach into Broughton from the Whitehaven direction may have been disused by this date.

Other changes during this period included enlargement and rebuilding of Barrow terminus in stone during 1856; opening of 'conditional stop' stations at Roose Gate (about 1850), Ireleth Gate (April 1851; closed October 1857) and Dunnerholm Gate; and, on the Whitehaven line, closure of Kirksanton Crossing and Whitbeck Crossing (September 1857) and Under Hill (1 January 1860). Doubling of much of the Furness system was also completed: from Roose Junction to Barrow in 1854; from Crooklands to Lindal, including widening of Lindal tunnel, in 1857; and on to Ulverston the following year.

Opening of the Ulverstone & Lancaster, and the various associated improvements, represented the end of the first phase of railway expansion in the region, a relatively straightforward story of somewhat hesitant growth in order to create adequate outlets for the mineral riches of the area. The next phase was infinitely more complex and dynamic, involving a whole series of interrelated factors which were to alter both the Furness Railway and its region out of all recognition. The remaining sections of this chapter deal first with the policies and events relative to this transformation and ultimate decline, and then with the story of developments on the ground, firstly within Barrow and then on the lines on either side of what became the company's metropolis.

THE TAIL THAT WAGGED THE DOG

The third quarter of the nineteenth century brought an economic revolution to Furness. Discoveries of vast deposits of iron ore were instrumental in turning Barrow from village into boom town and creating one of the most impressive dock complexes in the country. The Furness Railway ceased to be primarily a small mineral line and vied with the London & North Western as the largest system in the Lake Counties, at the same time having its territorial limits firmly defined by its more powerful neighbour. The catalyst for this remarkable change was a discovery made in 1850 by H. W. Schneider, a speculator and dealer in metalliferous ores who had been prospecting in the district for some time. At Park, north-west of Dalton alongside the Broughton line, he found what proved to be the second largest haematite deposit in British history, extending to some 9 million tons. By 1856 it was producing 120,000 tons per annum; in the same year some 445,000 tons of ore was shipped from Barrow, almost all of it conveyed over the Furness which paid an 8 per cent dividend and was for its size one of the most successful lines of the period.

With a view to providing additional outlets for this ore in County Durham and Cleveland, Furness interests took a leading role in promoting the South Durham & Lancashire Union Railway, which as noted in Chapter II was incorporated in 1857 and opened from Tebay to Barnard Castle in 1861. The subscribers included Schneider, as well as Buccleuch and Burlington who each put up £5,000. In the event the main traffic flow proved to be in the reverse direction, following a decision by Schneider and Robert Hannay to open an ironworks at Barrow, the first two furnaces coming into blast during 1859. No suitable coal was available locally, and so it was necessary to transport hard-structured coke 130 miles from ovens in South Durham, the extra cost being counterbalanced by the richness of the Furness ores. These developments, together with growth of the Bessemer process of steel-making for which the local haematite was ideally suited, brought much extra traffic to the Ulverstone & Lancaster. A proposal to purchase this line was accordingly approved by Furness shareholders on 21 January 1862, actual vesting on a 6 per cent basis taking place on 26 May under provisions of an Act of 12 July 1858. The Ulverston Canal was bought at the same time for £22,000, this transaction being authorised by an Act of 30 June 1862. A further acquisition to receive Parliamentary sanction a few days later, on 7 July, was the Coniston Railway (see Chapter VII).

A third railway amalgamation quickly followed, resulting from a chain of events starting in 1864 when the Whitehaven & Furness Junction agreed to participate in construction of a line from Egremont to Sellafield, thus providing a new southern outlet for West Cumberland ore. A second factor bringing change to this company's ailing fortunes was the discovery at Hodbarrow, on the north side of the Duddon estuary, of a deposit of haematite which was to prove the largest in the world until the opening up of the Lake Superior deposits in Canada later in the century. These two developments focused attention on the inadequacies of the existing route to the south between Holborn Hill (later Millom) and Ulverston, the distance by rail being over 17 miles compared with the 7 miles of a straight-flying crow. James Brunlees was engaged to report on the feasibility of a direct line across the Duddon to Park, the Furness offering tentative support to these proposals. The situation changed in October 1864 when the Whitehaven company announced its intention to extend this route to Lindal, a move which came as a severe blow to the Furness at a time when it was just embarking on a massive docks project at Barrow for it would clearly increase the isolation of the town. It countered with its own Bill for a direct line from Barrow via Sandscale Haws and across the Duddon to Hodbarrow, but this interfered with access to Borwick Rails harbour and was thrown out in favour of the Whitehaven company's scheme, which was sanctioned on 29 June 1865. The Furness was now left with little option but to acquire the Whitehaven line and thus become very much a case of the tail wagging the dog, this latest merger meaning that in only four years from 1862 amalgamations had increased the company's route mileage from 23 to $64\frac{1}{2}$. Terms for purchase on an 8 per cent basis were authorised by an Act of 16 July 1866 to take effect from 1 July of the previous year. W. B. Kendall, a civil engineer with the Furness, undoubtedly reflected local opinion when he noted that this was 'a preposterous price, having regard to all the circumstances'.

Kendall was also able to comment that the London & North Western had his company 'in the nut-crackers', for in 1866 it absorbed the Whitehaven Junction and thus, as a result of its 1859 lease of the Lancaster & Carlisle, now controlled both ends of the Furness system. This control was made more absolute through skilful opposition to two further lines authorised during this period. The first of these was initiated by the Midland, which was finding that expansion of its steamer services from Morecambe was being hampered by tidal difficulties and was also keen to get better access to the Lake District. Agreement was thus reached on 1 October 1862 that, if the Furness would provide half the capital for a connecting line from Wennington on the 'little' North Western to Carnforth, then the Midland would put up the other half and transfer its Isle of Man and Belfast traffic from Morecambe to Piel Pier and Barrow. The agreement, which prevented the Midland from constructing any railways west of the Lancaster & Carlisle, also provided for that company to work the new line and for an exchange of running powers, to Leeds and Bradford on the one hand and to Barrow, Piel and Coniston on the other. The joint line offered the Furness a more direct route for its considerable ore traffic with the West Riding of Yorkshire, a fact not unnoticed by the London & North Western which would lose its share of these workings between Carnforth and Lancaster. As a result of 'vigorous opposition' it secured a clause in the authorising Act of 22 June 1863 to the effect that it would enjoy the same running powers over the Furness as the Midland. The latter company then became decidedly cool over the Wennington–Carnforth link, attempting to put off participation and only agreeing to proceed as a result of strong pressure from Barrow. The London & North Western in turn tried to talk the Furness into abandoning the project, but it was not to be swayed and construction went ahead.

The second new line stemmed from the nominally independent promotion in 1864 of the Furness & Yorkshire Union Railway, running from Arnside to Kirkby Lonsdale on the Clapham–Low Gill route. It formed part of a cross-country project involving other proposed lines extending eastwards from Sedbergh to the North Eastern via Garsdale and Wensleydale. The London & North Western at first opposed the Bill, but by agreement of 16 May 1865 it was resolved that the Furness should take over the scheme which would extend eastwards only as far as a connection with the West Coast main line at Hincaster Junction, $3\frac{3}{4}$ miles south of Oxenholme, thus offering a much shorter route for the coke trains from South Durham than that via Carnforth. The agreement also gave the Furness running powers to Tebay, the London & North Western being granted reciprocal powers to Arnside and at the same time undertaking not to indulge in new construction in this area west of its existing main line. The

Furness and Lancaster & Carlisle Union Railway was accordingly incorporated on 5 July 1865, but dissolved by a further Act of 20 June 1867 which conferred the powers on the Furness company. This time the boot was on the other foot, the Furness attempting abandonment which was successfully opposed by the London & North Western as well as Kendal and Durham coke interests. As noted later in this chapter, these two lines were respectively completed in 1867 and 1876.

With the boundaries of its territory thus determined, the Furness was left in peace by the London & North Western and other larger companies to exploit and develop its own district. This it did to some purpose, going far beyond the activities normally associated with a railway company. Its driving aim was nothing less than an attempt to make Barrow an international trading port by expanding seawards and at the same time developing numerous ancillary enterprises in the town. The company paid its first 10 per cent dividend in 1864 at a time when most railway shareholders only received 4 per cent. The previous year 600,000 tons of ore were conveyed, two-thirds of which was exported through Barrow, as well as some 250,000 tons of coal, coke and pig iron. With expansion taking place on all fronts it was no longer possible for James Ramsden to run the company virtually single-handed on autocratic lines. His powers were more clearly defined in 1865 when he was made managing director, the only such appointment on a major English railway in the nineteenth century. Eight years earlier it had been decided to provide him with a house worthy of his position at a cost 'not exceeding £2,000'. This was duly built at Abbots Wood, overlooking Furness Abbey station, where a special siding housed the 'General Manager's Saloon' in which Ramsden travelled daily to and from Barrow. He was knighted in 1872.

Furness Railway affairs were at their zenith in the early 1870s, with haematite prices booming and the various Barrow developments coming to fruition. Ironworks had been opened at several points along the main line, meaning that the primary role of the company was now to convey ore for smelting rather than shipment through Barrow. In 1873 total minerals carried soared to over 3½ million tons, traffic receipts were £478,000, gross profit £230,000 and a 9½ per cent dividend was declared, the investment value of the company and its associated enterprises being close on £6½ million. Yet within only a few years more chilly economic winds were blowing. The national slump of the mid 1870s caused a catastrophic drop in ore prices which affected the local economy so drastically that sale of the Furness to the Midland was seriously considered in 1875. By the end of the decade development of the Gilchrist Thomas method of steel-making had ended dependence on haematite, and it was also clear that the local reserves of ore, apart from those at Hodbarrow, were being worked out. In 1882, 2,132 vessels entered the port of Barrow and local ore production totalled 1,408,000 tons, both peak figures which were not to be equalled. Thereafter it was a story of gradual economic decline, with railway expansion in the region virtually at an end, as it became all too apparent that the attempt to create a new industrial centre of world importance based on Barrow had failed. The town was just too far away from the manufacturing centres of Lancashire and Yorkshire to become a great port for general commerce, its position being further undermined by construction of the Manchester Ship Canal. The shareholders became increasingly bitter and noisy, typical of this period being the Annual Meeting of 1891 when the dividend touched a new 'low' of 1½ per cent and a motion was put down that Ramsden should retire.

A CHANGE OF DIRECTION

Decline of its staple haematite traffic forced the Furness to consider ways of increasing revenue from passenger services. These had hitherto not really been taken seriously; in 1870 only one-fifth of receipts came from this source and the *Northern Echo* noted: 'The number of trains running daily are reduced to such a minimum as to leave ample time for reflection and meditation after the dispatch of business at any town on their route.' The tourist potential of a railway skirting the Lake District and running virtually alongside the sea for much of its length had long been recognised, as shown by the early Fleetwood–Piel steamers and connecting trains, but the phenomenal growth of mineral traffic pushed into the background any ideas of development in this field. There was a flurry of activity in the late 1860s with the building of the Windermere Lake Side branch (Chapter VII) and the planned development of Grange as a small resort, and this trend gained momentum in the latter part of the nineteenth century as instanced by the unsuccessful attempt to create an 'Eastbourne of the North' at Seascale. A major stimulus to such changes followed the death of Sir James Ramsden in 1896 and the appointment of Alfred Aslett, previously secretary and general manager of the Cambrian Railways, as his successor. Within three years a 12 per cent increase in passenger traffic had been achieved, strenuous efforts being made to attract custom by introduction of much-needed new rolling stock (including some electrically lit corridor coaches with a patent system which automatically discharged an aromatic disinfectant into the lavatory compartments every time the doors were opened or closed!), combined road/rail/steamer services (see Chapter VIII), an impressive range of cheap-fare facilities, and pace-setting publicity devices such as full-colour posters, pamphlets, postcards and guidebooks. (The ultimate was the publication in 1908 of *Voyages circulaires à itinéraires fixes dans la Région des Lacs de l'Angleterre*.) Station gardens were made to look as attractive as possible with nasturtiums, zinnias, geraniums, sunflowers and dahlias being grown on the platforms. No detail was overlooked, as shown at Furness Abbey where the signal posts and backs of the signal arms together with squared and finial-capped telegraph posts were painted green to harmonise with the surroundings. Aslett's enthusiasm even went as far as the purchase of High Cocken, the former residence on the outskirts of Barrow of the eighteenth-century portrait painter George Romney, which was turned into a Romney museum, a typically Edwardian-style refreshment pavilion with dome and flagpole being erected in the grounds.

Fostering of tourism by the Furness, helped by the rise of a holiday-making middle-class, reached its greatest heights in the golden years of the Edwardian age and then came to an abrupt halt on the outbreak of World War I. It had perhaps tended to present a rosier image than was actually the case. In 1856 the railway had been a mineral line conveying less than

200,000 passengers and yet paying a dividend of 8 per cent; in 1913 there were well over 4 million passengers, but the dividend was only 2½ per cent and the following year it shrank to a mere 1 per cent. When in 1901 the Midland took one of its periodic looks at the company with a view to amalgamation, it concluded that financially it had poor prospects – the capital account was overdrawn by £152,000 and most of the track needed strengthening. The Furness in fact managed to retain its independence, homespun nature and distinctive 'Indian red' locomotive livery up to the Grouping in 1923, when its leading directors were descendants of men who had founded the line, a Cavendish remaining chairman assisted by the son of James Ramsden. The Cavendish motto, *Cavendo Tutus*, loosely translated as 'Achievement through Caution', was used by the company to the last. During the succeeding decades of continuing decline there was caution but little achievement, the LMS and later British Railways understandably showing a lack of enthusiasm to develop the region. The Furness Railway, despite its occasional misjudgement of priorities, had served its district well and its demise was locally regarded as a great loss.

BARROW: THE 'ENGLISH CHICAGO'

The almost patriarchal image of the Furness was in considerable measure due to its role in stimulating the growth of Barrow on a scale that has few parallels in mid-Victorian history in so isolated a location. In 1854 the company invested £7,000 in purchasing the 160 acre Hindpool Estate, on the north-west side of the existing village, and plans were drawn up by Ramsden for a new town on this site with wide streets, extensive wharfage along the Barrow Channel and spacious sites for new industry. Development along these lines began to take place following the 1859 opening of Hindpool ironworks, connected to the existing railway terminus at Rabbit Hill by a tramway. This was incorporated into a 2½ mile branch, authorised on 30 June 1862 and completed in 1864, which extended beyond the ironworks through Ormsgill to Hawcoat sandstone quarry and provided the means of transporting vast amounts of stone for the town's building programme. The

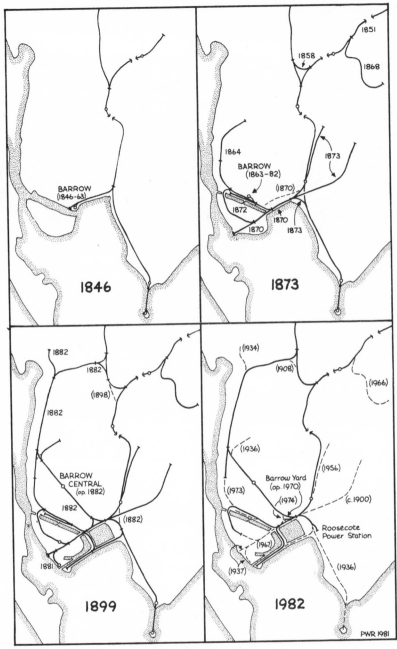

Map 4. Barrow: Chronological diagrams

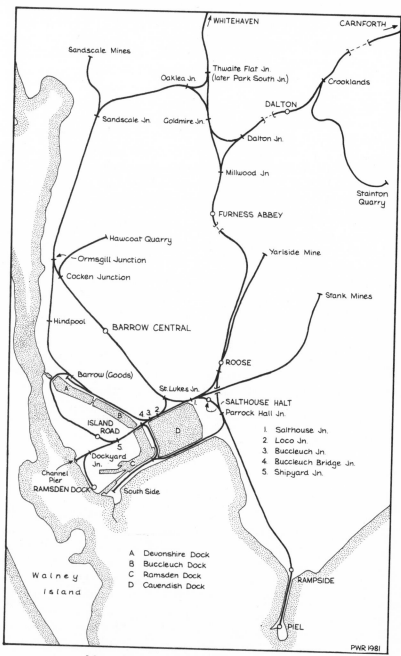

Map 5. Barrow: Maximum development

Furness at this stage ceased to be purely a railway company and became the *de facto* government of Barrow, building a church, town and market halls, police offices, gasworks and waterworks, schools, mechanics' institute and houses facing on to streets laid out on a gridiron pattern. Its transport monopoly meant it had a high degree of control over the local economy which was exercised to the extent that the distinction between railway and urban affairs became blurred, as shown by the new Barrow Corporation deciding to hold its meetings in the railway offices until the town hall was completed. Major expansion stemmed from the establishment in 1864 of a steelworks adjoining the ironworks at Hindpool, the two enterprises merging to form a new company with a capital of £1 million, much of this sum being put up by Furness Railway interests. Specialising in steel-rail production, it declared an unprecedented 30 per cent dividend in 1867. The population of Barrow increased from 3,135 in 1861 to 8,176 only four years later, the town being dubbed the 'English Chicago' because of its rapid growth, industrial boom and general lawlessness.

By this time the Furness directors had grasped the limitations stemming from lack of an industrial hinterland and realised that hopes of attracting additional traffic lay seawards. J. R. McClean, the company's engineer, conceived an audacious plan to produce two of the largest dock basins in the history of British port construction by enclosing the channel between Barrow Island and the mainland in its

---

FURNESS LANDMARKS

Top: Ex Furness Railway 4–4–0 No 10186 poses against the distinctive backcloth of Barrow Central's overall roof, destroyed by enemy action in 1941. *(H. C. Casserley) Middle:* An 1890s view of the goods lines running up to Hindpool from Barrow Yard, with the steam cornmill on the left. In the foreground is Furness Railway 0–4–0 No 14 and two 'Sharpie' 0–6–0s. *(K. J. Norman collection) Bottom:* The now-demolished Beela viaduct on the Arnside–Hincaster Junction line is crossed by Jubilee No 45712 *Victory* with empty coaching stock of a school excursion in July 1960. *(Derek Cross)*

entirety. Encouraged by the extra revenue which would stem from the decision of the Midland to transfer most of its Irish traffic from Morecambe, the Furness Railway & Barrow Harbour Act was duly obtained on 22 June 1863. This vested the harbour in the company and authorised raising £137,000 of additional capital towards construction of the 32½ acre Devonshire Dock and 31 acre Buccleuch Dock, with a combined wharfage of 1½ miles, as well as a timber pond. In the same year the company acquired Barrow Island, thus gaining valuable space for future warehouses, shipyards and timber yards.

The southern end of Barrow Channel was enclosed by a long embankment stretching south-westwards from Salthouse, enabling land to be reclaimed alongside the 1846 station and utilised for workshop extensions. The original terminus was converted into an engine shed and the line taken round the outside of the enlarged works to a new Strand station, opened on 29 April 1863 and described as 'light, airy and spacious'. Its twin-arched entrance faced St George's Square, where the Furness Railway headquarters with its central sandstone tower was built in 1866. Improved freight and warehousing facilities were provided by the establishment of Barrow Yard, situated close to Devonshire Dock which was completed at a cost of £133,000 by Messrs Brassey and Field and opened with enormous ceremony on 19 September 1867 before a crowd of 10,000 people. The celebrations commenced with a procession headed by three brass bands arriving at a dock full of specially decorated ships and ended with large-scale illuminations and the igniting of a huge bonfire by means of 120 gallons of gas

---

FURNESS STATIONS

Top: Ulverston, with its richly decorated roofwork and tower, built in 1873 when the affairs of the Furness Railway were at their zenith. The unusual platform arrangement was to permit easy exchange of passengers between the main line and Lake Side branch trains. (*K. J. Norman collection*) *Bottom:* Grange-over-Sands, arguably the best small station surviving in Cumbria. (*Peter W. Robinson*)

tar, 36 gallons of crude petroleum, 20 gallons of inflammable spirits and two gallons of naptha! The railway carriage shed was transformed into a vast banqueting hall for 1,350 diners; it was here that W. E. Gladstone, the chief guest, made his oft-quoted remark: 'Some day Barrow will become a Liverpool. Let it become a Liverpool if it will and can, the old Liverpool will be none the worse, but better for it.' On the other hand, *Punch* reported the event by lamenting that Barrow had:

> ...swelled almost within the memory of the youngest inhabitant from the quiet coast-nest of some five-score fishermen, into the busy, bustling, blazing, money-making, money-spending, roaring, tearing, swearing, steaming, sweltering seat of twenty thousand iron workers, and the crime and culture, dirt and disease, the hard-working and hard-drinking, the death and life, the money and misery they bring along with them.

No doubt some of the visiting dignitaries stayed at the Furness Abbey Hotel, which the previous year had been brought under direct management of the company, enlarged and connected to the station by a covered approach. In the days long before Trade Descriptions Acts, it was boldly advertised as being 'in the centre of Lakeland'! Earlier in 1867, following the opening of the Wennington–Carnforth line, the Midland's Isle of Man steamer services were transferred on 1 July to Piel Pier, which was rebuilt to allow trains to go alongside the boats. They were joined by the Belfast sailings on 2 September, both routes being operated by vessels owned by the Furness, Midland and Messrs James Little & Co in equal shares, the combine being known as the Barrow Steam Navigation Company.

Another development of 1867 saw Barrow gain borough status, its first mayor perhaps inevitably being James Ramsden, who seemed to take to heart the town's motto of *Semper Sursum* – ever upwards. Under his guidance it went through a period of almost uncontrollable expansion and was described by the Bishop of Carlisle as 'one of the miracles of our time'. The population soared to 18,911 in 1871, an estimated 35,000 just three years later and reached 47,259 in 1881, the Furness helping to accommodate this influx by erecting large areas of working-class housing on Barrow Island. Immigrants poured in from London, Staffordshire, Cornwall and Cheshire, houses were bought as soon as the foundations were laid and the beds in lodging houses were never cool. Enterprises of this period backed directly by the Furness board or its directors included the important Barrow Iron Shipbuilding Company, the Barrow and Calcutta Jute Company and the Barrow Steam Corn Mills Company, all forming part of the concept of making the town an international trading centre. Continuing to set the pace was the Haematite Iron & Steel Company, which by the early 1870s was the largest Bessemer plant in the world, consuming 450,000 tons of coal and coke per annum and producing 3,000 tons of rails per week, much of this output going to the USA and Canada.

In order to improve the approach to Strand station, a deviation of the main line was made in 1870 from a point south of Roose Junction across the new Salthouse–Barrow Island embankment. It then ran alongside Buccleuch Dock, inaugurated on 14 February 1873 and incorporating the original Furness Railway pier in its east wall. At the same time an extension was built from Buccleuch Junction to a steamer pier in Walney Channel, this being joined at Shipyard Junction by a line completed in 1872 which ran from Barrow Yard across the north end of Devonshire Dock and along the full length of Barrow Island so as to serve various timber yards.

Strand station was enlarged in 1873 to cope with rapidly expanding traffic, but hardly had this been completed when the decision was made to build a new central station at the point where the main road out of the town crossed a projected Barrow Loop. Authorised on 18 July 1872, this loop extended from Salthouse Junction to the Hawcoat branch and was intended to ease congestion on the dockside lines. Work was delayed by the recession, and when finally commenced it was decided to form a through route to the north by reviving the Park Loop, a line from Hindpool to Park which formed part of the company's abortive 1865 Duddon viaduct project. Acts of 27 June 1876 and 21 July 1879 sanctioned these arrangements, whereby a 5¼ mile loop extended from Salthouse Junction to

Thwaite Flat Junction, approached by an extremely sharp curve of only 11 chains radius. It bisected the Hawcoat branch which now diverged from sidings alongside the new line at Cocken Junction, leaving the remaining part of the branch from Barrow Yard to join the loop at Ormsgill Junction. Two spurs were also constructed, one from St Lukes Junction to Buccleuch Junction (later combined with and renamed Loco Junction) to allow through running between the central station and docks lines, and the other at the north end of the loop between Oaklea and Goldmire (formerly Park) Junctions so that trains from Carnforth could approach Hindpool works and the new station in either direction. All these lines were opened on 1 June 1882 when the former terminus (known as Barrow Town from June 1881) was closed and passenger services transferred to Barrow Central, a curiously rustic structure for an industrial town with its distinctive timber-framing, high ridge-and-furrow roof and deep concave awning over the outside platform. Joseph Fisher, writing in 1891, commented that it was 'situated in a bleak and cold position, and is not quite satisfactory as regards warmth and comfort in the wild and windy weather often experienced in the district during the winter months'. Virtually all Carnforth–Whitehaven passenger trains now followed this new route through Barrow, giving the crow flying its 7 straight miles between Millom and Ulverston an even greater advantage as the rail distance was increased to almost 25 miles!

Another loop planned in the early 1870s to relieve traffic congestion extended from Barrow through Gleaston and Urswick to a junction with the main line east of Lindal. During its parliamentary passage this shrank to a 2 mile single-track branch from Salthouse Junction to Stank Mines, authorised on 18 July 1872 and opened the following year. Other mineral branches of this era included one extending for $1\frac{3}{4}$ miles from Crooklands to Stainton quarry, providing limestone for Hindpool iron and steelworks, which was sanctioned on 16 July 1866 and brought into use in February 1868. In the same year the Furness approved construction of a siding from Roose to provide exchange facilities with an experimental horse-worked monorail from mines at Yarlside, which was built in 1868 by John Barraclough Fell, inventor of the famous 'Fell centre rail' and earlier a contractor of the Whitehaven & Furness Junction as well as a partner with John Abel Smith. After two years it was replaced by an equally experimental 8in gauge system, which in turn gave way in 1873 to a conventional standard-gauge line. A $\frac{1}{4}$ mile branch from Sandscale Junction, a mile west of that at Oaklea, to Sandscale Mine was opened on 2 October 1882.

Despite the economic difficulties of the 1870s, expansion of the docks continued following authorisation on 18 July 1872 of the 67 acre Ramsden Dock and the even more massive 146 acre Cavendish Dock, both sited on the south side of the Salthouse–Barrow Island embankment. Ramsden Dock, inaugurated on 24 March 1879, was connected to Buccleuch Dock by a passageway through this embankment, the Walney Channel Pier line being carried across the gap by an 80 ft span swing bridge (replaced by a Scherzer rolling lift bridge with interlaced tracks on 12 October 1907). This carried passenger traffic from 1 June 1881 with the opening of a short branch from Dockyard Junction to a new Ramsden Dock station close to deep-water steamer berths. The Isle of Man boats were transferred here from Piel on the same date, the Belfast ships following suit in October, although the station with its long covered platform and short bay was not completed until 1885. As a result Piel Pier fell into decay and was finally removed in

Ramsden Dock Station, Barrow-in-Furness.

Barrow Ramsden Dock station

1891, a local service being instituted between Barrow and Piel using a direct curve between Salthouse and Parrock Hall Junctions which was opened in 1873 but did not receive Parliamentary·sanction until 21 July 1879. The original line from Roose Junction to Parrock Hall was then closed to all traffic on 27 March 1882. A new station at Roose was completed in 1875, and the intermediate station of Concle on the Piel branch was renamed Rampside in September 1869.

By the end of the 1880s the Furness had spent no less than £2,149,000 on docks covering an almost incredible 294 acres and only exceeded in size by those of London and Liverpool. The belated recognition that the port would not achieve world importance resulted in Cavendish Dock remaining·incomplete and becoming merely a feeder for its three neighbours, although a line was built alongside it from Parrock Hall to link up with a branch from Buccleuch Bridge Junction (altered in 1901 to commence at Loco Junction) to South Side sidings near the main entrance to Ramsden Dock. In order to reduce its liabilities during the difficult closing years of the nineteenth century the company allowed control of the iron- and steelworks to pass to outside interests and disposed of its more embarrassing industrial assets such as the jute works and steam corn mill. The shipyard was taken over by Vickers Sons & Co in 1896, from which date Barrow was dependent on shipbuilding rather than the iron trade. A station was opened at Island Road, near Shipyard Junction, on 1 May 1899 to handle unadvertised trains carrying workmen to and from Vickers.

In 1892 the confidence of the Furness was further undermined when the Midland decided to forsake Barrow in favour of a more conveniently sited port at Heysham, and accordingly gave three years' notice of termination of its share in the Barrow Steam Navigation Company partnership. In fact it was not until 1 September 1904 that Isle of Man and Belfast services began operating from Heysham, and even then the Midland agreed to buy out the shares of the other two partners and maintain limited sailings from Barrow, those to Belfast being reduced to three boats a week from 1 January 1907. As noted in Chapter VIII, the loss of traffic was to a considerable extent countered by a second Fleetwood–Barrow steamer service (the first had ceased about 1869). All regular boat services from Barrow ceased after the outbreak of World War I, resulting in closure of Ramsden Dock station which made its last appearance in the timetables in April 1915. It continued to handle occasional excursion traffic after the war, the approach lines from Dockyard Junction being officially closed on 8 December 1937 and the station demolished the following year.

By this time other little-used lines and connections had been abandoned, beginning with the spur between Millwood and Goldmire Junctions (part of the original 1846 route) on 12 December 1898 and followed by the adjoining curve linking Goldmire and Oaklea Junctions on 4 December 1908. The surviving Dalton Loop between Dalton Junction and Thwaite Flat Junction (combined with Park South Junction on 14 September 1890) was by this stage normally used solely by goods trains and market-day specials avoiding Barrow. The Stank Mines branch was reduced to a short siding in about 1900. Complete closure of the Piel line took place on 6 July 1936, apart from a short stub at the Salthouse end (extended in 1954 to serve the new Barrow power station at Roosecote). An earlier demise on this branch was Salthouse Halt Platform, which had been brought into use on 22 May 1920. Lesser casualties in this period were the direct connection between Ormsgill Junction and Hindpool (taken out 28 August 1933); the Sandscale Mine branch (closed 9 July 1934 after being disused from 1916); and the Cocken Junction access to the Hawcoat branch (closed 23 December 1936).

Air raids of May 1941 destroyed Barrow Central station, the blast shattering the 'glass cage' which had entombed *Coppernob*, one of the early copper-domed Furness locomotives, since shortly after its withdrawal in 1899. The engine was moved to Horwich Works for safe keeping and today is in the National Railway Museum at York, still bearing the scars of its wartime experience. Eighteen years elapsed before a new station, renamed Barrow-in-Furness, was completed, its materials including multicoloured rustic bricks, slate window sills and fascia over the front entrance and generous amounts of glass and polished hardwood. Other post-war renewals included relining of both Dalton and Furness Abbey tunnels, the latter work involving installation of interlaced track and a temporary signal-box. Services were withdrawn from Furness Abbey station on 25 September 1950, the greater part of the hotel here having been demolished following its earlier closure in May 1938 and subsequent use as a military barracks.

In 1966 the lift bridge over Buccleuch Dock passageway was declared unsafe, resulting in abandonment of all remaining lines on the north side of Ramsden Dock and closure on 3 July 1967 of Island Road station along with concurrent diversion to Central station of workmen's services to Grange and Millom (the official date of 7 October 1968 relates to substitute bus services). These workings had reached their peak in World War II when there were five trains, of ten or twelve coaches, each morning and evening. The other approach to Barrow Island via the north side of Devonshire Dock was cut back to Michaelson Road Crossing, the rails south of this point having been covered with tarmac for a royal visit! Further east, the Stainton branch was closed on 12 October 1966 and the Yarlside branch last used ten years earlier. As part of a rationalisation scheme, a new Barrow Yard was established in 1970 just off the St Lukes Junction–Loco Junction spur, removal of which took place in February 1974 when both the yard and the nearby running shed were connected directly to Salthouse Junction. Usage of the line between the old Barrow Yard (closed 31 December 1971) and Hindpool had declined following closure of the ironworks in 1963, and in 1973 it was largely lifted in order to improve road access to Barrow Island. The steelworks was served by means of a new connection on the site of the former Ormsgill Junction brought into use on 13 August. Thus, by 1974 all that remained of Barrow's once vast railway network was the main passenger line, the Dalton Loop, the lines radiating from Salthouse Junction to Roosecote power station, Barrow Yard, the south side of Ramsden Dock and Vickers Works via Devonshire Dock and Walney Ferry, and the branch into the steelworks from Ormsgill.

This left little scope for further cut-backs in the 1980s, the relatively modest changes that have occurred being noted in the postscript.

CARNFORTH TO ULVERSTON

Development outside Barrow during the peak years very much took second place but was far from being insignificant. At Carnforth a new and 'most commodious' station was built to coincide with completion of the Ulverstone & Lancaster in 1857. Major growth followed the opening in 1866 of an ironworks (closed 1929), sited in the 'V' of the Carlisle and Barrow lines, which with the parallel expansion of railway facilities caused the population to increase from 393 in 1861 to 1,091 in 1871 and 1,879 ten years later. The ironworks was well placed in relation to the transport facilities of the region, being able to receive ore from Furness and coke from South Durham via Tebay, and to dispatch its products direct to the West Riding by the Furness & Midland Joint. This $9\frac{3}{4}$ mile line from Wennington approached Carnforth by passing through the 1,230 yd Melling tunnel, crossing the old and new courses of the Lune on separate viaducts and then swinging south-westwards to follow the valley of the River Keer. It opened to freight on 10 April 1867 and passengers on 6 June, with intermediate stations at Melling, Arkholme and Borwick. A further station known as Carnforth (F&M) was provided at the junction with the Furness for use by the 'boat trains' to Piel and other through services, although the majority of workings were propelled into the main station. Here, as with the separate goods depot, the premises were jointly owned by the Furness and London & North Western, the Midland being admitted as tenant in its capacity as working company of the joint line. Direct running from the Wennington direction into the main station came about with authorisation on 21 July 1879 of the 'Carnforth curve', sited on the west side of the Lancaster–Carlisle line and thus giving an approach from the Midland well described by E. L. Ahrons as 'a sort of contortion after the manner of a partial logarithmetic spiral'. The curve was opened on 2 August 1880, as was a rebuilt joint station incorporating some fine company motifs in its ornamental ironwork. Carnforth (F&M) was closed on the same date, the practice now being for through services to stop at the east end of the new curve. The Midland engine would then take two or three coaches into Carnforth station, the main portion of the train travelling direct to Barrow in charge of a Furness locomotive. The 1880 station had a single through platform capable of holding two Furness trains, a situation that created operating difficulties and lasted until as late as 1939–40 when the LMS constructed a second platform on the down side. Additional traffic stemmed from diversion of Wennington–Lancaster–Morecambe services through Carnforth from 3 January 1966, but a counterbalancing setback was closure of the station's main-line platforms on 4 May 1970. Two years earlier Carnforth motive power depot was acquired by private interests to form Steamtown, a 'live-steam museum' which held its inaugural open day on 1 June 1969 and has since become a major enthusiasts' and visitor attraction in the North West.

Apart from its ironworks traffic and importance for the exchange of mails between a succession of night postal trains,

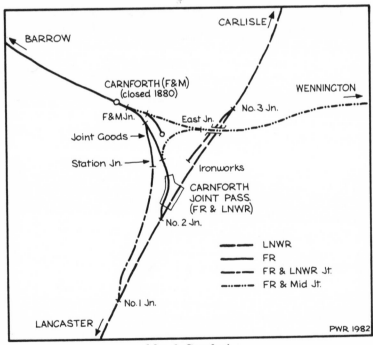

Map 6. Carnforth

Carnforth at one time saw much activity as the reversal point for coke trains from South Durham to Lindal and Barrow. These workings were diverted via the Hincaster Junction–Arnside cut-off on its completion but soon reverted to their original route. It was not until World War I, when traffic volume proved too much for the exchange sidings at Carnforth and there was a need for more efficient use of motive power, that the cut-off was again followed. There had earlier been problems with this 5$\frac{1}{4}$ mile single line, largely due to one George Wilson who felt that the route as originally proposed cut through the grounds of his seat at Dallam Tower 'in a Manner very objectionable and injurious'. He was a powerful enough figure to have several clauses included in the authorising Acts of 1865 and 1867 compelling diversion of part of the line on 'Arches and Pillars in order to obstruct view from Estate as little as possible', the erection of a weir across the River Beela and the building of a station close to the Tower at which at least one train per day would stop. This feudal intervention resulted in the two finest structures on the branch, the imposing twenty-six arch Beela viaduct (not to be confused with Belah on the Stainmore route) and the exquisitely proportioned station at Sandside with its deeply overhanging roof in the Swiss-chalet style. After a contract had been let in 1871, there were delays owing to a case in Chancery between Wilson and the Furness but opening ultimately took place on 26 June 1876. A second intermediate station was opened on 1 July 1890 at Heversham, situated on the steeply graded portion of the branch climbing some 200 ft from sea level at Sandside in only 2 miles. The regular passenger service, primarily operating between Grange and Kendal and known locally as the 'Kendal Tommy', ceased on 4 May 1942. Following withdrawal of the South Durham coke trains, the line was closed completely north of a quarry at Sandside on 9 September 1963, the remaining portion following suit on 31 January 1971.

The opening of the Furness & Midland Joint brought considerable benefits to Silverdale and Arnside, which were placed within three hours of the West Riding conurbation and developed as small resorts. The same change was even more marked at temperate Grange, where the Grange Hotel, promoted by a separate company formed by James Ramsden, was the largest in the region when opened in 1866. It attracted a clientele who undoubtedly would approve of the *Westmorland Gazette*'s description of the resort as 'not gay, not fast, not boisterous, nor overcrowded'. The Furness made a modest attempt at creating a Lancashire Riviera by laying out ornamental gardens and constructing a short length of promenade near the station, which was rebuilt in a pleasing style of architecture intentionally matching that of the hotel. Together with neighbouring Kents Bank, the growth of Grange was further accelerated by the coming of the hydropathic movement in the 1880s, the population increasing to over 1,200 compared with only 135 some thirty years earlier. Development of a different kind saw a siding being provided at Wraysholme as part of a World War I project for an airship factory at Flookburgh, a halt platform having earlier been erected for territorials using the nearby army camp.

Kent and Leven viaducts were renewed in the 1880s and completely rebuilt in the early years of World War I, prolonged exposure to salt water having caused serious deterioration of some of the cast-iron columns. As part of the doubling of the Carnforth–Ulverston line completed in 1866, they had been widened in 1863 when the Marine Department of the Board of Trade agreed to a fixed span being substituted for the original opening span on the Kent viaduct. This prevented sea-going boats reaching Milnthorpe and caused considerable controversy, only resolved when following a Chancery Court case the Furness agreed to build a stone jetty at Arnside and a connecting shore-side road. More involved measures were necessary to eliminate the opening span on Leven viaduct as the river at this time was used by boats plying to and from the small port of Greenodd. As part of the project for the Lake Side branch (see Chapter VII), which passed through this port, a short siding from the Ulverston Canal basin to a trailing connection with the down main line was concurrently authorised on 16 July 1866. The Furness undertook to convey traffic from the basin to Greenodd at special rates; the opening span was accordingly fixed in the same year, although it appears the siding was not brought into use until about 1869. It was extended on the opening of North Lonsdale ironworks alongside the canal in 1874, and then superseded by the 2 mile Bardsea branch under Acts of 27 June 1876 and 11 August 1881. Making an east-facing connection with the main line at Plumpton Junction and crossing the canal on a sliding bridge, the branch was double track as it formed the initial part of a proposed new route along the coast to Barrow which would have eliminated the expensive banking of freight trains in both directions up to Lindal. This laudable scheme failed to materialise and the line never in fact reached Bardsea, terminating a mile short of the village at a station near Conishead Priory Hydro. A service of two mixed trains each way from Ulverston commenced on 27 June 1883, an intermediate halt at North Lonsdale Crossing being opened in June 1888. Passenger traffic soon shrank to just one daily train, which left Ulverston at noon and returned after a six-minute wait at the terminus – local folk insisted it was a ruse to compel travellers to spend a night at the Hydro! Services ceased altogether on 1 January 1917 when complete closure of the southern part of the branch took place as a World War I economy measure. The remaining portion, retained to serve the ironworks until its closure in 1938 and later the Glaxo works, was singled and converted into a siding in 1952.

Ulverston gained what was perhaps the architectural *pièce de résistance* of the Furness with the building of a new station on the west side of Urswick road bridge in 1872–4. With its Italianate flamboyancy of scale, tall clocktower incorporating corner urns, elaborate roof and richly monogrammed ironwork, it symbolised the company's pinnacle of achievement. Successfully tendered for at £9,025, it was unusual in having platform faces on both sides of the down line to facilitate easy exchange between through services and Lake Side branch trains. The architects were Paley and Austin of Lancaster who designed most of the company's stations during this period.

Iron-ore trains once formed the mainstay of operations between Carnforth and Barrow but these gradually dwindled from the 1920s. In World War I diversity was provided by 'Jellicoe Specials' taking coal to the Home Fleet based at

Scapa Flow, several of these trains being diverted via the coast route to relieve pressure on the main line over Shap. They were worked throughout by London & North Western engines, no strangers to Furness metals at this time, as in common with North Eastern locomotives they appeared on the coke trains from south Durham when these were re-routed via the Hincaster Junction–Arnside line. Unusual originating traffic has included sea-washed turf for bowling greens from Meathop siding, near Grange, and cockles from Kents Bank and Cark & Cartmel. Carts would make trips on to the Morecambe Bay sands between tides to collect the cockles which were then bagged to be put on a special nightly fish train for the towns of Lancashire and Yorkshire. Cark station also handled racehorses for the Whit Monday races at Cartmel and witnessed many illustrious passengers coming to and from Holker Hall.

NORTH OF BARROW

Furness folk have a saying that 'nowt good comes round Black Combe'. It certainly applied to the acquisition of the Whitehaven & Furness Junction Railway, for not only was an exorbitant price paid but the entire system had virtually to be rebuilt. Wooden stations were renewed in stone and timber trestles replaced by cast-iron viaducts, beginning with those over the Rivers Esk (1867), Mite and Irt (both 1868). Work was also started by the Furness on its inherited scheme for a viaduct directly across the Duddon estuary, but after a contract for £29,736 had been let in February 1867 it was resolved later that year to suspend operations. A detailed financial study had found that the cost of the scheme and the consequent reduction in mileage rates could not be offset by increased traffic. The decision has been described as the most regrettable in the history of the Furness Railway, but it was perhaps equally unfortunate that vast expenditure was allowed to continue at Barrow, the ultimate result being that the company found itself with a main line too circuitous and docks too large. Abandonment of the cut-off between Park and the north side of the Duddon was sanctioned by an Act of 9 August 1869, which imposed the 'onerous condition' that rates charged on the existing line should henceforth be calculated as if the viaduct had been completed. Materials already assembled on the foreshore were used in rebuilding Spile Bridge near Foxfield (1871) and the trestle across the Calder (1872).

Powers obtained for the northern approach to the viaduct were used for a 1¾ mile branch from Holborn Hill to Hodbarrow mines, construction of which was in hand in April 1866 and was completed by the following year. The size of the ore deposits led to erection alongside the branch of an ironworks, also opened in 1867, and associated building of 'a sort of model town' named Millom, which soon transformed Holborn Hill, a village with only 163 inhabitants in 1861, into the largest settlement in the district, housing close on 4,000 people by 1876. The station adopted the name of the new town on 1 June 1866. It was a similar story at Ireleth, where Askam ironworks commenced smelting ore from nearby Park mines in 1867, growth of an adjoining industrial colony taking the number of inhabitants up to about 3,000 in 1873 compared with some 400 eight years previously. A new station at Ireleth was opened on 1 April 1868 and renamed Askam on 1 January 1875. The ironworks closed in 1918 after several years of only intermittent use, having been taken over by the Millom concern which survived tenaciously in its remote location. Its days were numbered when Hodbarrow mines closed on 31 March 1968 after raising the colossal total of over 25 million tons of haematite, and in fact it lasted only another six months. The Hodbarrow branch was closed beyond the ironworks on 12 August 1968.

Widening of the main line north from Askam was carried out in 1872–4, by which time double track extended all the way from Carnforth to Sellafield. In 1870 the Furness acquired a sizeable tract of land at Seascale, plans for a large resort with a grand hotel, marine walks, promenades and villas being drawn up by Edward Kemp of Birkenhead. Building began in 1879, but as in the 1850s the distance from any major centre of population proved a drawback. Only a few crescents were completed, together with apartment houses, shops and limited sports facilities, although in a spirit of optimism a refreshment pavilion with a balcony overlooking the sea was built on the station's down platform. The railway also stimulated limited resort development at St Bees which from 1908 to 1918 had a separate halt platform for the golf course. Construction that could hardly have been more different occurred a few miles to the south with the opening in 1897 of Vickers' gun-testing range at Eskmeals, served by a single-track branch as well as Monk Moors Halt, built for the use of workmen's trains from Barrow and Millom.

Peaceful deployment of the forces of war saw completion in 1956 of the first full-scale nuclear power station in the world at Calder Hall, adjoining the Windscale reprocessing plant on the site of an earlier Royal Ordnance Factory which had been built close to the railway. This much needed injection of new life-blood into south-west Cumberland brought with it the rebuild-ing of nearby Sellafield station, construction of a short branch serving the works of what became British Nuclear Fuels (BNFL) and also probably saved the Barrow–Whitehaven line from closure. It also created some of the most interesting – and controversial – freight workings over the route. These consist of specially constructed 50 ton 'Flatrol' wagons conveying ir-radiated nuclear fuel elements in steel flasks from Magnox power stations in this country and from overseas via Barrow docks.

Withdrawal of passenger services and singling of the track on this straggling line have both been proposed, local traffic potential being minimal, as indicated by the decision to make all intermediate stations apart from Askam and Millom

---

CONTRASTS IN BRIDGES

Top: Kent viaduct, with a Furness Railway 4–6–4T and a LNWR 2–4–0 about to pass. *(K. J. Norman collection) Middle:* Ingleton viaduct which once formed a 'no man's land' between the feuding LNWR and Midland Railways. This photograph is thought to depict the train used by the Board of Trade inspector on 27 August 1861. *(J. B. Hodgson collection) Bottom:* Keekle viaduct, on the 'main line' of the Cleator & Workington Junction Railway, under construction about 1878. *(Cumbrian Railways Association–Pattinson collection)*

request stops from 2 May 1977. As an underutilised but scenically attractive backwater, the route was thus an ideal choice for the weekly Cumbrian Coast Express from Blackpool (later London Euston) to Sellafield, steam-hauled beyond Carnforth, which was introduced with immense success by British Rail in summer 1978. It ceased on a regular basis at the end of the 1985 season, although in more recent years BNFL itself has chartered similar steam-hauled Pullman specials from around the country, the all-in fare including a 'video bus tour' of the nuclear recycling plant.

SOLWAY FAREWELLS

Top: The final run of England's last horse-drawn passenger service from Port Carlisle to Drumburgh in April 1914. *(Templeton collection) Bottom:* Last day on the Silloth branch in September 1964, with Type 2 No D5310 awaiting departure with a Carlisle train. *(Derek Cross)*

Chapter VI

West Cumberland

There is nowhere else in England quite like West Cumberland. Cut off from the rest of the country by the great barrier of the Lake mountains, it would have remained isolated and insignificant had it not been for its rich mineral resources. These, coupled with the resourcefulness of a people noted for their independence, enabled the region to overcome its geographical handicaps and develop strong maritime trading links with Ireland and the Americas.

Outcrop coal mining around Whitehaven began as early as the thirteenth century, but was not systematically developed until some 400 years later when the area came into possession of the Lowthers, later the Earls of Lonsdale. Successive members of the family built a harbour, expanded the mines and initiated development of what Nikolaus Pevsner has described as 'the earliest post-mediaeval planned town in England'. These changes gathered momentum at the beginning of the eighteenth century when Whitehaven already had over 2,000 inhabitants and was the third largest town in the north of England after Newcastle and York. It entered a golden age as shipping, initially developed to take coal to the Isle of Man and Ireland, brought in its wake the growth of a Continental and American trade in wines, spirits, tobacco and timber. In 1725 Daniel Defoe noted that the settlement had 'grown up from a small place to be very considerable by the coal trade, which is increased so considerably of late, that it is now the most eminent port in England for shipping of coals except Newcastle and Sunderland'. By 1762 its population had soared to 9,063.

Under the guidance of the Lowthers' celebrated mining

engineer, Carlisle Spedding, the mines spread under the sea and were soon to be described as 'perhaps the most extraordinary of any in the known world'. Spedding received his initial training on Tyneside, reputedly adopting a disguise for the purpose, and was able to 'borrow' several ideas, one of which related to the concept of wooden wagonways for moving coal from pit to port. A ½ mile wagonway from Ravenhill pit in Howgill to staiths beside the harbour was laid down to a gauge of 4 ft 10 in in 1735, apparently being brought into use on 15 November. This was followed by the nearby and almost parallel ¾ mile line from Parker pit to the harbour, opened on 4 August 1738, when the *Cumberland Pacquet* commented that it 'was considered as only something less than magic, was hailed by the acclamations not only of all the inhabitants which the town then contained, but by people from every part of the adjoining county'. A third line built in 1754 ran for ¼ mile from Whingill to Bransty, from where the coal was initially carted to the harbour. Spedding began work on an ornamental arch to carry the wagonway over a turnpike road to the water's edge, but progress was halted by his death and was long delayed. It was not until 9 August 1803 that the Bransty Arch, 27 ft high and 20 ft in span with flanking pedestrian ways, was finally opened 'with great eclat'. (It was demolished on 10 March 1927, having become a notorious traffic bottleneck).

The Whitehaven wagonways were initially gravity-operated with horse-haulage of returning empties. From about 1810 they were rebuilt with cast-iron fish-bellied rails. Although evidence is conflicting, it would appear that in 1816 John Peile, the then colliery agent, took the remarkable step of ordering an eight-wheeled geared locomotive from Ouseburn Foundry, Newcastle. The following year it was tried on the Ravenhill wagonway, which by this time had been extended to Croft pit, but it broke up the cast-iron track and before July 1818 it had been decided to abandon the experiment with locomotive haulage.

The spectacular growth of Whitehaven from the mid-seventeenth century was repeated a hundred years later at other ports as development began in earnest of the extensive West Cumberland coalfield stretching from St Bees almost to Wigton. Workington had four pits by the 1740s, a 3 mile wagonway from Seaton to the north side of the harbour being constructed by Sir James Lowther about 1732. It was certainly in use by 1734, and was followed by two other Lowther lines, both 2½ miles long, from St Helen's colliery and from pits at Clifton. During the 1770s the local Curwen family built two short lines to the south side of the harbour from their collieries at Moorbanks and Chapel Bank. A few miles down the coast Henry Curwen laid out a wagonway from his pits to Harrington harbour soon after it was completed in 1760. To open up the northern part of the coalfield, Humphrey Senhouse of Netherhall began to develop a harbour at the mouth of the River Ellen in the 1750s and, in honour of his wife, bestowed the name Maryport on the associated settlement. It was soon well established, with a population of 1,300 by the 1770s, a 2½ mile wagonway having been constructed to the harbour from pits near Broughton Moor in 1755.

'THE GREAT THOROUGHFARE'

Under the guiding influence of the Senhouse family, Maryport's prosperity increased to the extent that by the late 1830s almost 100,000 tons of coal per annum was being exported through the harbour. It was Humphrey Senhouse (1773–1842) who took the initial steps to build a railway from Maryport to Carlisle, these coinciding with rival proposals from Lowther interests which advocated a larger scheme extending down the coast to Whitehaven. Attempts were also made to interest the Newcastle & Carlisle in a westward extension, but the company feared a loss of its market for North-East and Brampton coals to West Cumberland colliery proprietors and also took the view that Port Carlisle was a better harbour than Maryport (see Chapter IV). The Whitehaven project failed to materialise, the upshot being the formation of the Maryport & Carlisle Railway with George Stephenson as engineer. In his report to the proprietors in October 1836 he pointed out, 'The nature of the country is such that it will not admit of any other line ever being made to compete with it; it must, therefore, ever remain the great thoroughfare through that part of Cumberland.' The prospectus set the tone for many rose-tinted documents characteristic of the railway age in stating that the line would pass 'through a country abounding in coal, lime, stone, slate and other minerals, already to a considerable extent advanced in manufactures, and teeming with agricultural produce and industrious population'. Even the Act of 12 July 1837, authorising the first incorporated line wholly in the Lake Counties, reflected the optimism of the period in referring to a route that would 'facilitate the Communication between the Continent of Europe and Ireland and the Western Coast of England by forming in conjunction with the Newcastle-upon-Tyne and Carlisle Railway and the Brandlings Junction Railway, One complete and continuous Line of Railway Communication from the German Ocean to the Irish Sea'.

In order to satisfy agricultural interests around Wigton, Parliament by means of a special clause in the Act put pressure on the promoters to finish the line throughout. The railway was to be built for 6 miles at the Carlisle end as soon as it was completed for 12 miles at the Maryport end, operations then proceeding forward from each extremity until the two sections met. Despite this staggered pattern and the fact that five-sixths of the £180,000 capital had been subscribed at the time of incorporation, progress was painfully slow as it proved difficult to extract the full amounts from shareholders in the ensuing slump and by August 1840 more than half the shares had been forfeited.

The first 7 mile section was opened on 15 July 1840. It extended from the South Quay at Maryport, curving sharply round an ox-bow bend of the River Ellen to a passenger station in front of what is now Jubilee Terrace, and then closely followed the river to an intermediate station at Bullgill and a terminus near coal pits at Arkleby. A $1\frac{1}{4}$ mile extension to Aspatria was completed on 12 April 1841. Although the arithmetic does not quite agree with that of Parliament, matters then turned to the Carlisle end with the $11\frac{1}{4}$ miles from a junction with the Newcastle & Carlisle at Bogfield to a terminus at Wigton being opened on 10 May 1843. There was an intermediate station at Dalston, with another at Curthwaite soon being added. 'Large and commodious' coaches bridged the gap between the two termini as well as

MARYPORT AND CARLISLE RAILWAY.

Times of Departure of the Trains on and after September 26th, 1842.

From MARYPORT,	6h. 30m. Morning	From ASPATRIA,	7h. 30m. Morning
	9h. 0m. Morning		10h. 0m. Morning
*Quick Train,	11h. 20m. Morning	*Quick Train,	12 at Noon
	1h. 30m. Afternoon		2h. 30m. Afternoon
	4h. 0m. Afternoon		4h. 45m. Afternoon

FARES.

MARYPORT to ASPATRIA,	.... First Class 1s. 6d.	Second Class 1s. 0d.
Do. ARKLEBY,	do. 1s. 0d.	do. 0s. 9d.
Do. BULL GILL	do. 0s. 9d.	do. 0s. 6d.
Do. DEARHAM BRIDGE,	do 0s. 6d.	do. 0s. 3d.

Passengers set down between any two of the above Stations will be charged the same as if they were taken to the next Station.

The time kept at the Railway Office is post office, or mean-time at London, being 13m. 14s. before mean-time at Maryport.——Note.—The Public are respectfully advised that most of the clocks at Maryport are kept half an hour behind London, or RAILWAY TIME.

* The Quick Train exchanges Passengers at Aspatria Station with the New Coach, "Engineer," between Carlisle and Whitehaven.

By Order, W. MITCHELL, Secretary.

J. OSTLE, PRINTER, MARYPORT.

Maryport & Carlisle Railway timetable of September 1842, when Maryport was still keeping local time.

providing connecting services from Maryport to Whitehaven and from Wigton to Keswick for visitors to the Lakes. Further delays were caused by a decision to build the central section of the line on a revised alignment, but ever so gradually the gap narrowed, a mere ¾ mile extension from Wigton to a temporary station at Brookfield being brought into use on 2 December 1844 at the same time as a more substantial 3½ miles from Aspatria to another temporary terminus at Low Row. The two threads of iron finally met with completion of the intervening section on 10 February 1845, an event that in local eyes must have equalled the driving of the last spike on the Canadian Pacific. Improved transport brought immediate benefits to communities along the line, but in contrast the once fashionable resort of Allonby a few miles up the coast from Maryport found itself bypassed and, despite an attempt to run a connecting coach service from Aspatria, it gradually faded into obscurity.

With the opening of the entire route, Brookfield was closed and on 2 February 1848 Low Row was replaced by a station at Leegate. For a brief period trains also called at Heathfield. Of the other stations, Dearham opened about 1842 (it was renamed Dearham Bridge on 1 June 1867) and Cummersdale in 1858; Arkleby closed in 1852. Indicative of the feudal nature of the line and the extent to which it was controlled by the local gentry was the existence of two private stations. Brayton was referred to in a directors' minute of 8 March 1845 when it was resolved, 'in consequence of the great pecuniary assistance rendered by Sir Wilfrid Lawson ... that all trains do stop to take up and put down, when a signal is displayed at the private station house ... called the Brayton Station, any passenger going to and coming from Brayton Hall'. Sir Wilfrid, one of the company's original directors, agreed on 1 March 1848 'to allow his station' to be used by the public. A slightly later symbol of privilege was Crofton, built for the Brisco family of Crofton Hall under an Act of 26 June 1855. The same Act authorised a new station at Maryport closer to the town centre; it was brought into use on 4 June 1860 and consisted of a single platform over a thousand feet long with impressive red sandstone buildings in castellated style housing the company's offices. Also authorised at the same time and completed in February 1861 was doubling of the line, an initial stretch from Maryport to Arkleby having been widened in 1846–7 to cope with heavy coal traffic which in turn increased following the sinking of pits close to the railway at Crosby in 1854 and Ellen (Bullgill) in 1859. The final development under the 1855 Act comprised branches to Maryport's new Elizabeth Dock, opened in 1857 when coal exports through the harbour totalled 341,068 tons.

The early years of the Maryport & Carlisle were far from smooth with a constantly changing procession of officials who were often incompetent. In March 1847 a Committee of Enquiry censured William Mitchell, the secretary and engineer, who was requested to leave his employment. It found that 'none of the servants of the company pay him the least attention, and in consequence of his laxity and indifference and entire want of system, the affairs of the company have got into the greatest discredit and disrepute'. At the annual meeting the previous year he had been described as 'the most disobedient, disobliging servant', and allegations had been made regarding 'plenty of drunken railway officers' at the Carlisle end of the system. In 1849 the secretary was Samuel Sale who is referred to in surviving correspondence as 'a swindler, previously in jail' and 'of indifferent moral character'. Instead of attending to his duties, he was seen at Carlisle watching a cricket match with the chief engineer and two head-bookkeepers!

Matters were not helped when George Hudson leased the line from 1 October 1848 at an annual dividend of 4 per cent, nominally on behalf of the York, Newcastle & Berwick Railway. As outlined in Chapter IV, the lease was never ratified and the company became independent again on 1 January 1850, leaving its affairs in such a state of confusion that a committee of investigation was appointed and the position brought to a head. It unravelled a sorry tale, finding that by 1844 the directors had borrowed £200,000 without legal authority and had charged salaries, travelling expenses and postage to capital. It criticised expenditure on buildings, for instance at Dalston where 'an old wooden house had been brought from Carlisle and erected at an expense exceeding the estimated cost of a good brick or stone building'. Debts amounted to £280,534 compared with a share capital of £167,612. After a 'long and angry discussion' extending over several hours at a special meeting of shareholders on 20 November 1850, the report of the committee was accepted and the former chairman and five directors replaced. *Herapath's Journal* commented in a leading article: 'It would appear that a worse state of things never was brought to light than this report has revealed to the public.' It blamed the shareholders for failing to safeguard their own interests, referring to 'their abominable laxity of conduct, their almost criminal state of indifference'.

Under new management the position began to improve, especially from 1857 with the appointment of John Addison who was to be secretary, general manager and engineer for the next twenty-seven years. He was to bring much-needed stability and to provide the basis for the company's amazing prosperity in the 1870s and '80s. When he came into post the railway was an amateurish concern, having to suffer such insults as the reference in *Bradshaw* to a mixed train on a Carlisle–Wigton service: 'Goods train—punctuality not guaranteed.' Under his guidance it became what Jack Simmons, the historian of the Maryport & Carlisle, has described as 'a perfect specimen of the small, independent local railway company'.

ALONG THE COAST

As the railway age gathered momentum, it became obvious that an extension southwards from Maryport to Whitehaven could not be long delayed. In 1843 Lord Lowther (later the 2nd Earl of Lonsdale) commissioned a detailed report from George Stephenson and F. Forster who strongly favoured construction at a cost of about £80,000: 'It appears to us to be of the greatest importance to the Town of Whitehaven that this line should be made. If it is not made there is no doubt in our minds that the Maryport Harbour will be so improved as to seriously affect the trade of Whitehaven.'

Lord Lowther quickly made up his mind, the Whitehaven Junction Railway being incorporated on 4 July 1844 with a capital of £100,000. With Stephenson acting as engineer, the first $5\frac{1}{2}$ miles from the then Maryport station to Workington were brought into use on 19 January 1846, services apparently being worked by Maryport & Carlisle locomotives and stock. A $2\frac{1}{4}$ mile extension to Harrington was completed on 18 May, the final $4\frac{3}{4}$ miles to a terminus at Bransty on the north side of Whitehaven being opened for goods on 15 February 1847 and passengers on 19 March. Apart from Workington and Harrington, there were intermediate stations at Flimby and Parton. Short branches were later constructed under an Act of 23 July 1858 to Elizabeth Dock, Maryport (opened 8 September 1859) and Merchant's Quay, Workington (completed about 1860). Although the journey time from Whitehaven to Carlisle was now reduced to 2 hr 10 min compared with six hours by coach, old habits died hard and many travellers southbound from Whitehaven still used steamer services. This was partly due to low fares; for instance, in 1854 it was possible to travel from Whitehaven to Liverpool by steamer for as little as 3s (15p) on deck or 6s (30p) in a cabin, compared with the 1850 rail fare of 10s 11d (59½p).

The Whitehaven Junction closely hugged the sea-shore

almost throughout; indeed, between Harrington and Parton the hugging was perhaps a little too intimate for comfort with the line being built on a sea-wall at the foot of notoriously unstable cliffs over 200 ft high. As early as August 1847 a critical letter in the *Carlisle Journal* claimed that this stretch was badly laid out, with its numerous sharp curves following every indentation of the shore at the base of 'frightfully dangerous rock in a constant state of mouldering away'. Over the years there were to be ceaseless problems with landslips and storm damage in what became locally known as 'avalanche alley', a difficulty repeated to a lesser extent between Parton and Whitehaven where in 1852 a stretch of line 30 yd long was entirely washed away during a gale and had to be rebuilt at a cost of £1,380.

At Parton the tracks ran alongside the famous Lowca Engineering Works, founded in the mid-eighteenth century and passing into the hands of Tulk & Ley in 1830. Its first two engines, built in 1840 for the Maryport & Carlisle, were transported northwards by raft owing to the poor state of the roads. The first nine locomotives were all for local lines and included two for the Whitehaven Junction, but by the 1850s the works had greatly expanded and was supplying railways throughout the world. Taken over in 1857 by Fletcher, Jennings & Co, Cumbria's pre-eminent firm of locomotive builders constructed or rebuilt 264 engines before closing in the early 1920s as the New Lowca Engineering Co Ltd.

At Whitehaven an extension from Bransty to the harbour was built under powers obtained on 22 July 1848. Further development came with construction of the Whitehaven & Furness Junction Railway (see Chapter V) with its separate terminus at Newtown (locally known as Preston Street, a name officially adopted about 1860). A line through the market place and alongside the harbour provided a primitive link for the exchange of mineral traffic between the two systems. The first locomotive for use on the Whitehaven & Furness Junction was being manoeuvred over this link by men and ropes on 14 July 1849, in readiness for opening of the initial section a week later, when it ran away and killed one George Cox. A second engine was successfully delivered in the same manner on 18 August but soon disgraced itself, the

Whitehaven Herald of 20 October noting: 'The No 2 engine got out of control and crashed into the schoolmaster's house at Preston Street killing a child.'

Construction of a more satisfactory link between the two companies was already in hand under a Whitehaven & Furness Junction Act of 3 August 1846. The early and close-knit development of Whitehaven posed problems, it finally being decided that the best practicable route was beneath the surface. The connection diverged ½ mile south of Newtown terminus and then ran under the grounds of Whitehaven Castle, town house of the Earl of Lonsdale who obtained a clause in the Act that a cutting should not be substituted for a tunnel without his consent. The gently curving single-line bore ended hard by Bransty station, its 1,333 yd creating the apparent contradiction that the longest railway tunnel in England's most mountainous county was almost at sea-level. After delays caused by encountering old coal pits, the new line was opened on 30 September 1852, trains being worked through by a 'tunnel engine' in charge of a pilotman.

Passenger trains from the south continued to terminate at Newtown, largely due to inadequate facilities at Bransty. Moves to improve this situation were no doubt helped by the Lonsdale patronage common to both lines into Whitehaven, a factor which bore results in 1854 when the two companies put control of their rolling stock under a joint committee and agreed to share staff. The following year alterations at the Whitehaven Junction terminus were completed and from 3 December 1855 all passenger services were concentrated at Bransty and all goods facilities at Newtown. With closure of Newtown to passengers, a station at Corkickle close to the south portal of the tunnel was opened on the same date. This early example of what we now term rationalisation had its drawbacks in that goods services from the north had to reverse into Newtown and passenger trains from the south had to stop opposite William Pit and then set back into Bransty. It was not until 24 December 1874 that through platforms were opened adjacent to the north portal of the tunnel under Acts of 2 June 1865 and 13 July 1868.

Concentration of freight traffic at Newtown made the lines from there to the waterfront exceptionally busy, various harbour branches having been authorised on 4 August 1853 and an extension to the Bulwark opened on 28 July 1856. The Act prevented the line through the market place being used on market days between 7 am and 3 pm, but otherwise strings of horse-hauled wagons trundled through the streets day and night with between 300 and 400 commonly being handled every twenty-four hours in the early 1860s. Despite all this activity, Whitehaven did not enter a second golden age and traffic through the ancient harbour relatively declined with the opening of more modern docks at Silloth, Maryport, Workington and especially Barrow. In the twenty years from 1851 the town's population grew only from 20,636 to 21,208, compared with an increase of almost a third at the newer industrial centre of Workington.

INLAND TO COCKERMOUTH

Promotion of the Whitehaven Junction meant that the only major town in West Cumberland without the benefits of railway communication was Cockermouth, an agricultural centre with a population around the 5,000 mark. Accordingly, the Cockermouth & Workington Railway was incorporated on 21 July 1845 with a capital of £80,000, the first directors including Henry Cecil Lowther as well as Sir Wilfrid Lawson of Brayton. Extending for $8\frac{3}{4}$ miles along the valley of the Derwent, it crossed the river five times before terminating close to Workington harbour where a sharply curved connection was made with the coast line at Derwent Junction. One major problem was that the route passed within 10 yd of Brigham vicarage, a difficulty undoubtedly made more acute by the fact that the incumbent was John Wordsworth, son of the poet William who castigated the railway for 'cutting between him and the river through his garden and little pleasure ground'. The younger Wordsworth certainly got his pound of flesh, clauses being inserted in the Act compelling the company to build a new vicarage within $\frac{1}{4}$ mile of the original with stable, offices, outbuildings, fixtures and a garden of not less than $\frac{1}{2}$ acre. The vicar was to be paid £5 for every month which elapsed between commencement of building the railway and completion of the vicarage plus the then relatively enormous sum of £50 for the expense of moving.

The line was opened on 28 April 1847, intermediate stations being provided at Brigham, Broughton Cross, Camerton and Workington Bridge. Under the Whitehaven Junction Act of 22 July 1848 the company was granted joint use of Workington station, but it was not until 1 August 1858 that through passenger trains were introduced to Whitehaven and Carlisle. A $\frac{1}{3}$ mile branch from Marron Foot to Bridgefoot was authorised on 26 June 1849 but not constructed. The Cockermouth & Workington seems to have been plagued with the same troubles in its early days as the Maryport & Carlisle, a report in February 1857 containing harsh words on the former secretary and general manager, John Dodds: 'Under the management of that official the permanent works and rolling stock had been permitted to get very much out of repair, and in consequence the board had been under the necessity of expending large sums of money during the last half-year in order to place the works on a satisfactory footing.' Earlier the company had come in for more august criticism from Henry Mayhew, one of the founders of *Punch*. In 1851, the year that saw publication of his great work *London Labour and the London Poor*, he also found time to write with George Cruikshank an account of *The Adventures of Mr & Mrs Sandboys . . .*, a Buttermere couple who decide to go up to London to see the Great Exhibition. The first stage of their journey from Cockermouth is described in devastating terms that one suspects would be applicable to many other small railway companies of the period:

The line being in none of the most flourishing conditions, every means for economising the 'working expenses' have been resorted to. The men engaged upon it have been cut down to boys; so that the establishment has very much the look of a kind of railway academy, where the porters on the platform are ever playing at marbles or leapfrog, where the policemen all wear pinafores, and where the clerks are taken to the station in the morning, and 'fetched' in the evening by the maids of their anxious parents ... Not a razor is used by the whole establishment; and the staff – we have it on the best authority – are allowed to give over work an hour earlier every Saturday evening, in consideration of its being 'tub-night'.

Mayhew reserves some further sarcasm for the decision by 'the frugal directors' to effect economies by using coal instead of coke in the locomotives:

> The result of this wise economy has been, that the engines on this line are perpetually smoking in the faces of the passengers, and pouring forth so lavish a volcanic eruption of 'blacks', that by the time the ladies and gentlemen reach the end of their journey, they are generally as dark complexioned as if they had been unconsciously working or reading by the light of the very best – patent – warranted infumable – camphine lamps.

No doubt coal was favoured because the line had opened up the coalfield in the Camerton area and received some three-quarters of its traffic from this source. To cater for the growing trade the Earl of Lonsdale obtained powers in 1861 to build a new dock on the north side of the Derwent, with an associated private railway, the Cockermouth & Workington being authorised on 8 June 1863 to connect to this line by means of a short spur crossing the Whitehaven Junction on the level just north of Derwent Junction. Lonsdale Dock was brought into use in September 1864.

PORT CARLISLE AND SILLOTH

West Cumberland's fifth independent railway had unusual origins. As outlined in Chapter IV, the Carlisle Canal, providing an important link from the 'Border City' to the Solway Firth at Port Carlisle, was opened in 1823. By the late 1840s it was in acute financial difficulties as a result of the network of railways converging on Carlisle from all directions, a further blow coming with the introduction of cheap rail/steamer fares from the city to Liverpool via Whitehaven in April 1850.

Local traders and manufacturers were determined to retain an outlet for their goods, independent of the control of outside railway companies, and in March 1852 the canal committee minuted: 'It appears highly desirable and indeed the only means of retrieving the affairs of the Canal Company that the Canal should be converted into a railway.' During the following year a grander concept evolved, largely because silting up of the Solway estuary was making it increasingly difficult for the growing number of steamships to enter Port Carlisle. It was thus decided not only to convert the canal but also use the greater part of the resulting railway as a springboard for a new line from a junction at Drumburgh (pronounced 'Drumbruff'), 2½ miles south-east of Port Carlisle, to a point further down the Solway at Silloth Bay, less affected by tidal conditions and with deep water closer to the shore, where a dock would be constructed. This, it was felt, was 'the natural and in every respect the most desirable terminus of the line and the most eligible Port for the City of Carlisle'.

Backed by Carlisle Corporation, the project materialised in two stages. The first involved reincorporation of the Carlisle Canal Company as the Port Carlisle Dock and Railway by an Act of 4 August 1853 which also authorised conversion of the waterway. In an attempt to retain trade, work went ahead as rapidly as possible with preparations beginning in June prior to passing of the Act. The canal was closed on 1 August and drained, ensuing operations involving the removal of six locks, the raising of sixteen overbridges and making a ½ mile diversion at Kirkandrews. The result was a rather curious 11 mile single-line railway almost entirely in cutting with long level stretches punctuated by short and relatively steep grades marking the site of former locks. In addition, there were numerous sharp curves which in later years were to create a permanent speed restriction of 25 mph. Goods traffic commenced on 22 May 1854 and passenger services on 22 June, the initial intermediate station at Burgh (renamed Burgh-by-Sands 9 July 1923) being joined shortly afterwards by Kirkandrews and Glasson. Locomotives and carriages were at first hired from the Newcastle & Carlisle Railway, but in January 1855 the company ordered its own engine which was delivered later the same year. Somewhat spasmodic steamer services were reintroduced from Port Carlisle to Liverpool in connection with the midday train and, in an attempt to make the bleak Solway shore more hospitable for waiting passengers, a pleasure ground with pavilion laid out adjoining the station.

The second stage, the extension to Silloth, proved more

difficult, attracting intense opposition from the Maryport &
Carlisle which understandably saw the project as a move to
develop another harbour at its expense. When the Bill for the
Carlisle & Silloth Bay Railway & Dock came before
Parliament in 1854, the secretary of the Maryport company,
Henry Jacob, stated in evidence: 'I cannot conceive the
necessity for a line passing over a district so utterly bare of
inhabitants, or anything else as this projected line. It ends in a
rabbit warren, and they can only hope for success by
abstracting the traffic from us; we are able to carry it all.'
Further opposition from the Earl of Lonsdale and the
Maryport Harbour Trustees led to the Bill being thrown out,
but the scheme was put forward again in the following session
when the company was successfully incorporated on 16 July
1855 with a capital of £68,000 for the railway and £80,000 for
the dock.

The Silloth project got deeply embroiled in local politics, its
chairman, P. J. Dixon, also being Mayor of Carlisle. The
Carlisle Patriot ran a sustained and highly vitriolic campaign
against the railway, referring to the promoters as 'a set of fools
for throwing their money away in moonshine' and furthering
'a mere speculative bubble'. Allegations were made that the
majority of shares in the Port Carlisle company were held by
the mayor's family, and the directors were censured for not
revealing to shareholders their true intentions with regard to
Silloth superseding Port Carlisle. With some justification the
paper maintained that the canal west of Drumburgh should
have been abandoned rather than converted, and correctly
prophesied that the existing port would become a white
elephant as soon as Silloth dock was completed. W. James,
chairman of the Port Carlisle company, admitted in 1856 that
the conversion project, if viewed in its own right, had been
something of a failure, and looked forward to the Silloth
extension 'to help a lame dog over a stile – as a man who was
about to be drowned looked forward to a swimming jacket'.

Fortunately the despairing chairman did not have long to
wait, for the 13 mile Silloth line ran across flat countryside
almost at sea-level and hence engineering works were minimal
and construction rapid. Formal opening took place on 28
August 1856, although it was the following year before

PORT CARLISLE RAILWAY.

PROPOSED ENTRANCE TO SILLOTH BAY DOCK

OPENING
OF THE
CARLISLE & SILLOTH BAY
RAILWAY

ON THURSDAY, 28TH OF AUGUST.

TRAINS will LEAVE CARLISLE at 12 o'Clock, calling at Burgh only.

A TRAIN will LEAVE DRUMBURGH for SILLOTH at 2 o'Clock calling at Kirkbride and the Abbey.

RETURNING from SILLOTH at 4 o'Clock for Carlisle, direct; and at 7 p.m., calling at the Abbey, Kirkbride, Drumburgh, and Burgh.

RETURN TICKETS—ONE SHILLING each; to be obtained at the PORT CARLISLE STATIONS; MR. DRAPE, Inn-keeper, ABBEY; MRS. SCOTT, Innkeeper, KIRKBRIDE; or at 48, CASTLE STREET, CARLISLE.

N.B.—No Tickets will be issued after 6 o'Clock on WEDNESDAY Evening. the 27th Instant

BY ORDER,

AUGUST, 21ST, 1856.

A. PIXTON, MANAGER.

A PUBLIC DINNER

Will be provided by Mr. HARDING, in a TENT adjoining the *Solway Hotel*, at SILLOTH.   P. J. DIXON, ESQ., Chairman of the Company in the Chair.—Tickets 3s. each to be had at 48, CASTLE STREET; and at the PORT CARLISLE STATIONS; and from MR. HARDING, Silloth.   Dinner on the Table at Three o'Clock—A Choice Musical Band in attendance.

HUDSON SCOTT, PRINTER, 11, ENGLISH STREET, CARLISLE.

Poster advertising the opening of the Carlisle & Silloth Bay Railway.

intermediate stations were completed at Kirkbride and Abbey (renamed Abbey Town August 1889). Plans for a platform at the junction at Drumburgh had been approved in March 1856 and a further station was subsequently constructed at Black Dykes (later Blackdyke Halt). During 1856 a jetty was partially completed at Silloth to enable the existing Liverpool steamer service to be transferred from Port Carlisle, the new harbour coming into its own with the opening of Marshall Dock on 3 August 1859.

From the opening a 'United Committee' was established for operating the Port Carlisle and Carlisle & Silloth Bay, the former providing the locomotives and the latter the rolling stock. In September 1857 the committee decided to purchase a horse for £35, the cost to be added to the locomotive stock, thus originating the famous 'Dandy' service on what was now the Port Carlisle branch from Drumburgh. Mixed trains had been the rule on the branch since opening of the Silloth line, but traffic was now so light it was resolved to economise on engine mileage by introducing a horse-worked passenger service and running locomotive-hauled goods trains as required. In the first quarter of 1858 it was estimated that the single industrious horse saved 1,887 engine miles. The original horse-drawn coach was replaced in 1859 by 'Dandy No 1', a quaint vehicle providing inside accommodation for first and second-class passengers only, the unlucky third-class having to perch outside with their backs to the carriage and their feet on footboards. Its similarity to a stage coach was emphasised by luggage being carried on the roof. In later years a notice at Carlisle warned: 'The accommodation on the Port Carlisle carriage is limited, and passengers will only be booked through to Port Carlisle on the understanding that they will wait for the Dandy to make a second trip if necessary, otherwise can only book through to Drumburgh.'

The relegation of Port Carlisle to the horse age coincided with a transformation at Silloth, where a unique attempt by the directors of a railway company to supervise and control the development of a resort began in September 1855 with the purchase of 46 acres of Blitterlees Common for building purposes. Their motive was to create a source of passenger revenue, Dixon at the inauguration ceremonies referring to the line opening up a 'sea-side or sea bathing place for the inhabitants of Carlisle' and anticipating establishment of a town which would enjoy mushroom growth comparable with that of West Hartlepool or Bradford.

By 1857 streets had been laid out in gridiron pattern and houses were being constructed over an area that had previously comprised just a few farms and cottages behind the dune-lined coast. The scale of activity soon went far beyond the powers granted by the company's Act, expenditure on estate development being carefully hidden in the published accounts. By 1861 it appears £4,000 had been spent on terraced housing, £7,000 on an hotel, £3,600 on baths and a gasworks, £13,000 on laying out and servicing the town, £2,400 on purchase of a further 160 acres of Blitterlees Common and, even more startling, £6,000 on the clearance of sandhills to improve the view across the Solway Firth! The company also gave land for a temperance hotel, created pleasure gardens with trees and shrubs, and supplied bathing machines to the boarding-house keepers. Silloth, optimistically described by the Bishop of Carlisle as 'the Torquay of the North', already had a population of around the thousand mark and was well on its way to becoming the ultimate railway resort.

Yet despite its flourishing start the Silloth project failed to realise the starry-eyed hopes of its promoters, largely because the established railways in Carlisle successfully prevented freight traffic flowing on to the line. The two local companies thus saw salvation in the North British Railway when, as outlined in Chapter IV, it conceived its ingenious project to create an independent rail/sea Anglo-Scottish route from Edinburgh to Liverpool via Silloth by building south from its existing railhead at Hawick to join the Port Carlisle just west of Carlisle. As soon as the North British had obtained powers for this intervening link, the two Cumberland lines attempted in August 1859 to ease their critical financial position by entering into a sale and leaseback scheme with the Scottish company for all their locomotives and rolling stock. Matters worsened and in 1861 the Silloth company was forced to seek more capital, thus exposing the extent of its continued unauthorised expenditure on resort development. The two local concerns were finally put out of their misery the following year when, as already noted, they were leased by the North British on completion of its Hawick to Carlisle 'Waverley Route'. At the time critical comment was made in Parliament as to excessive spending on 'those splendid baths and wash houses' at Silloth by 'a rotten and ruined concern'.

Under its indefatigable English-born chairman, Richard Hodgson, the North British at first showed great interest in its inheritance. The company purchased its own ships for sailing from Silloth to Liverpool, Dublin and Belfast, beginning with *Ariel* in August 1862. A later ship was named *Waverley* to symbolise the marine continuation of the Edinburgh–Carlisle line. The company opened an office in Dublin, but owing to mounting losses soon withdrew from the Irish trade in favour of the Liverpool route which proved remarkably successful and profitable. Exports of coal from Canonbie, on the Langholm branch, and imports of store cattle and horses from Ireland as well as wheat for the Carlisle biscuit industry helped to put Silloth dock on a sound footing. The town increasingly became a Scottish colony ruled from Edinburgh, the company donating land for a new church and arranging for the granite stone to be brought in free as ballast in a ship from Newry. Silloth Cricket Club was also given ground, but the strange English game which involved propelling hard balls close to waiting passengers proved too much for the Scottish directorate and local sportsmen were told to play bowls instead! When the townspeople had a disagreement with the North British over paying their share of street lighting, the company gave instructions that lamps were not to be lit between sunset and 11 pm. Hodgson, ever seeking ways of attracting more traffic, was influential in the building of a sanatorium with its own private.platform which was opened in 1862. He also determinedly set about making the resort known to Scotsmen living close to the North British system, and was soon telling shareholders: 'So popular has that sea-bathing place on the Solway become that it is difficult to obtain accommodation for those who seek it.' Hodgson even went as far as personally writing a guidebook to Silloth in which he could not resist comparing its high 'ozone content' with the much inferior amount at Maryport! Here he touched on one of the flaws in the seemingly all-conquering Scottish invasion, namely the antagonism it created among hitherto loyal English customers of the line, who simply switched their traffic to the Maryport & Carlisle. Silloth never fully overcame this drawback, remaining a useful port and resort for a Scottish railway company – which even went as far as operating passenger services on a Sunday – but failing to compete with more established harbours further down the Cumbrian coast. Once the North British had its own outlet to England via the Settle–Carlisle line, the company seemed to lose interest in Silloth and even declined to maintain the sewers or provide a urinal! The town became an arrested community and a symbol of the unfulfilled ambitions of the original promoters who had expected so much of their brave new venture by the Solway.

Even so, by the turn of the century there had been a modest recovery, aided by the growing number of West Cumberland workers arriving by excursion train, and in 1901 Silloth boasted more lodging-houses than either Windermere or Keswick. The resort was especially popular on Carlisle race days when the city's Sunday school managers would send out their charges in the thousand to avoid any possible temptations of the sport of kings. On the other side of the coin, the Barony Races held at Burgh to celebrate the accession of a new Lord of the Manor could attract vast crowds; on 29 August 1883 some 8,000 passengers arrived on twelve trains, the normal branch service having been suspended and the tiny station platform specially lengthened for the occasion.

THE BOLTON LOOP

In an attempt to increase traffic through Silloth, the North British backed proposals in both 1861 and 1862 for a branch running south-east from Abbey across the Maryport & Carlisle near Leegate to tap the northern tip of the coalfield around Mealsgate in the upper Ellen Valley. Although unsuccessful, the proposals provoked retaliatory action from the Maryport company which on 30 June 1862 obtained powers for its 7¼ mile Bolton loop, so named because it ran through the large parish of Boltons. It was always regarded as two separate branches which met at the elevated village of Mealsgate over 300 ft above sea-level, one climbing from Aspatria on gradients including 1¾ miles at 1 in 70 and the other from Aikbank Junction, north of Leegate, involving 2 miles at 1 in 60 easing to a further mile at 1 in 90. Goods traffic from both ends commenced on 2 April 1866, but delays in developing the coalfield caused the loop to be 'worked with the utmost regard for economy' and the eastern end from Aikbank Junction soon became disused with 1½ miles of track being removed in September 1869. It was not until 1 October 1877 that this was reinstated and coal traffic worked off the east end of the loop for the first time.

Passenger workings from Aspatria to Mealsgate commenced on 26 December 1866, a choice of date not as strange as might seem as Boxing Day was then still very much part of the normal working week. Branch travellers were reputedly at one time directed from the main-line connection by a discriminating porter who called out to first-class passengers, 'Aspatriah, change heah for Mealsgate'; to second-class, 'Speattry, change 'ere for Mealsyat'; and to third-class, 'Spatthry, git oot'. Trains called at an intermediate station at Baggrow, giving rise to the local nickname 'Baggra Bus' for the branch service. Once the eastern end of the loop had been relaid an intermediate station was opened at High Blaithwaite, but the sole passenger service consisted of one mixed train each way from Wigton deliciously described by E. L. Ahrons as 'an "omnium gatherum" of assorted passengers, goods and minerals'.

TAPPING THE ORE-FIELD

Although developments centred on Silloth caused great local excitement in the late 1850s and early '60s, they were largely eclipsed by events further south which were to have a more momentous effect on the destiny of West Cumberland. In 1841 the Whitehaven Iron & Steel Company had been formed in the first major attempt to exploit the local iron-bearing outcrop of limestone, a narrow strip little more than a mile wide extending for some 9 miles from south of Egremont to Lamplugh, south-west of Loweswater. The following year it began to construct an ironworks at Cleator Moor, in the fork formed by the Rivers Ehen and Keekle, production increasing so rapidly that by the early 1850s the need to cart ore and pig-iron to Whitehaven for shipment by sea or rail was proving a severe constraint.

The result was incorporation on 16 June 1854 of another Lonsdale-backed line, the Whitehaven, Cleator & Egremont Railway, with a capital of £50,000. It left the Whitehaven & Furness Junction at Mirehouse Junction, a mile south of Corkickle, and then by means of sharp curves and gradients as steep as 1 in 52 climbed for 2 miles to reach Moor Row in the Keekle Valley. Here the main line continued southwards for a further 2½ miles through Woodend (where an intermediate station was opened on 1 March 1880) to the historic market town of Egremont, a 2¼ mile branch diverging at Moor Row to serve Cleator Moor before terminating at Frizington more than a mile south of the village of the same name. Initial construction was a single line on earthworks built for double track, although it was agreed that the Mirehouse Junction–Corkickle section should be doubled in order to handle the additional traffic. Mineral trains commenced on 11 January 1856, but owing to shortage of siding accommodation at Corkickle and delays in finalising various working arrangements it was 1 July 1857 before passenger services were inaugurated. At first all trains ran through to Bransty, but in August the Whitehaven & Furness Junction demanded a toll of 2s (10p) for passing through the tunnel and Corkickle soon became the enforced terminus.

Completion of the line had an immediate and dramatic effect, ushering in a new era of industrialisation and enabling West Cumberland to take full advantage of its unique con-centration of iron ore, coal, limestone and sand. Ironworks could now be built on more convenient sites away from the ore-field, a trend that began as soon as mineral traffic was flowing with the development of Oldside Works, Workington, from 1856. Here Henry Bessemer conducted experiments which helped to perfect his process for making 'semi-steel' and in turn led to an unprecedented demand for the local haematite so suitable for producing low phosphorus pig-iron. Oldside was followed by the establishment of an ironworks at

Harrington in 1857 and five years later the much larger West Cumberland Iron & Steel Company commenced operations at Workington. It had Charles Vignoles, designer of the flat-bottomed rail, as one of its first directors, and locally inaugurated the manufacture of steel rails which was soon to make West Cumberland a leading supplier to world markets. At Cleator mineral branches spread in all directions to serve the various mines, the old village being superseded in the early 1860s by the new planned town of Cleator Moor, a unique social monument to the age of iron mining. The population of the two communities more than doubled from 1,779 in 1851 to 3,995 in 1861 and again almost doubled to 7,061 ten years later. During its first six months the railway conveyed 54,000 tons of ore and 11,000 tons of coal and coke, and brought comparative prosperity to the ailing Whitehaven & Furness Junction which saw its weekly receipts increase by over 30 per cent.

Growth of the iron industry and expansion of the railway system now went hand in hand. The next development was authorisation on 7 June 1861 of a $5\frac{1}{4}$ mile extension from Frizington to the head of the Marron Valley at Kidburngill, designed to tap further deposits of iron ore and also limestone at Eskett and Rowrah. Mineral trains commenced running in November 1862, loaded traffic flows fortunately being downhill over the ferocious maximum gradient of 1 in 44 which took the line to a summit level of over 550 ft above sea-level near Rowrah. In order to provide a more direct route from this northern end of the ore-field to Workington which would avoid the congestion created by the single-line Whitehaven tunnel, powers were obtained on 8 June 1863 to continue from Kidburngill alongside the River Marron to a triangular junction with the Cockermouth & Workington just north of Bridgefoot. This $6\frac{1}{2}$ mile line, again notable for its curves and gradients, was opened for mineral traffic on 15 January 1866. Although the single-track route avoided settlements of any importance, the existing passenger service to Frizington was extended to Rowrah on 1 February 1864 and over the remainder of the line to a station at Marron Junction, on the western apex of the triangle, on 2 April 1866. Apart from Rowrah, there were intermediate stations at Eskett,

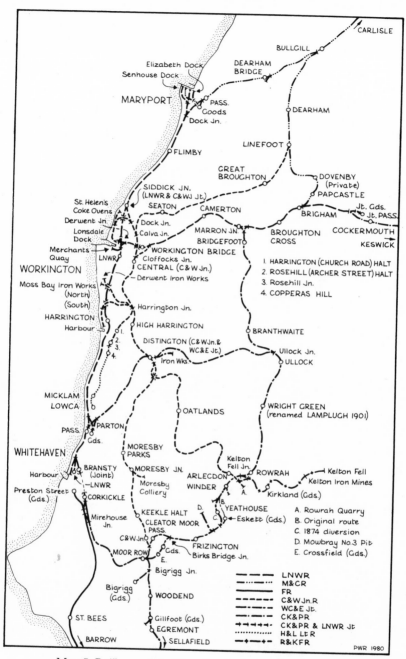

Map 7. Railways of the West Cumberland Ore-Field

Winder, Wright Green (the new name for Kidburngill which the company agreed to adopt on 15 March 1866; it was again renamed on 14 August 1901 when it became Lamplugh, even though this village was 2 miles away!), Ullock (opened May 1866), Branthwaite and Bridgefoot.

The railway through the heart of the ore-field between Moor Row and Rowrah was perpetually plagued by problems as deposits began to be worked out beneath the track. The first major difficulties occurred as early as 1863 when fears that subsidence near Cleator Moor could affect traffic over a long period caused powers to be obtained on 8 June for a $1\frac{1}{4}$ mile loop running to the north of the existing line from Moor Row to Birks Bridge Junction. At the half-yearly meeting in August 1864 it was reported that the loop, including a new station for Cleator Moor, was virtually complete, but owing to a protracted dispute with the Board of Trade over signalling it was not until 19 April 1866 that passenger trains were diverted on to what was locally known as the Bowthorn line. The original stretch of line now became the Crossfield loop, remaining in use for freight and mineral traffic with the former station becoming a goods depot.

The second serious problem occurred at Eskett in 1872 when the company was compelled to take quick action by obtaining sanction on 6 June for a $\frac{3}{4}$ mile deviation under a Board of Trade certificate rather than the normal Act of Parliament. It involved difficult construction in cutting, and erection of a new station at Yeathouse, the original line being truncated as a through route but retained as a feeder to various mines and the former station at Eskett which survived as a goods depot. The half-yearly meeting in August 1874 was told the deviation had been opened the previous April, presumably for minerals only as it was 10 June before the Board of Trade sanctioned it for passenger traffic. In the following year a subsidence occurred at Frizington and, 'in order to prevent danger', powers for a $\frac{1}{2}$ mile deviation were obtained on 2 August 1875. Apart from this almost continual battle with ground sinking beneath its feet, the company was also involved in doubling the line from Mirehouse to Marron Junction, the work being completed as far as Cleator Moor by 1863 but not finished throughout until ten years later. Today it seems scarcely credible that a railway through this remote region should ever have required double track, but for several years traffic volumes were enormous with, for instance, a single mine such as that at Parkside, near Frizington station, producing 150,000 tons of ore in 1874.

Traffic from the ore-field developed not only northwards to Workington but also southwards to Barrow, creating considerable congestion at Whitehaven where trains had to reverse or be remarshalled. To overcome this problem the Cleator company decided to build an extension south from Egremont to join the coast line but met intense opposition from the Whitehaven & Furness Junction which saw the ore traffic as a major source of revenue and itself proposed to complete the intervening link. After a protracted struggle, agreement was reached on 14 November 1864 to construct the line jointly, the Whitehaven, Cleator & Egremont making the most of its bargaining position and obtaining an undertaking that all its passenger services could again terminate at Bransty from 1 January 1865. Arrival and departure times were to be arranged to suit those on the Whitehaven & Furness Junction unless the Cleator company agreed to pay 6d (2½p) for the 'expense of a special engine' through the tunnel. (Despite the apparent reconciliation, this was not the end of the matter for the Cleator company's working timetable of 1 May 1875 noted that all trains would henceforth terminate at Corkickle.) An Act of 28 June 1866 authorised a 5 mile line from Egremont to Sellafield and established the Cleator & Furness Railway Committee for its joint operation, opening taking place on 2 August 1869 with an intermediate station at Beckermet. Trains were worked by the Cleator company under an arrangement with the Furness Railway which had by now absorbed the Whitehaven & Furness Junction. Further north a 1 mile freight branch from a junction just south of Moor Row to ore workings and a goods depot at Bigrigg was authorised on 19 June 1865 and by August 1867 was almost complete.

RAILS OVER THE SOLWAY

Development of the West Cumberland ore-field coincided with the working-out of ore deposits around Coatbridge supplying ironworks in Ayrshire and Lanarkshire. As a result, by the early 1860s over 100,000 tons of ore was being dispatched annually from the Cleator area to Scotland by rail with a further 20,000 tons being shipped from Whitehaven to Ardrossan. All the rail traffic was of necessity routed through Carlisle, it being calculated that the cost of transport would fall by 1s (5p) a ton if a direct line could be built across the Solway Firth. Hence the promotion in 1863 of the Dumfriesshire & Cumberland (Solway Junction) Railway under the guidance of Alexander Brogden, a South Wales ironmaster and a member of the family responsible for forming the Ulverstone & Lancaster Railway. As might be expected with a line which again involved a major estuary crossing, James Brunlees, designer of the Kent and Leven viaducts, was appointed engineer.

Under the shorter title of the Solway Junction Railway, the company was incorporated on 30 June 1864 with a capital of £320,000, most of the backing coming from Scottish interests although two of the directors were from Cumberland. Opposition was led by the Maryport & Carlisle, directly affected by loss of traffic, with further hostility coming from the North British and Glasgow & South Western. The Scottish portion of the line extending from a junction with the Caledonian at Kirtlebridge south to Annan, together with what was then the longest railway viaduct in the world stretching across the Solway to Bowness, is fully described in Volume 6 of this series (Scotland: The Lowlands and the Borders). In England the route as originally authorised ran south from Bowness, where a branch diverged to Port Carlisle, crossing over the River Wampool and connecting with the Carlisle – Silloth line at Kirkbride by means of a west-facing spur. It then continued almost due south to a triangular junction with the Maryport & Carlisle at Brayton. Matters were complicated by the North British making another attempt to gain access to West Cumberland's mineral wealth by an Abbey to Leegate line, largely duplicating the Solway Junction south of Kirkbride. This branch was authorised on 23 June 1864 but powers were suspended until the following year, Parliament decreeing that the Solway Junction should then apply to deviate its line via Abbey and that, if it was successful, the North British route should not proceed. The resulting Solway Junction Act of 29 June 1865 provided for a deviation running parallel with the Silloth line from Kirkbride to Abbey before continuing to Brayton as previously proposed. A west to south curve was to be built at Abbey for the benefit of the North British which was granted running powers from this point to Brayton in respect of mineral traffic.

In the following session the Solway Junction attempted to penetrate further south towards the ore-field by promoting a line from Bromfield, 2 miles north of Brayton, through Allonby to Maryport. Although thrown out, it succeeded in what was probably its prime purpose of persuading the Maryport & Carlisle to grant the company traffic facilities and full use of Brayton station in return for an undertaking that it would not again promote a similar extension. This agreement was confirmed by the Solway Junction Act of 15 July 1867 under which the line assumed its final form, the company being granted running powers from Kirkbride to Abbey and thus avoiding the necessity of constructing a parallel route between these points. The north to east curve at Brayton, the west to south curve at Abbey and the Port Carlisle branch were not built.

Opening of the $17\frac{1}{4}$ mile single-line route was delayed, surprisingly not by the giant viaduct over the Solway but by enormous difficulties in crossing the 2 miles of peat moss south of Bowness which for many years had been a swamp in places over 50 ft deep. It was first necessary to dig 10 ft deep ditches at 33 ft intervals with a further series of transverse dykes before a cart road could be laid on a 4 ft bed of faggots. The piles for the bridge over the Wampool had to be sunk 30 ft before reaching a boulder bed, and the line itself was laid on faggots, ballasted with ashes and strengthened with 18 ft sleepers. Goods traffic began on 13 September 1869 and passenger services south from Kirtlebridge to Bowness on 8 March 1870, but the Board of Trade refused to sanction the remainder of the route until the embankment over the moss was properly consolidated. The first passenger train over the whole line, an excursion from Aspatria to Dumfries Agricultural Show on 28 July 1870, was followed by full opening through to Brayton on 8 August. Under an agreement of 22 March 1867 the line was worked from the outset by the Caledonian Railway. An intermediate station at Whitrigg was opened on 1 October 1870, and at Abbey Junction, indicative of the mutual suspicion between the Caledonian and North British, there were separate platforms for the Solway and Silloth lines, the former opening on 31 August 1870. On the Abbey to Brayton section, Broomfield station made its first appearance in the timetables in April 1873 (it was more correctly renamed Bromfield on 1 November 1895).

WHEELING AND DEALING

With the formation of the Solway Junction in 1864 there were no less than eight railway companies in West Cumberland, the majority of them extremely prosperous as a result of the iron-ore boom. In the period 1863–6 the Maryport & Carlisle paid an average dividend of $9\frac{1}{2}$ per cent, the Whitehaven, Cleator & Egremont 9 per cent and the Whitehaven Junction $11\frac{1}{4}$ per cent, compared with a norm throughout the country of 4 per cent, and it was thus inevitable that outside companies should begin to take an interest in the region. A major factor was the incorporation in 1861 of the Cockermouth, Keswick & Penrith Railway, designed to provide a more direct link via Stainmore between the ore-field and County Durham with its blast furnaces and superior supplies of coking coal, the one essential resource lacking in West Cumberland. As outlined in the next chapter, the London & North Western soon gained a strong influence over the affairs of the new company and was thus only separated by the tiny Cockermouth & Workington from a potentially lucrative source of traffic.

Impending completion of the Cockermouth–Penrith line in 1864 initiated some involved negotiations which culminated in October with the Whitehaven Junction agreeing to take a lease of the Cockermouth & Workington at a figure of 10 per cent but being unsuccessful in its bid to lease the Whitehaven, Cleator & Egremont on a similar basis. The next move towards local consolidation in the face of powerful invasion came from the Maryport & Carlisle which promoted a Bill in the session of 1865 to amalgamate with or lease a total of five companies, the three serving Whitehaven plus the

Cockermouth & Workington and the Solway Junction, or one or more of them. At the same time, no doubt more than a little alarmed at London & North Western support being given to the Solway Junction in general and its proposed Maryport extension in particular, it decided to strengthen its defensive position by promoting the 6 mile Derwent branch. Extending from a south-facing junction with the existing main line near Bullgill, it negotiated some pronounced reverse curves before joining the Cockermouth & Workington by an east-facing junction at Brigham, thus providing a more direct northern outlet for the ore-field and a shorter route from Cockermouth to Carlisle.

The Derwent branch was authorised on 19 June 1865, but the Whitehaven Junction Bill for the lease of the Cockermouth & Workington was thrown out. The Maryport & Carlisle's Bill for a more comprehensive local merger met with such little support that it was withdrawn, several companies taking the parochial view that current high dividends meant there was no need for amalgamation. The *Railway Times*, in expressing great disappointment, commented: 'These disjointed associations are now almost entirely hemmed in by closely compacted and united systems, and they must either cohere in self-protection or fall a prey, one by one, to the snare of the fowler.' With the field now wide open for such intervention, this prophecy was soon realised and by July the London & North Western had stepped in and secured absorption of both the Whitehaven Junction at a fixed dividend of 10 per cent and the Cockermouth & Workington at 7 per cent, rising to 10 per cent in 1869. Sir Richard Moon, severe and hard-headed chairman of the 'Premier Line', later stated that it was the best bargain his company had ever made.

The Maryport & Carlisle immediately sought to protect its interests by depositing a Bill for various compulsory running powers, but this was withdrawn following conclusion of an agreement with the London & North Western on 2 April 1866. Under its terms the Maryport company was granted running powers from the southern end of its Derwent branch at Brigham east to Cockermouth and west to Marron Junction, and there was also a provision that a minimum of four passenger trains each way must be operated between

Maryport and Whitehaven in connection with services from Carlisle. Under further arrangements, the Whitehaven, Cleator & Egremont was granted running powers for passenger traffic from the northern end of its system to Brigham. Finally, it was agreed that one half of the mineral traffic from the ore-field to Scotland should be routed via Marron Junction, where it would be exchanged with the Maryport & Carlisle, and the other half via Whitehaven. The Cockermouth & Workington and Whitehaven Junction companies were dissolved and vested in the London & North Western by an Act of 16 July 1866, the same day as the Furness Railway received powers to absorb the Whitehaven & Furness Junction.

The Derwent branch was opened to goods traffic on 12 April 1867 and passengers on 1 June, a Maryport to Cockermouth service involving reversals at Bullgill and Brigham commencing on 1 November. Running powers into Cockermouth for freight traffic were exercised from 1 December; in reciprocation, the London & North Western worked limestone trains through to quarries at Papcastle by arrangement. Intermediate stations were at Dearham and Papcastle and, indicative of the slow decline of feudalism in West Cumberland, another Maryport & Carlisle private station came into being at this relatively late date. Situated at Dovenby, it was used exclusively by the Ballantine-Dykes

---

SCENES ON THE COCKERMOUTH, KESWICK & PENRITH

Top: A 'Cauliflower' 0–6–0 ambles through the countryside near Keswick with a scarcely-credible array of rolling stock in May 1936. *(L&GRP) Middle:* Having attached extra coaches, the up *Lakes Express* prepares to leave Keswick on 20 August 1960 hauled by Fowler 2–6–4T No 42314. *(John Marshall) Bottom:* By 1966 Keswick had become the terminus, a single track from Penrith terminating at a dead-end. A two-car diesel unit stands forlornly amid the desolation. Complete closure of the only railway to be built through the Lake District followed in 1972. *(Peter W. Robinson)*

family of Dovenby Hall, one of whom had been chairman of the company from 1842 to 1850.

Gradually the 'disjointed associations' continued to be ensnared. A peak demand for haematite led to a reduction in the amount of ore sent out of West Cumberland as ironworks sprang up all along the coast: the Maryport and neighbouring Solway works in 1868 and 1871 respectively; Moss Bay, Lowther and Derwent plants at Workington in 1872–4; Parton Ironworks in 1873; and the Lonsdale Iron & Steel Co at Whitehaven in 1872. The result was catastrophic for the Solway Junction which came close to writing its own obituary when it stated: 'The erection of numerous furnaces in Cumberland for smelting the Hematite iron ore has had a most prejudicial effect upon the company, as the ore raised in the district being now mostly consumed there, the great staple traffic which the line was constructed to carry is gone.' Its intriguing announcement that it hoped to bring 'important passenger traffic over the line' did not bear fruit, and instead it attempted to satisfy its creditors by arranging for the Scottish portion of the system to be transferred to the Caledonian in 1873. By 1881 arrears of interest on the company's debenture stock totalled £11,771, but even so the Solway Junction continued to indulge in some extraordinary flights of fancy such as its attempt in 1883 to build a line from Brayton to Bassenthwaite Lake as well as refreshment rooms at Abbey Junction and an hotel at Bowness! It at last gave up the unequal struggle when on 6 July 1895 it was fully vested in the

---

LAKELAND TERMINI

Top: Lake Side, purpose-built for passengers transferring from rail to Windermere steamers. A 5MT 4–6–0 awaits departure in July 1965, the last year of BR operations, though thanks to the Lakeside Railway the transfer from train to ship may still be made. (*Derek Cross*) *Middle:* Approach to Windermere, showing the once-extensive layout. (*L&GRP*) *Bottom:* Coniston, a jewel of a station in an incomparable mountain setting. Note the ground signals and the push-and-pull coach in this 1937 view. (*L&GRP*)

Caledonian. Another Scottish saga in Cumberland entered its final chapter on 12 August 1880 when the Port Carlisle Dock & Railway and the Carlisle & Silloth Bay Railway & Dock were fully amalgamated with the North British.

It was a different story with the Whitehaven, Cleator & Egremont, which in the fifteen years from 1860 paid an average dividend of $10\frac{3}{4}$ per cent and resisted several offers of amalgamation from the London & North Western. The advent of a competitive route (see below) finally caused it to succumb in 1877 when shareholders accepted a perpetual dividend of 10 per cent, vesting taking place on 1 July under an Act of 28 June. By this time the Furness Railway, anxious to strengthen its foothold in West Cumberland and resentful of penetration south of Whitehaven by the 'Premier Line', had mounted a strong campaign of opposition to the merger which culminated in agreement being reached in February 1877 that each company should have a half-share in the line. A further Act of 17 June 1878 accordingly amended the terms and provided for vesting in the North Western & Furness Joint Committee to take place from the following 1 July. The general pattern of operations from this date was that the London & North Western handled most passenger trains, many services now being extended to operate to and from Workington via both Whitehaven and Marron. It was also responsible for goods and mineral traffic north of Rowrah, the Furness generally working freight south of this point.

'TRACK OF THE IRONMASTERS'

Had the building of Britain's railways proceeded on any logical basis, the construction of lines in West Cumberland would in essence have ended with the opening of the Solway Junction in 1870. As it was, a whole new network of routes was yet to be superimposed on an area which already had close to saturation coverage. Behind this development lay the 1866 amalgamations which removed some key lines from local control and created immense dissatisfaction among many industrialists who maintained that Euston's sole interest in the region was to charge as high rates as possible. Yet even the local companies were not blameless in this respect, the position being well summed up by the local press when it made a blistering attack on the policies of the London & North Western:

The history of the L.N.W.R. in the district proves how extremely undesirable it is that the public should be placed at the mercy of a body of men whose only aim appears to be to get as much as they can, and give as little as possible in return . . . As for the travelling public, they have been humbugged to all intents and purposes, and rickety carriages, condemned for the main line, are considered good enough for West Cumberland.

Unpunctuality, defective management, high fares, exorbitant rates for traffic, scarcity of rolling stock, and second class passengers treated as so much rubbish – these are the leading features of L.N.W.R. policy in West Cumberland. But the North Western is not the only sinner, in respect of excessive rates. Both the Whitehaven, Cleator & Egremont and the Furness Railways are as deep in the mud as in the mire. The West Cumberland Blast Furnaces have to pay £9,000 more than a similar company in South Wales for hauling the same traffic over the same distance.

It was a round of price increases initiated by the Whitehaven, Cleator & Egremont in 1873 which proved the last straw and sparked off moves to find an alternative solution, culminating in the autumn of 1875 when a meeting was called by the West Cumberland Iron & Steel Co, the Moss Bay Hematite Iron Co and James Bain & Co of Harrington Ironworks. It was resolved to find the best route for a new railway to connect the ore-producing area around Cleator with Harrington, Workington and Maryport, a provisional committee being appointed with the 3rd Earl of Lonsdale as chairman and H. F. Curwen as vice-chairman. As the obvious route along the coast was already occupied by the London & North Western, it was necessary to adopt a high-level course diverging from the Whitehaven, Cleator & Egremont just south of Cleator Moor station and then climbing steeply to a summit 460 ft above sea-level near Moresby Parks before descending on long stretches of 1 in 70 through Distington and Workington to a junction with the London & North Western at Siddick. Despite strenuous opposition from the established companies, the Cleator & Workington Junction Railway was incorporated on 27 June 1876. Most of the £150,000 capital was put up by parties connected with the iron industry, hence the popular reference to the company as the 'track of the ironmasters'. Apart from the 11½ mile double-track 'main line', powers were also granted for a 1¼ mile branch at Workington from Dock Junction to Lonsdale Dock and for two lines diverging at Harrington Junction, the 1 mile Derwent branch to Moss Bay (North) and Derwent ironworks and the 1½ mile Harrington branch connecting at Rosehill Junction with a private mineral line serving James Bain & Co's colliery at Lowca.

Later in the year a Bill was promoted to enable the Furness to work the system and to authorise extensions from Cleator Moor to Egremont in the south and from Siddick to Dearham in the north. These would have given the Barrow company an independent outlet to the Maryport & Carlisle but were abandoned when it gained a half-share in the Whitehaven, Cleator & Egremont. Agreement was then reached on 6 April 1877 for the Furness to work the main line and the Lonsdale Dock branch for 33⅓ per cent of receipts on passenger and goods traffic and 35 per cent in the case of minerals, a joint committee being appointed to put these arrangements into effect. The agreement was confirmed by an Act of 28 June, and under a further Act of 21 July 1879 the Furness was authorised to purchase shares in the company up to a maximum of £25,000. A tripartite agreement was also concluded with the London & North Western regarding traffic from the Cleator Moor end of the system. Mineral workings over the main line and branches commenced in July 1879 with full opening to goods taking place on 4 August. Apart from ore from the Cleator area, the line also handled pig-iron in connection with the various ironworks, coal from local collieries, coke from the North East and at a later date manganese ore *en route* from Barrow to Workington. A passenger service between Moor Row and Workington (known as Workington Central from 10 July 1880) was inaugurated on 1 October 1879, trains calling at the company's own station at Cleator Moor as well as at Moresby Parks, Distington and High Harrington, these workings being extended to an exchange station at Siddick Junction from 1 September 1880. The footbridge here provided direct access to the sand dunes and beach, popular with rail-borne picnickers who gathered a local shellfish delicacy known as 'covens' which were taken home, boiled and then winkled out on the end of a pin and eaten. Halt platforms were provided at Keekle and Moresby Junction for workmen's services, the latter appearing in the public timetables from July 1910 until 2 January 1911 and from June 1913 until 1 October 1923.

The next line to be built by the Cleator & Workington Junction displayed a common West Cumberland characteristic in that it had strong Scottish associations. In the early 1870s the Glasgow ironmasters, William Baird & Co, decided to open up haematite veins in the Skiddaw Slates around Knockmurton, obtaining powers on 16 July 1874 for the 3 mile Rowrah & Kelton Fell (Mineral) Railway. As a result of its Scottish parentage the directors of this most obscure of minor railways included such famous names as Andrew K. McCosh and William Whitelaw, later chairman of the London & North Eastern Railway. Climbing east from Rowrah on a ruling gradient of 1 in 40, the line served several limestone quarries as well as a small coal depot at Kirkland before terminating at Knockmurton mine over 850 ft above sea-level and within 2 miles of Ennerdale Water. Locomotives and rolling stock were provided by Baird's and the line laid with 'slightly defective steel rails' supplied by Barrow Haematite Steel Co. Owing to disagreements regarding the junction with the Whitehaven, Cleator & Egremont at Rowrah, opening had to be postponed from the intended date of 11 November 1876 and it was not until mid-January 1877 that the line was considered operational. Under these circumstances the company turned to the Cleator & Workington Junction which on 5 May 1877 agreed to build a 6½ mile connecting branch from Distington to an end-on junction with the mineral railway at Rowrah. Authorised on 4 July 1878 and opened on 1 May 1882, 'Baird's Line' as it was always known had gradients which even by West Cumberland standards were ferocious. Two miles of 1 in 44 and a further mile of 1 in 52 took the branch past Oatlands to Whillimoor Top where it turned through more than ninety degrees and descended at 1 in 60 into Brownrigg Gill; here a magnificent horseshoe curve of 14 chains radius was followed by an abrupt climb out of the valley at 1 in 46, the final approach to Rowrah being preceded by a station at Arlecdon. Apart from providing an outlet for haematite and limestone traffic, the branch also served a small colliery near Oatlands station, terminus for a passenger service from Workington from 3 July 1883 until July 1892. In common with the Derwent and Harrington branches, the Cleator & Workington Junction worked the line to Rowrah with its own locomotives which from 1889 also ventured on to the mineral railway for limestone traffic.

The company made renewed attempts in the early 1880s to eliminate its dependence on the London & North Western for traffic to the north. It finally seemed to be on the point of creating an independent route to Scotland when on 16 July 1883 it obtained powers for a line from Calva Junction, just north of Workington, to Brayton, connecting directly with the Solway Junction which thus abandoned proposals for an extension from Bromfield to Brigham. The line would have entirely duplicated existing routes and in an era of increasingly difficult trading conditions proved to be beyond available resources. On 16 March 1886 an agreement, confirmed by an Act of 25 June, was concluded with the Maryport & Carlisle under which construction was not to extend beyond a junction with that company's Derwent branch at Linefoot, traffic facilities being granted forward to Brayton. Mineral trains, mainly conveying coke from the North East, commenced to run over the $6\frac{1}{2}$ mile steeply graded single-track route on 24 March 1887; at a later date some of these were worked through to Harrington Junction by Maryport & Carlisle locomotives. It was not unknown for trains to 'take off' when descending the gradient, suitably banked buffer stops being sited near Calva Junction for just such a contingency. Goods depots were provided at Seaton, Great Broughton and Linefoot and the line stimulated the development of new coal mines at Camerton and Buckhill. A passenger service from Workington to Seaton began on 4 January 1888, the route also becoming popular for excursions from Cleator Moor to Carlisle which were worked throughout by Furness Railway locomotives and carriages.

Powers for a number of short lines were also obtained in

1883. These included a spur from Workington Bridge to Cloffocks Junction, providing a direct link for coke traffic from the North East via Cockermouth when brought into use on 16 March 1885. A mile-long line diverging from the company's existing Derwent branch was opened as far as Moss Bay Ironworks (South) on 19 December 1885 and continued along the shoreline to Harrington harbour on 7 July 1893, but a further authorised extension to Harrington Ironworks was not constructed. A later development was the completion in May 1908 of a ½ mile line, diverging from the Lonsdale Dock branch, to serve St Helen's Colliery Coke Ovens.

BOOM TIME TO DEPRESSION

The 'track of the ironmasters' helped to take the West Cumberland iron industry to even greater heights. Ore production peaked at 1,725,438 tons in 1882, when there were no less than forty-five furnaces in blast at the various ironworks producing some 12 per cent of the country's pig-iron and 19 per cent of UK steel. The new line was directly responsible for the building of an ironworks inland from the coast at Distington in 1879, a choice of site also influenced by the activities of the Whitehaven, Cleator & Egremont which just prior to absorption had been making renewed efforts to open up fresh mineral reserves. On 2 August 1875 it obtained powers for its Gilgarran branch running westwards from Ullock Junction to Gilgarran colliery, supplemented on 27 June 1876 when authorisation was given for the Gilgarran extension to Distington and the Whitehaven branch descending a precipitous 250 ft in 2½ miles to a junction with the coast line at Parton. Opening of the entire 6¼ mile single-track route for goods traffic took place on 23 October 1879, a short-lived passenger service between Whitehaven and Distington surviving from 1 June 1881 until 8 December 1883. Lines now converged on Distington from five directions, the station being made joint, with three-quarters of the expenses born by the Cleator & Workington Junction and a quarter by the North Western & Furness Joint Committee. The line from Ullock Junction passed through the ironworks yard, thus providing a direct link for ore and limestone from the Rowrah area and enabling pig-iron to be dispatched to Whitehaven harbour via Parton (the Cleator & Workington Junction obtained running powers to the works rather than building its own branch as authorised by an Act of 3 June 1881). Two ½ mile long mineral lines were also added to the Whitehaven, Cleator & Egremont system at this time: the Mowbray branch near Frizington, authorised on 27 June 1876 and opened on 11 November 1879; and the Gillfoot branch, serving Helder mine, brought into use on 1 June 1880 after receiving powers under a London & North Western Act of 3 July 1879.

The tide of expansion rippled the full length of West Cumberland's coast. At Workington the population dramatically increased from 14,361 in 1881 to 23,749 ten years later following a decision in 1883 by Charles Cammell & Co to transfer its existing plant and work-force from Dronfield to its recently acquired Derwent Ironworks. It was a development which virtually forced the London & North Western to do something about its decrepit and much abused Workington station, a completely new structure at a higher level so as to eliminate two busy level crossings being opened on 7 November 1886. Maryport, which also enjoyed its maximum growth during this decade, became the main port for the West Cumberland iron and steel trade – and especially for the export of rails – with the completion in 1884 of Senhouse Dock, an associated London & North Western branch being brought into use on 16 June and a connection also being built by the Maryport & Carlisle. This latter company maintained its unbridled prosperity with dividends averaging 10½ per cent until the mid-1880s, although it did not proceed with branches proposed in 1882 from Maryport to Allonby and from Mealsgate to the heart of John Peel country at Caldbeck. Further north, there was a growth in rail traffic at Silloth following opening in June 1885 of the 6 acre New Dock flanked by Carr's colossal flour mill.

Perfection of the Gilchrist process of steel-making and consequent erosion of the monopoly enjoyed by haematite, coupled with importation of cheaper Spanish ores, meant that West Cumberland's heyday followed the pattern of Furness in being extremely short lived. A gradual decline from the late 1880s was coupled with virtual cessation of railway expansion, although one locally significant event followed the formation in 1909 of the Workington Iron & Steel Co which brought into a single concern the Harrington, Derwent, Lowther, Moss Bay and Solway ironworks, Harrington harbour, Lowca colliery and a part interest in Workington dock and harbour. The new company immediately expanded the colliery at Lowca and commissioned a coke and by-product plant, and on 7 June 1911 reached an agreement that its own locomotives could work through to this point from Derwent Ironworks using the Cleator & Workington Junction's Derwent and Harrington branches to reach the existing private mineral line at Rosehill. Difficulty was encountered in getting employees to Lowca, an awkward location perched directly on top of the unstable cliffs above the Parton–Harrington stretch of the coast line, and it was therefore arranged for workmen's trains to be operated from Workington. These proving successful, it was then decided to make them public by transforming the 2 mile private line from Rosehill Junction into the Harrington & Lowca Light Railway, the necessary Order being confirmed by the Board of Trade on 16 May 1913. A service of four trains each way, with one running through from Seaton, commenced on 2 June, the Furness Railway providing the locomotive and one coach which was attached for passengers other than workmen who were 'confined exclusively to their own coaches' owned by the Iron & Steel Co. Basic stations, akin to the 'bus shelters' of more recent times, were erected on the Cleator & Workington Junction at Harrington (Church Road) Halt. (opened November 1913) and Rosehill (Archer Street) Halt, and on the light railway at Copperas Hill, Micklam and Lowca. This obscure service has one claim to fame in that it ran over what is almost certainly the steepest gradient in Britain to have carried adhesion-worked passenger trains, a cruel 13 chains at 1 in 17 immediately following the stop at Archer Street. In bad weather trains had to set back from the halt towards Harrington Junction in order to have a run at the bank.

World War I brought a renaissance in industrial activity with the ironworks mostly operating at full capacity. The atmosphere of these years on the Cleator & Workington Junction, when very heavy mineral trains from the North East were picked up at Linefoot or, as a wartime expediency, at Maryport and taken to Harrington Junction or Distington, is well recalled by a former employee:

> More often than not, a Furness Railway 0–6–0ST would head a first train, followed perhaps by a Furness 0–6–0T banking, and at the same time hauling its own train, which in turn was banked by one or other, and sometimes both, of the above mentioned engine classes, all banging away up the bank – the long continuous incline of the Cleator & Workington main line. Smoke, steam and yes, flames roared out of the chimneys, and hundreds of pieces of fire shot up into the air and in falling often started lineside fires. The din was deafening, and some youngsters actually ran away at the sight and sound of such fury.

The need during this period to achieve savings in locomotive power saw through working of passenger trains between Whitehaven and Carlisle by both London & North Western and Maryport & Carlisle engines, the latter also running as far south as Millom with the 'evening mail'. On the freight side, coal trains from the North East were picked up by Furness locomotives at Workington because of the paucity of exchange-siding accommodation at Whitehaven, and on the 'track of the ironmasters' a turn was worked by the Maryport & Carlisle right through to Cleator Moor.

At Silloth, construction of a gun-testing range in 1886 and the opening, in 1905, of Solway Flour Mills augmented traffic flows on the branch. At the same time progress at last caught up with the Port Carlisle line. The track had deteriorated to such an extent that the spasmodic locomotive-hauled goods service had ceased on 1 January 1899, matters then remaining in limbo until modest freight operations resumed on 1 May with horse traction. Finally, the need for major renewals could be postponed no longer and as a result locomotives ousted animal power, England's last surviving horse-hauled passenger service ceasing on 4 April 1914. There was widespread lamentation with picture postcards and even a three-verse poem being produced to commemorate the event. 'Dandy No 1' was relegated to use as a pavilion for the local bowling club, but was rescued and restored by the LNER for the 1925 centenary celebrations and was then displayed at Edinburgh Waverley and later Carlisle Citadel before becoming an immaculately preserved exhibit in the National Railway Museum. The replacement passenger workings were withdrawn as a wartime measure from 1 January 1917 until 1 February 1919.

Demand for steel during the war enabled the West Cumberland economy to hold its own into the 1920s, but then changed conditions quickly brought disaster to an area so far removed from an industrial hinterland and so totally dependent on haematite and coal. Even before the war, local reserves of ore had begun to be worked out, causing many miners to go overseas in search of work and leading to the introduction of the through Friday-night carriage from Whitehaven to Southampton referred to in Chapter VIII. Virtual cessation of ore traffic to Scotland, coupled with the unsafe condition of the Solway viaduct, brought complete closure of the Solway Junction system south of Annan on 20 May 1921, passenger services having earlier been withdrawn from 1 January 1917 until 2 March 1919. In May 1922 the Abbey Junction to Brayton section was reopened for goods trains, worked by the Maryport & Carlisle by agreement with the Caledonian, the line also being used by excursions from West Cumberland to Silloth until closure was effected on 13 February 1933. Another casualty from lack of traffic to Scotland was the Calva Junction to Linefoot line which was closed beyond Buckhill colliery on 22 August 1921 (official date 1 September). Passenger services as far as Seaton had been withdrawn in July 1897, restored in February 1907, briefly extended to Linefoot between 1 September and November 1908 and were finally taken off in February 1922.

The Grouping of 1923 brought all lines in West Cumberland apart from the Port Carlisle and Silloth branches under the aegis of the London Midland & Scottish Railway. There were immediate repercussions for the Cleator & Workington Junction, which ended its independent days with 95 per cent of the shares being held by the United Steel Company as successor in 1919 to the Workington Iron & Steel Co. Its locomotives were reallocated to the ex London & North Western shed at Workington, where early one morning the shed master's clerk was not amused when he found a

'Cauliflower' of the non-vegetable variety resting on his desk. One of the newly transferred drivers had misjudged the engine's braking power with the result that it had demolished the buffer stop and carried on through the office wall! Most ore traffic over the 'track of the ironmasters' from the Cleator area was now diverted via Whitehaven, although in any event there was a trend for more ore to be imported by sea following replacement of Lonsdale Dock at Workington by the much larger Prince of Wales Dock in 1927. In addition, with recession biting ever deeper, all iron- and steel-making facilities were concentrated on the Moss Bay/Derwent site at Workington, the ironworks at Maryport, Distington, Harrington and Cleator Moor having all been closed by the end of the 1920s. As a result the Workington Bridge to Cloffocks Junction spur was no longer required and was removed on 26 March 1930, its use for coke traffic having gradually declined from the early 1900s following erection of coke ovens at most local collieries. The Dock branch at Workington was shut down on 27 July 1936 and the line from Moss Bay (South) to Harrington harbour lapsed into disuse prior to closure of this small port in 1928. Limestone from Rowrah Hall Quarry kept 'Baird's Line' open until 8 August 1938 when traffic was rerouted via Marron Junction over a modified connection at Rowrah. Passenger services as far as Oatlands had been reintroduced in November 1909 and from 5 October 1912 to 1 January 1917 were extended to Arlecdon (there had earlier been workmen's trains to this point) before being withdrawn in September 1922. Ore traffic over the connecting Rowrah & Kelton Fell line had ceased by 1 April 1917 when Baird's handed over operations to the Salter Quarry Co which purchased the railway on 1 November 1919; the greater part of it then became derelict, a fate which befell the remaining section when the quarry ceased production in 1927, although it was another seven years before the track was lifted.

Other closures to mineral traffic included the Ullock Junction–Distington line on 14 February 1929, the continuation on to Parton ceasing to handle trains north of the connection with Lowca colliery lines at Bain's siding on 2 May 1932. This route had again carried passenger workings between Whitehaven and Distington from 1 October 1913 until 1 September 1914, followed by a service exclusively for workmen as far as a newly opened Parton Halt some 100 yd up the branch which commenced on 11 January 1915 and ceased on 1 April 1929. The run-down of mineral extraction in the Cleator area brought closure on 21 July 1923 of the Mowbray branch and on 11 February 1931 of the Gillfoot branch and also the line to Eskett. At Maryport, the ex London & North Western line to the docks had been disconnected by the late 1930s.

Further changes on the passenger front saw the General Strike bring an end to public services over the Lowca Light Railway on 31 May 1926, workmen's trains surviving until 1 April 1929. With the number of unemployed at Maryport reaching an appalling 76.7 per cent of the insured population in June 1931, and lesser but still alarming figures being recorded throughout West Cumberland as the great depression of the 1930s brought desolation and poverty to a once thriving area, the LMS decided that the majority of local rail services could be replaced by road transport. No doubt influencing this decision was the fact that the company became a major shareholder in Tillings, which absorbed Cumberland Motor Services, the local bus operators. Passenger traffic between Aspatria and Mealsgate ceased on 22 September 1930, the line on to Aikbank Junction having been closed entirely on 1 August 1921 (an official notice refers to High Blaithwaite station reopening as required from 5 September 1921). The most drastic move came on 13 April 1931 with the withdrawal of passenger trains over the former Cleator & Workington Junction between Moor Row and Siddick Junction and also over the line through Rowrah from Moor Row to Marron (the station at Marron Junction had been closed as early as 1 July 1897, latterly having been used for 'exchange' purposes only, the east curve at this point being taken out on 5 October 1902). Services from Whitehaven to Egremont and Sellafield followed suit on 7 January 1935, and complete closure of the ex Maryport & Carlisle's Derwent branch on 29 April left only the lines along the coast and inland to Cockermouth and Penrith as LMS passenger-carrying routes. On LNER metals it was a rather more optimistic story with Silloth retaining its popularity as a seaside resort, steamer services surviving to Douglas and Dublin and through summer Saturday trains being put on from Newcastle. The Port Carlisle branch did however close to all traffic on 1 June 1932, despite attempts at a revival with the introduction on 9 July 1928 of a steam railcar service.

RECENT TIMES

It was not until just before the outbreak of World War II that concerted efforts at national level began to bring an improvement in the economic plight of West Cumberland, a trend that gathered momentum after the war with the injection of new industries. The spirit of optimism was reflected in the reintroduction of passenger trains between Whitehaven and Sellafield via Egremont from 6 May 1946, but it was perhaps a portent of things to come that they survived only until 16 June 1947 (workmen's services from Winder to Drigg via Egremont had earlier been operating from 11 March to 8 April 1940). One of the most important new industries was the Marchon chemical plant, built on a cliff-top site at Kells just to the south of Whitehaven. Considerable rail traffic in cement and sulphuric acid soon developed, leading to reopening in 1955 of the Mowbray brake, a rope-worked incline connecting the works with the coast route near Corkickle. By 1964 it was handling almost 500,000 tons of freight per annum and powers were sought for what would have been an expensive direct rail link from St Bees climbing some 250 ft in 3 miles. It was not constructed, the incline continuing as one of the very few examples of its kind in Britain. Its inability to handle large tankers and the need to make major renewals brought about its closure in early 1987.

A protracted improvement in the same area was the relining of Whitehaven tunnel, commenced in 1932 and finally completed in 1958, progress being limited because the necessary total possession could only be granted for some five hours during the night. The Corkickle end was opened out, reducing the length of the tunnel to 1,291 yd 2 ft. The 1950s brought an attempt to revitalise the Silloth branch, the first in Britain to have its steam passenger trains entirely replaced by diesel multiple units on 29 November 1954. DMUS also appeared on the Workington – Cockermouth – Keswick – Penrith route at this time (see next chapter), and were introduced on the coast line north of Whitehaven on 7 February 1955, from which date passengers for the south tended to travel via Carlisle rather than Barrow. Dieselisation failed to save the Silloth branch, which in the full flood of post-Beeching 'executions' was completely closed on 7 September 1964 amid scenes of unprecedented hostility. An angry and jeering crowd of an estimated 9,000 people packed the terminus and delayed departure of the last train for half an hour, with stones being thrown at the locomotive inspector, detonators placed on the track and dozens of teenagers staging a sit-down on the line. Allegedly to prevent any possibility of reopening, the track was lifted so quickly that several carriages were left stranded at Silloth and had to be dismantled where they stood. Eighteen months later complete closure on 18 April 1966 of the Workington–Cockermouth–Keswick line reduced West Cumberland's once extensive passenger network to just a single thread linking Barrow with Whitehaven, Workington, Maryport and Carlisle.

On the freight side, early post-war closures included the Bigrigg branch on 10 September 1951 and the Aspatria–Mealsgate line on 1 December 1952. The spur giving direct access from the Cockermouth–Workington route to the Prince of Wales Dock was taken out of use on 21 February 1953. Limestone from Rowrah Hall Quarry to Workington was rerouted via Moor Row from November 1953, causing the Rowrah–Marron Junction line to be closed from 3 May 1954 (official date 6 November 1960). At Cleator Moor the diverted trains ran over the Crossfield loop, the greater part of the Bowthorn line being abandoned about 1954 after a period of use for stabling condemned coaches. It survived at its western end to feed the former Cleator & Workington Junction main line, which lost its major traffic-producing point in 1961 when winding ceased at Walkmill colliery at Moresby Parks. Owing to continuing problems with landslips on the coast line between Parton and Harrington, the one-time 'track of the ironmasters' was maintained as a diversionary route until 1

July 1963 when it was closed between Cleator Moor and Distington. The next section northwards to Harrington Junction ceased normal operations on 16 September 1963, although the southbound line was retained as a 'through siding' to serve the High Duty Alloy works at Distington, opened during World War II on a site close to the former ironworks. This use ceased on 26 September 1965 when a further section of main line as far as Calva Junction was also closed, thus ending BR access to the Derwent branch which had been retained as far as Wilkinsons' Wagon Works just short of the bridge over the coast line. Harrington Junction did however still see trains, the United Steel Company (British Steel Corporation from 1967) continuing to work traffic from Moss Bay (South) to Lowca via the 1 in 17 up Copperas Hill until 23 May 1973, when the surviving portion of the Parton–Distington line giving access to Lowca was likewise closed.

At Maryport the company offices at the impressive passenger station were demolished in 1960, the remainder of the buildings being swept away about ten years later in favour of a 'bus shelter'. Further south, the end of British Steel operations at Rowrah Hall Quarry placed the Moor Row–Rowrah line in a state of suspended animation from which it never recovered, the last train running in February 1978 and track-lifting operations taking place in the summer of 1980.

FREIGHT LINES

Top: A pair of British Steel Corporation diesels surmount the incline up Copperas Hill on the Harrington & Lowca Light Railway. Its 1 in 17 gradient is the steepest in Britain to have carried adhesion-worked passenger trains, the service between Workington Central and Lowca surviving from 1913 to 1926. *(Peter W. Robinson) Middle:* A Whitehaven Junction Railway 0–6–0 at Lonsdale Dock, Workington, in the 1860s. On the left is a coal drop for lowering chaldron wagons into the ship's hold. *(Cumbria County Library) Bottom:* Roadside tramway at Burneside. A diminutive motor rail tractor with time to spare on the line linking the station with the Cowan Head paper mill of James Cropper & Co. *(W. S. Garth)*

West Cumberland's sole surviving haematite mine, at Becker-met, closed on 3 October 1980, thus ending the only traffic that remained from Mirehouse Junction through Moor Row and Egremont to Beckermet Mines Junction. Beyond this point the section to Sellafield was closed on 18 January 1970, a work-men's service from Moor Row having been withdrawn on 6 September 1965. The cumulative effect of all these closures is that the West Cumberland freight network has been reduced to almost the same skeletal form as the passenger system, the only remaining branch from the coast route being the ex Cleator & Workington Junction line from Siddick Junction to Calva Junction, where occasional trains reverse to reach the NATO arma-ments depot at Broughton Moor, traffic to the Buckhill colliery at this point having ceased in 1939.

Ironically, traffic levels on the coast line at first benefited from continued rationalisation of the local coal and steel industry. Gradual closure of the remaining collieries in the 1960s and early '70s left just Haig pit at Whitehaven. This was unable to meet the needs of the coke oven plant at Workington Iron & Steelworks, and thus some 4,000 tons of coal per week had to be brought in from Yorkshire plus a further 1,000 tons from South Wales. Similarly, cessation of steel-making at Workington in 1974 meant running daily train loads of steel blooms from Teesside, ore also being brought by rail from East Coast ports as the Prince of Wales Dock is too small for modern supercargo ships. Then in 1981 came the virtual shut-down of the Iron & Steelworks, leaving just the rail mill, an event that not only marked the end of iron-making in West

---

Cumberland after over 130 years but also decimated
Workington–Carlisle freight traffic. Some compensation was
provided in the same year with the opening of an opencast
depot between Maryport and Flimby, leading to an upsurge of
rail-borne coal to Fiddlers Ferry terminal near Widnes.
Another blow was the closure of Haig pit in 1986. This further
reduced traffic flows on the coast route, which would have an
insecure future were it not for the existence at Sellafield of
British Nuclear Fuels with its commitment to moving 'hazard-
ous' freight by rail.

CHAPTER VII

The Lake District

'RASH ASSAULT'

Until the second half of the eighteenth century the Lake District belonged to the people who lived and worked there and who neither perceived nor cared that their surroundings formed England's most spectacular stretch of countryside. Then the age of the early travellers who gazed with a mixture of awe and horror at the high peaks and deep lakes merged with the Romantic era which revered mountains as stimuli to the emotions and symbols of natural order. Visitors came in rapidly growing numbers, drawn by the flowery prose of the pioneer guidebooks and the outpourings of the Lake Poets, which captured popular imagination and turned the region into one of literary pilgrimage. Wordsworth spearheaded the movement which saw the Lake District as a place of national heritage, the epitome of arcadia where the countryside and its inhabitants could be preserved as if in aspic, protected from the growing industrialisation of the outside world.

Such attitudes inevitably tended to cast railways in the role of creeping blight; as early as 1838 Wordsworth's wife, Mary, could suggest that they would have to leave their home at Rydal Mount every August and September once the West Coast route reached Lancaster because visitors would overrun the Lakes. When in August 1844 proposals were announced for a line extending from the Lancaster & Carlisle at Oxenholme to a terminus at Low Wood, on the Windermere shore between Bowness and Ambleside, the wrath of the poet was both impassioned and immediate. He launched a concerted attack on the proposals, writing letters to the most influential newspapers and people of the day, including Gladstone: 'The project, if carried into effect, will destroy the staple of the country which is its beauty, and on the Lord's Day particularly, will prove subversive of its quiet, and be highly injurious to its morals.' In October he penned his now famous sonnet, beginning 'Is there no nook of English ground secure from rash assault?', which 'breathed into his hearers a contagious fire' when first read at Rydal.

The propaganda and lobbying successfully created an opposition movement among affected landowners but in November this was dissipated when it was announced that the line was to be cut back to Birthwaite (now Windermere). Yet Wordsworth and his allies still feared it would be extended over Dunmail Raise to Keswick. In December the poet wrote two patronising letters to the *Morning Post*, accompanied by his earlier sonnet and another one infinitely worse (see Appendix II).

Most of the poet's predictions have to some extent proved correct, although not necessarily as a result of the railway age, but in the mid-1840s they were years ahead of their time and out of step with prevailing Victorian ideals of *laissez-faire* expansionism and free trade. Wordsworth was accused in the national press of unrivalled snobbery and attacked for his 'spirit of exclusiveness'. Without the support of the landowners, his protests had little effect and the Kendal & Windermere Railway Bill passed through Parliament with remarkably little fuss during 1845. So too did the next four lines to penetrate the Lake District – the Coniston and Lake Side branches, the Ravenglass & Eskdale and even the Cockermouth, Keswick & Penrith, cutting through the heart of northern Lakeland – none of which drew what we would now term environmental objections.

It was not until changing attitudes in the second half of the Victorian age began to question traditional economic dogma that there was another wave of protest against railway expansion. Proposals for a link from Windermere to Keswick had been frequently canvassed since completion of the Cockermouth–Penrith line in 1865 and in the winter of 1875–6 it seemed these were about to come to a head. There was a feeling, particularly in intellectual and professional circles, that the Lake District was now adequately served by railways and that any further growth would destroy the unique peace and wildness of the untouched central region. A powerful editorial in the *Saturday Review* of 22 January 1876 referred to the Lakes as being the one part of Great Britain 'which can be said to be held in trust for the whole nation'. Echoing the sentiments of Wordsworth, it commented: 'If the ascent of Helvellyn or Fairfield had to be begun amidst the smoke of chimneys, the roar of furnaces, and the shrieks of railway engines, the special charm of the Lake scenery would be gone.'

With the support of Tennyson and Browning, the campaign against the line had as its figurehead John Ruskin, the distinguished painter, art critic and social historian who in 1871 had moved to Brantwood near Coniston. He regarded the Lake District as a haven from the worst evils of the industrial revolution and made no secret of the fact that he detested railways. His pleadings had a familiar ring:

> The stupid herds of modern tourists let themselves be emptied, like coals from a sack, at Windermere and Keswick. Having got there, what the new railway has to do is to shovel those who have come to Keswick, to Windermere – and to shovel those who have come to Windermere, to Keswick. And what then? All that your railroad company can do for [the tourists] is only to open taverns and skittle grounds round Grasmere, which will soon, then, be nothing but a pool of drainage, with a beach of broken gingerbeer bottles; and their minds will be no more improved by contemplating the scenery of such a lake than Blackpool.

Yet it is doubtful if such views would have triumphed over the argument that the line would tap valuable mineral resources, and it was perhaps as well for the conservationist lobby that the scheme was laid aside when both estimated costs and traffic projections proved discouraging. It was a very different story less than a decade later when in 1882 a Bill was deposited for the Braithwaite & Buttermere Railway, an 8 mile mineral line climbing above the west side of Derwentwater and Borrowdale to serve the slate quarries on top of Honister Pass. The result, coming close on the heels of Manchester Corporation's success in brushing opposition aside and acquiring Thirlmere for reservoir purposes, was the formation in 1883 of the Lake District Defence Society which attracted an impressive array of elite support and claimed to have 'members of national weight and power in every department of English life'. Its secretary, Canon Rawnsley was at pains to avoid the divisive arguments of Wordsworth and Ruskin and fought a careful campaign designed to appeal to local commercial and tourist interests:

> Are the proprietors who work the slate quarry up in Honister to be allowed to damage irretrievably the health, rest and pleasure ground of the whole of their fellow countrymen who come here for needed quiet and rest? Let the slate trains once roar along the western side of Derwentwater, and Keswick as a resort of weary men in search of rest will cease to be.

The Bill was withdrawn, the new society going on in the same year to oppose the Ennerdale Railway, a 6¼ mile line diverging from the Whitehaven, Cleator & Egremont at Esket Junction and intended to tap iron-ore deposits in the upper part of the valley. Similar proposals had already been put forward the previous year, but the 1883 hearing was notable for the case advanced by James Bryce, MP, chairman of the Commons Preservation Society, who felt that the Lakes should be kept 'free from the intrusion of railways altogether'. He obtained an instruction that the Commons select committee had 'to enquire whether the proposed railway will interfere with the enjoyment by the public who annually visit the Lake District by injuriously affecting the scenery in the neighbourhood'. Thus, for the first time amenity objections were heard in Parliament against railway development in the region, although the House was able to sidestep the issue by rejecting the Bill on financial rather than aesthetic grounds During its passage the chief promoter became insane and murdered his wife, but this did not stop the scheme once more reappearing in the session of 1884. By this time Canon Rawnsley was able to state that 'public opinion throughout the country has been aroused by the fact that there is this threatening of one of the finest valleys in the lovely Lakeland which every year is more and more dependent on tourists'. He deplored suggestions that the railway would take excursionists into the valley, claiming that they would want 'drink shops whirligigs and donkeys'. Further opposition came from M. J Baddeley of guidebook fame, and more extremist views were put forward by Alfred Hunt of the Royal Society of Painters in Water Colours who insisted that to build the line 'would be a very wicked thing to do, and would injure the course of English Art very deeply'. The Bill was again thrown out on its financial demerits.

A similar pattern was followed in 1886 when a Bill was put forward for the Ambleside Railway, an independently promoted extension of the Windermere branch. James Bryce and Canon Rawnsley orchestrated what was by now the almost traditional opposition campaign, receiving support from the national press as instanced by the *Daily Telegraph* of 15 November 1886: 'If the ultimate object of the proposed railway be to drive the railway through ... to Keswick, the stoutest resistance to any such scheme should be offered by every lover of splendid natural scenery in the three kingdoms.' The project collapsed when the London & North Western refused to work the line. It was the last Lake District railway scheme to come before Parliament, the conservation movement gathering further strength in 1895 when Rawnsley played a leading role in the formation of the National Trust. The following year an Ambleside Light Railway was quickly suppressed as were proposals in 1899 by the British Electric Traction Company for a 3 ft 6 in gauge tramway along the shores of Windermere from Bowness to Ambleside.

Down the years different ventures continued to be put forward with little real chance of success. In 1921 a £150,000 scheme was floated for an Ambleside–Keswick line worked by specially designed petrol-electric engines to meet anticipated objections over noise and smoke emission. Surviving LMS internal correspondence shows that in 1934 the company considered establishing 'aerial transport' to the summit of either Wansfell or Coniston Old Man. The Wansfell project involved twenty-five cable cars, the estimated cost being £34,760 plus an extra £3,000 for a tea-house at the summit. The possibility of a link between the Dalegarth terminus of the Ravenglass & Eskdale Railway and the top of England's highest mountain was also canvassed: 'The question of providing transport to the summit of Scafell, either by rack railway or aerial ropeway, is one which is attended by great possibilities, and once this is established it will attract large

numbers. The laying of a suitable railway up Scafell would b
a much simpler undertaking than up Snowdon.'

The post-war era of motorways and massive destruction c
the environment caused the wheel to come full circle with th
Lake District's railways now being seen by comparison as
relatively harmless feature of the landscape. Acceptance gav
way to endearment as they drifted into decline but little wa
done to resist closure and in 1958 the Coniston branch cease
operations to be followed in the mid-1960s by the Lake Sid
and Keswick–Cockermouth lines. The surviving link betwee
the West Coast route and Keswick slipped away in 1972
ironically at a time when amenity interests were in full cry ove
proposals for the new A66 trunk road from Penrith t
Cockermouth, closely paralleling the railway and indeed usin
part of its track-bed alongside Bassenthwaite Lake. Th
project went ahead, despite a protest meeting on Latrig
summit on 14 October 1973 when Colin Speakman for th
Ramblers' Association stated:

> The road – a juggernaut highway – will dominate one of the
> most beautiful and delicate landscapes in Britain. In the future
> someone will realise that the little railway line that once ran so
> unobtrusively below us could have carried all those people and
> all those heavy loads at a tiny fraction of the cost and damage to
> the environment.

After more than a century railways had clearly been forgive
for their 'rash assault', although the former arguments agains
them lived on in a new guise. Wordsworth and Ruskin woulc
have relished the *Daily Telegraph*'s comment on the road: 'Thi
is a crime, make no mistake. It is a matter of commercial greec
against humanity, of God and Mammon.' Modes of transpor
may change but the basic issues tend to remain the same. Jus
as the Cockermouth, Keswick & Penrith was the only railwa
to be built through the Lake District, so it seems probable tha
the A66 will be the only new highway to penetrate the region
A Windermere–Keswick rail link was constantly resisted, ir
the same way as have been 'improvements' to the roac
between the two towns. Heavy lorries are now barred from thi
route and have to make a devious journey very similar to th
one freight was compelled to take in the railway age.

KENDAL AND WINDERMERE

The first railway to serve the Lake District had its origins in the complex genesis of the West Coast main line as outlined in Chapter II. When it became clear that the Lancaster & Carlisle was to pass no nearer Kendal than Oxenholme, a full 2 miles distant, the inhabitants of Westmorland's largest town soon decided to form a local company. Rather than build just a short link with the main line, the provisional committee took the then bold step of promoting a branch which would continue to the shores of Windermere and thus serve a dual function by also catering for the developing tourist trade. The 10¼ mile Kendal & Windermere Railway was incorporated on 30 June 1845 with a capital of £125,000 and had as its leading light Cornelius Nicholson who had earlier led the unsuccessful campaign for a West Coast route through Kendal via Longsleddale. Work was initially concentrated at the eastern end of the line between Oxenholme and Kendal so that it could be opened to passengers at the same time as the southern portion of the Lancaster & Carlisle on 22 September 1846.

Viaduct over the River Kent, Kendal

Goods traffic to Kendal commenced on 4 January 1847 and on 21 April the double-track branch was opened throughout to its Windermere terminus, a mile north of Bowness. It was both a gala occasion and a beautiful spring day with many passengers strolling down to the lake to take a trip on the steamer service to Newby Bridge and Waterhead (Ambleside), introduced two years earlier.

The line descended at 1 in 80 from Oxenholme to Kendal and then followed the Kent Valley to intermediate stations at Burneside (closed from January 1855 to May 1857) and Staveley. A 2½ mile climb at 1 in 80 took the branch to its bleak and barren summit at Blackmoss, almost on the 500 ft contour, which preceded the abrupt 1 in 65 plunge to Droomer crossing, just short of the terminus. Until the summer of 1850 locomotives and rolling stock were provided by the London & North Western as part of the pool it made available to the Lancaster & Carlisle. The branch was then worked under contract by E.B. Wilson & Co of Leeds until November 1851 when the company itself assumed control. Unfortunately its trains were so often late in arriving at Oxenholme that eventually the Lancaster & Carlisle despaired of the situation and issued instructions that its services should no longer wait for those off the branch. There were many other causes of friction between the two concerns, as instanced by the occasion when the Kendal & Windermere was ejected from the main-line company's telegraph office at Oxenholme because it was using it as a booking office without consent. The last straw occurred when the Lancaster & Carlisle started to run its own goods collection and delivery service in the Kendal area. Surrender came when the Kendal & Windermere agreed to be leased in perpetuity by the Lancaster company from 1 May 1858, the terms being included in the latter's Act of 13 August 1859. Owing to continuing controversy, matters were not finalised until after the Lancaster & Carlisle had itself been leased by the London & North Western in the second half of 1859 (the Kendal & Windermere, like the Lancaster company, survived as a legally separate entity until 21 July 1879).

The new influence was soon felt. In May 1860 the *Westmorland Gazette*, lamenting Kendal's reputation of having 'the worst railway station in the kingdom', welcomed the announcement that the London & North Western was to build at a cost of £7,000 a 'handsome and substantial' structure to replace 'the wretched wooden sheds which have long done duty'. Duly completed the following year, the station symbolised changes the railway had brought to the town, shoe manufacture and a whole host of new industries having to a large extent superseded the declining wool trade. The branch also had a profound influence at Burneside, a new village being built to cater for the developing paper mills of James Cropper & Co which received huge consignments of coal and paper pulp by rail. From the 1870s the three mills were linked to the station by a 1½ mile narrow-gauge tramway (converted to standard gauge in 1927). Charles James Cropper was a director of the London & North Western Railway; as a perk the company was allowed to have the station painted in colours of its own choice and expresses would make a special stop to pick up or set down the firm's representatives.

Yet, as Wordsworth had feared, it was at Windermere that the line brought the most dramatic transformation. At the opening in 1847 the station existed in glorious isolation high above the lake, its colonnaded *porte-cochère* forming the railway gateway to Lakeland. From here connecting coach services departed to Coniston, Hawkshead, Ambleside, Keswick and Cockermouth. The only nearby building was the Windermere Hotel, constructed to coincide with completion of the line and linked to the station by a private drive. The railway attracted increasing numbers of long-stay holiday-makers and also opened up the immediate area to people at two very different ends of the all-important Victorian social spectrum. The wealthy, especially 'cotton kings' from the Manchester and Liverpool areas, were able to use Windermere as a weekend and summer refuge, building large houses in even larger grounds which both offered splendid views across the lake and isolated their occupants from the other type of visitor who came by train. This was the working-class day-tripper, who in the time available was unable to venture far from the station and thus even at this early date caused the promenades at Bowness to be thronged with jostling crowds. The inaugural excursion to Windermere ran in August 1847 and in its first full year the line carried 120,000 passengers, two-thirds of them between May and October.

Within a decade the original isolation of the terminus was over. In 1855, Harriet Martineau noted in her book *The Complete Guide to the English Lakes*: 'A few years previously the area was so secluded that it was some distinction even for the most travelled man to have seen it. Now there is a Windermere railway station, and a Windermere post office and hotel – a thriving village and a populous locality.' Gradually the village turned into a town which by the mid-1880s had over forty lodging houses, a college, school, church and small shopping centre. The combined population of Bowness and Windermere more than doubled in the second half of the century from 2,085 in 1851 to 4,613 in 1891, and by 1887 it was being stated that 'the property around Windermere station is over crowded with villas'. Rising wages and increasing free time now brought growing numbers of excursionists; on Whit Monday 1883 some 8,000 of them arrived at the terminus.

At the opening ceremonies Cornelius Nicholson had prophesied the day would come when express trains from Manchester to Windermere would 'bring the merchant and manufacturer after he has finished his correspondence or left the Exchange, down to the shore of that beautiful lake, and if he likes carry him back next morning in time for breakfast'. By the turn of the century these hopes had been realised. In 1910 the Windermere Express, as it was proudly designated in *Bradshaw*, was covering the down journey between the two centres in just two minutes over two hours, stopping only at Preston and Lancaster. At first it was limited to a northbound working on Friday evenings with a return on Monday mornings but later became a regular weekday service in both directions. The London & North Western catered for the cotton barons by providing an exclusive club carriage, available only to holders of first-class season tickets who had to apply to the club committee for admission which was by election and involved payment of a hefty annual subscription. This exotic vehicle, with a comfortable armchair for each member, writing desks, sherry cabinets and a big clock on the wall, survived on the service until the outbreak of World War II.

Excursion traffic reached peaks in the 1930s and 1950s when on occasions empty stock had to be stabled as far away as Milnthorpe. There was outward as well as inward business, a very popular evening excursion to Morecambe including admission to the Winter Gardens as part of its 1s 1d (5½p) return fare! Decline set in abruptly in the 1960s, by which time many trains were carrying fewer than ten passengers in the winter. The Manchester 'club train', as it was still often called, ceased in 1966, and by 1968 there were no services beyond Preston apart from one London train which lasted another two years. Goods facilities at Windermere were withdrawn on 28 April 1969 and at Kendal on 1 May 1972, and in 1973, despite strong local opposition, the branch was reduced to nothing more than a long, single-track siding as part of the rationalisation preceding electrification of the West Coast route. This created the bizarre situation of excursions having to terminate at Oxenholme and disgorge their passengers on to droves of road coaches while the trains were worked empty over the 50 miles to Carlisle for turning and servicing. A campaign by the Friends of the Lake District for restoration of run-round facilities at the terminus was not successful, but at least Lakeland's only remaining branch line has tenaciously survived with a quite respectable diesel unit service. In 1985 the original Windermere station was tastefully converted into a supermarket, a new 'chalet'-style terminus slightly up the line being formally opened on 17 April 1986.

THE CONISTON BRANCH

Among the most famous of Lake District industries have been the Coniston copper mines where large-scale working began in 1599. Two hundred and fifty years later, in 1849, when the Coniston Mining Company was employing 400 men and producing 250 tons of ore per month, a 3 ft 3 in gauge line was proposed from Coniston to the newly completed Furness Railway at Broughton in an attempt to solve transport problems which were severely restricting expansion. Although the project did not then proceed, it was revived seven years later as a standard-gauge line following the same route. Incorporated on 10 August 1857 with a capital of £45,000, the

Coniston Railway was nominally independent but closely allied with the Furness, the chairman being the Duke of Devonshire and the secretary James Ramsden. The Furness agreed to take shares to the value of £10,000, an identical amount also being purchased by the owners and lessees of the mines. Despite the original contractors, Messrs Child and Pickle of Bradford, becoming bankrupt, the 8½ mile single-track branch was opened to passengers on 18 June 1859. It climbed steeply from an end-on junction at Broughton, almost at sea-level, past intermediate stations at Woodland and Torver before brushing the 350 ft contour and gradually descending to Coniston Lake terminus (known simply as Coniston from 1914). Goods and mineral traffic did not begin until 1860 when a short extension to Copper Mines Wharf was also brought into use. The line was worked by the Furness from the outset and amalgamated with it by an Act of 7 July 1862.

Unfortunately completion of the branch coincided with the peak period of the copper mines which entered a slow decline from the mid-1860s and a swifter one from the mid-'70s as the ores were worked out. The railway, like so many others, was increasingly forced to rely on tourist traffic. It found itself at a grave disadvantage, facing west away from both central Lakeland and civilisation, and with its terminus having been built high above Coniston village and lake in order to allow access to the mines. Had the branch been designed primarily with tourism in mind, like the earlier Windermere and later Lake Side lines, it would almost certainly have diverged from the Carnforth–Barrow route near Ulverston and followed the Crake Valley due north in order to run alongside Coniston Water. The indirectness of the rail journey featured in a fine piece of satire by Ruskin, writing in 1875 in typically bombastic tones from nearby Brantwood:

> In old times, if a Coniston peasant had any business in Ulverston he walked . . .
>
> But now he would never do such a thing. He first walks three miles in a contrary direction to a railroad station, and then travels by railroad twenty-four miles to Ulverston, paying 2s fare. During the twenty-four miles transit, he is idle, dusty, stupid; and either more hot or cold than is pleasant to him. In

either case he drinks beer at two or three of the stations; passes his time between them with anybody he can find, in talking about anything to talk of; and such talk always becomes vicious.

He arrives at Ulverston, half-drunk and otherwise demoralised, and 3s at least poorer than in the morning. Of that sum 1s has gone for beer, 3d to a railway shareholder, 3d in coals and 1s 6d has been spent in employing strong men in the vile mechanical work of making and driving a machine, instead of his own legs, to carry the drunken lout. The results, absolute loss and demoralisation to the poor on all sides, and iniquitous gain to the rich.

Attempts had been made to develop tourist traffic as soon as the line opened, a group of Furness Railway directors instituting steamer services on Coniston Water which were later formalised by an Act of 18 July 1872. The famous *Gondola* was commissioned at a cost of £1,100 and built in sections by Jones, Quiggin & Co of Liverpool before being transported by rail and cart for assembly at Coniston Hall; she was launched in October 1859 and commenced regular summer services in June 1860. Described as 'the perfect combination of the Venetian gondola and the English steam yacht', her graceful lines and unique appearance captured public imagination in a remarkable way. In 1906, during the golden age of Lakeland tourism, she carried over 22,000 passengers, a 50 per cent increase on the figure of ten years earlier. As a result it was decided to provide a more modern replacement vessel, *Lady of the Lake*, which was built at Southampton and similarly transported in sections prior to being launched in May 1908. Sentiment for the *Gondola* proved so strong that she was recommissioned and both vessels continued in service until the outbreak of World War II when sailings ceased. The *Lady* was broken up in 1950, but *Gondola*, after being converted into a houseboat and later submerged, was acquired by the National Trust. Following a £100,000 appeal, she was magnificently restored by Vickers of Barrow and recommenced public sailings on the lake in July 1980, thus providing a direct link with the early days of the Furness Railway.

The normal branch service was based on Foxfield, although in the 1870s and '80s there was a daily through train via the Dalton Loop to Furness Abbey where it was combined with a

Barrow–Carnforth working. From September 1891 it was rerouted through Barrow. By 1913 traffic justified the provision of a 'large tea pavilion' at the terminus, a facility which fortunately did not blemish a particularly attractive station with its Swiss cottage style of architecture, overall roof and gabled drystone walls. During this period the station goods yard handled quite sizeable quantities of slate from quarries on Coniston Old Man and near Elterwater as well as timber traffic, all brought in by teams of horses.

Although regular excursions continued in BR days, the branch never overcame its inherent drawbacks and with annual losses put at over £16,000 became the first Lake District line to close to passengers, on 6 October 1958. Thereafter traffic beyond Broughton was slight, consisting of a thrice-weekly goods which survived until 30 April 1962 when complete closure north of Foxfield took place. Withdrawal of passenger facilities almost coincided with the opening of a central secondary school at Coniston, thus creating extra bus traffic on an inadequate road system and leading to much ill feeling in the locality. In his *Lake District Transport Report*, published in 1961, David St John Thomas noted:

> Coniston people find it hard to look at the matter dispassionately... To add hurt to their pride, the bus – though paid for by British Railways and running in some kind of connection with trains at Foxfield – is not honoured with a mention in the railway timetable. Euston has forgotten, Coniston is disappointed, disillusioned.

THROUGH NORTHERN LAKELAND

The relatively low-lying route through northern Lakeland created by the River Derwent and its tributaries first attracted attention during the Railway Mania period when unsuccessful ventures included the Cumberland Union, a Cockermouth–Keswick–Penrith line which proposed to use atmospheric traction. Seemingly more promising was the Cockermouth & Workington Extension Railway, incorporated on 3 August 1846 as part of an intended through route from West Cumberland to Windermere. Nominally independent, it was

nevertheless closely connected with the Cockermouth &
Workington (see Chapter VI) which it sought to continue
round the north and east sides of Bassenthwaite Lake as far as
Keswick. The project became stillborn when both the
Windermere line and another associated scheme for a link to
Penrith, the East & West Cumberland Junction Railway,
failed to progress.

Matters then rested until the formation in 1857 of the South
Durham & Lancashire Union Railway and a year later the
Eden Valley Railway. This left only a relatively short gap
between Penrith and Cockermouth to be bridged in order to
create an alternative cross-country route to the existing
Newcastle–Carlisle–Maryport lines for the transit of pig-iron/
iron ore eastwards and coke westwards, thus enabling South
Durham coal owners to compete on more equal terms with
those in North Durham and Northumberland for West
Cumberland markets. In 1860 a scheme was put forward for a
line from Maryport to Penrith via Caldbeck, designed to serve
the additional function of tapping deposits of coal, lead, silver
and copper in the fells north of Skiddaw. Backed by the
Maryport & Carlisle as a defensive measure, it was soon
quashed in favour of the Cockermouth, Keswick & Penrith
Railway which had the more certain virtue of tourist potential
and was incorporated on 1 August 1861 with a capital of
£200,000. The route was engineered by Thomas Bouch, who
had also been responsible for the Stainmore line, the contract
price of £267,000 for the $31\frac{1}{4}$ miles of single track including the
exceptionally high total of 135 bridges.

The London & North Western quickly gained a strong
influence over the company through its controlling position at
the Penrith end. An Act of 29 June 1863 provided that it was to
work all traffic except mineral; this was to be handled by the
Stockton & Darlington Railway which at the beginning of that
year had absorbed both the South Durham & Lancashire
Union and Eden Valley lines. The two operating companies
were each authorised to subscribe up to £25,000 and appoint
two directors to a joint committee of management. Opening to
minerals took place on 26 October 1864 with an initial
passenger service of three trains each way commencing on 2
January 1865, the intermediate stations being Blencow,

Penruddock, Troutbeck, Threlkeld, Keswick, Braithwaite, Bassen-thwaite Lake and Embleton. In addition there were at one time platforms at remote Highgate, near Mosedale, where from 1908 until 1928 trains stopped twice a day to take children to and from school. Between Threlkeld and Keswick, the LMS provided a platform to serve Briery Bobbin Mill, and this was used by workmen's trains until the mill's closure in 1958.

By the time the line had been completed the Stockton & Darlington had become part of the North Eastern Railway which on 23 June 1864 received powers to build a 1 mile spur from Eamont Junction on the West Coast route to Redhills Junction on the Cockermouth line. Promoted to eliminate the need for mineral traffic to reverse at Penrith, the Redhills curve was brought into use on 5 September 1866. At the opposite end of the line, it had proved impossible to commence construction at the existing Cockermouth & Workington terminus which was left at the end of a ½ mile branch and became the town's goods depot. Livestock and all passenger services were handled at a station on the new route on the south side of the town, the incorporation Act of 1861 providing that both stations should be placed under control of a joint committee. These arrangements continued with only slight legal modifications after 1866 when the Cockermouth & Workington was absorbed by the London & North Western, an event that brought in its wake a standard pattern of through Penrith–Workington train services.

Although seldom heralded as such, the line was one of the outstanding scenic routes of England. It climbed steeply away from Penrith for over 4 miles at 1 in 70 and near Blencow traversed a gradual but complete horse-shoe which included the impressive St Andrew's Cutting blasted through solid rock. By this means it gained sufficient height within 9½ miles to reach a summit level of 889 ft, a mere 26 ft lower than Shap, at a point east of Troutbeck. The line then dropped abruptly at 1 in 62½ to just short of Threlkeld, falling almost 400 ft in 4 miles and offering splendid views of the striking peak of Saddleback, especially from the twelve-arch Mosedale viaduct. The character of the route now changed completely as it plunged into the Greta gorge, a miniature canyon so thickly wooded that from above there was little indication of a railway in the bottom apart from eight slender bow-string girder bridges criss-crossing the river. Emerging suddenly at Keswick, the floodplain of the Derwent was crossed before the line swung northwards and hugged the western shore of Bassenthwaite Lake for a full 3 miles, this final spectacular burst with broad panoramas of Skiddaw preceding more gentle surroundings on the approach to Cockermouth.

Prior to the coming of the railway Keswick had stagnated, as indicated by a fractional population decline in the ten years from 1851 and the fact that in 1862 it retained the heaviest stage-coach traffic still surviving in England. From the outset the railway's directors appreciated the advantages of promoting the tourist trade in the town, with its superb situation in almost Alpine style among high mountains encapsulating the ideals of visitors who wanted to share the uplifting power of the scenery as publicised by Wordsworth and his contemporaries. Easter Monday of 1865 brought 1,200 day visitors from Carlisle, Penrith and West Cumberland, and in May 1866 the *Carlisle Journal* noted that the first excursion trains of the year had conveyed between 3,000 and 4,000 people from Preston for a fare of 3s (15p) each. This latter invasion apparently caused some second thoughts for the following month it was resolved: 'The Board ... do not see .... how Excursion traffic can be avoided, but the secretary is instructed not to promote such Traffic by Special Trains.' Throughout the remainder of its existence the company was at pains to maintain the middle-class image of Keswick as a haven of peace among the mountains, justifying its failure to maximise tourist traffic on the grounds that only a relatively limited number of discerning visitors preferred the town to the more accessible Windermere and Ambleside. Prior to opening the line, it did however decide that 'a large First Class Hotel' next to the station was 'imperatively required'. Completed in 1869 at a cost of around £11,000, this 'substantial pile' with seventy-six guest rooms and its own covered entrance from the platform was regarded as one of the finest establishments in the north of England. It was leased to the Keswick Hotel Company, whose chairman Isaac Fletcher also became chairman of the railway in 1870. Co-operation between the two concerns was thus fostered, the hotel owning a fleet of horse-drawn coaches which were used to operate combined road and rail tours through the northern half of the Lake District.

As with other lines in the Lake Counties, passenger revenue became increasingly important as mineral traffic declined. In the early 1870s the Franco-German war put an end to the profitable trade in pig-iron which was conveyed to Teesside for shipment to Rotterdam, eastbound loadings as a whole shrinking to almost negligible proportions due to increased local consumption of iron ore by the growing number of West Cumberland ironworks. Westwards, coke traffic slumped dramatically in the period prior to World War I with the establishment of coking plants at most of the furnaces. By 1921 there were just two coke trains per day, and even these soon ceased with the last working over the Redhills curve taking place on 18 February 1926. A few intermittent coke trains in the 1928-9 period reversed at Penrith, although the Redhills curve continued to be used for turning engines too long for the Penrith turntable until its official closure on 11 June 1938.

Thus ended one of the most fascinating and formidable of cross-country freight operations, involving taxing climbs to the summits of Stainmore and Troutbeck on a route that nowhere permitted fast running. In taking North Eastern engines to what that company must have regarded as the remote western outpost of Cockermouth, it involved West Auckland crews in a gruelling out-and-back turn that normally took sixteen hours but could be as long as twenty! Coke and iron ore were not the only minerals to be seen on the line, as at different times it also handled granite from quarries at Threlkeld and Embleton, lead from mines near Troutbeck, Threlkeld and Braithwaite, limestone from quarries and kilns at Blencow and Flusco and Buttermere green slate which was brought down to Keswick from the Honister quarries. More general freight traffic has included cattle to the Monday markets at Cockermouth, sheep to and from the famous auctions at Troutbeck and pit props from the forests around Bassenthwaite Lake station.

Seasonal passenger traffic increased to the extent that the line was doubled between Troutbeck and Threlkeld in 1894 and from Redhills Junction to Troutbeck in 1901. An Act of 1 June 1894 sanctioned the financing of this work. Despite this

A page from *Bradshaw*, October 1885

improvement, the average journey from Penrith to Cockermouth still took 1¼ hours, and at the half-yearly meeting of the
company in February 1911 a shareholder launched a stinging
attack on the service provided. Taking his text from Genesis,
'God hath made everything that creepeth upon the Earth', he
claimed the line was the only one to be mentioned in the Bible.
Further, the 'dreadful rolling stock' was antiquated, un-
comfortable, dirty and practically 'the refuse' of the London &
North Western.

Matters gradually improved, but it was not until a four-year
strengthening programme began in 1935 that locomotives of
any reasonable size could reach Keswick. The ancient
'Cauliflowers' had many a struggle with the heavy Sunday
trains introduced in the 1920s (see Chapter VIII). A local
through coach working from Keswick to Carlisle via Brigham
and Bullgill survived until closure of the ex Maryport &
Carlisle Derwent branch in 1935. Apart from regular
operations, there was also an additional traffic surge each July
when those seeking closer communion with God among the
mountains flocked to the evangelical conference known as the
Keswick Convention. The numerous special trains included
'The Budd', a through express from Euston named after the
London businessman who promoted it.

Diesel units took over the basic Penrith–Workington service
on 3 January 1955, the wave of optimism leading to the
reintroduction of summer Sunday trains and the reopening of
remote Blencow station which had been closed on 3 March
1952. Yet by 1960 the line was losing an estimated £50,000 per
annum, an independent survey at that time being critical of
the retention of 13½ miles of double track, lavish signalling
facilities and fully staffed intermediate stations and seeing
little hope of any increase in traffic and indeed arguing the case
for a replacement integrated bus service. Through goods
workings were withdrawn on 1 June 1964 and the section west
of Keswick completely closed on 18 April 1966. Vociferous
objections from Keswick's hoteliers and tradesmen led to the
Minister of Transport refusing to confirm the closure order for
the remaining part of the line which then became a single-
track extended siding with all stations being reduced to
unstaffed halts from 1 July 1968. In this skeletal form it

lingered on until withdrawal of the diesel-unit shuttle service on 6 March 1972, mineral trains continuing to operate from Penrith to Flusco quarry west of Blencow for a further few months until 19 June.

THE LAKE SIDE BRANCH

From the opening of the Furness Railway in 1846 coaches were run in connection with trains from Dalton to Newby Bridge where passengers transferred to the newly established Windermere steamer service to Bowness and Waterhead (Ambleside). The following year the company contemplated building an extension to the southern end of the lake, but matters were shelved until promotion of the Wennington–Carnforth line, creating a direct route from the Midland Railway to the southern fringe of the Lake District, led to a reappraisal of possible routes northwards to Windermere. A line from Cark was considered in 1863, but in the same year the Furness reached agreement with the merchant traders of Greenodd that the opening span of the Leven viaduct might be permanently closed if a rail link was provided to the port from the Ulverston Canal (see Chapter V). It was therefore ultimately resolved to extend this link from Greenodd to Newby Bridge, the final decision being taken on 26 October 1865 at a board meeting significantly held at the Midland Hotel, Derby. An Act of 16 July 1866 authorised the 7 mile 'Newby Bridge Branch' from Plumpton Junction, 1½ miles east of Ulverston, together with the ¼ mile Leven curve from Leven Junction to Greenodd Junction to permit direct running on to the new line from the east. From the outset the lake steamer service was seen as an essential element in fostering tourist traffic on the branch, the Act allowing the Furness to buy shares to the value of £10,000 in the Windermere United Steam Yacht Co Ltd which operated the boats. A further Act of 18 July 1872 permitted outright purchase of the company, an operation completed three years later.

In the meantime the double-track triangular junction with the main line together with the single-track branch north from Greenodd Junction had been opened for goods to Greenodd on 18 March 1869 and Newby Bridge on 23 April. This last was a temporary terminus for during construction it had been decided that the existing steamer berth here, involving vessels in a risky voyage down the headwaters of the Leven, was not ideal for rail/ship interchange. It was resolved to continue the branch for a further ½ mile to a purpose-built quay at Windermere (Lake Side), the extension being opened on 1 June 1869 to coincide with the introduction of passenger services and retrospectively authorised on 9 August. An additional intermediate station at Haverthwaite was brought into use on 1 September.

Undoubtedly the most famous passenger to use the branch was H. W. Schneider, the Furness ironmaster, who coincidentally with the opening of the line bought Belsfield House at Bowness. Each morning he would leave the house preceded at a discreet distance by the butler carrying a covered and heated silver salver. The solemn procession would board Schneider's graceful steam yacht *Esperance*, and during the 6-mile sail down the sylvan reaches of the lake the salver would be uncovered to enable the butler to serve a lavish breakfast on board. At Lake Side the industrialist transferred to a reserved first-class compartment to complete the journey to his office at Barrow. *Esperance* later became immortalised as the houseboat in Arthur Ransome's *Swallows and Amazons* and is now preserved at the Windermere Steam Boat Museum.

The first part of the branch ran hard by the side of the Leven estuary and offered superb panoramas of green fells and rugged mountains. Greenodd up platform was virtually lapped by the high tide, the company thoughtfully providing windows on all sides of the shelter building so that passengers could at least enjoy the view while patiently waiting for the train to arrive! North of this point the line twice crossed the river on bridges built for double track and then entered Haverthwaite, where the station was sandwiched between two short tunnels with the passing loop actually beginning inside the southernmost bore. The remaining stretch was densely wooded and most picturesque, especially on the final approach to Lake Side where the waters of Windermere seemed almost to touch the wheels of the train and the peak of Gummer's How provided a spectacular backdrop. The

Furness went to town with the station buildings on its new tourist line to the extent of causing mutterings among shareholders about extravagant opulence. It used 'patent white bricks' – they were actually yellow – in a decorative and expensive style of Flemish bonding, offset by horizontal bands of vitrified purple-black stretchers, the whole effect looking rather out of place in such rural surroundings. Lake Side, carefully laid out as a combined railway terminus and steamer pier, boasted a ridge-and-furrow overall roof and a slender pointed tower. Running parallel with the lake and platforms was a long veranda, on top of which was built a 'Palm Court' type restaurant and refreshment room where tourists, suitably soothed by an orchestra complete with harp and bass viol, could contemplate their surroundings as they dined. The splendour of the terminus was somewhat marred by a functional coal dump, providing essential fuel for the steamers but unhappily situated right in front of the main buildings.

Tourist and excursion traffic on the branch expanded steadily in the years prior to World War I. A significant development was the introduction in 1905 of a steam rail-motor service, a new halt known as Newby Bridge Motor Car Platform being opened at the same time. Even in the depths of winter the line could be busy, for if Windermere froze then special trains were run to bring in skaters from a wide radius. A setback occurred in 1920–1 when mounting losses forced the company to withdraw winter steamer sailings on the lake and instead borrow two single-deck buses from the Great Western Railway to provide a substitute Newby Bridge–Ambleside connection. A similar operation took place the following winter but thereafter the Lake District Road Traffic Co took over the service.

Local traffic gradually declined and on 26 September 1938 the branch service went the same way as that of the steamers when all-year-round passenger workings were withdrawn. A summer service was operated in 1939 and 1940, the latter year being the last on which the Leven curve was used on a regular basis (it was not officially closed until 23 March 1952). In the summer of 1941 traffic shrank to a Millom–Lake Side train on alternate Sundays, passenger operations then ceasing until 3 June 1946 when they were restored on a seasonal basis with local services from Ulverston and a through train from Morecambe. By the early 1960s the branch was under threat of closure, the end coming on 6 September 1965 when passenger services were withdrawn, regettably just after most of the line had been relaid with experimental concrete sleepers and BR had announced its decision to expand the Windermere steamer business.

Freight traffic ceased beyond Haverthwaite on 6 April 1964, surviving to this point for another three years until the shutdown of the nearby pioneer Backbarrow Ironworks brought complete closure of the branch on 24 April 1967. In its time the line had handled a wide variety of goods including coal for the steamers, ore for the ironworks, bobbins from Stott Park Mill near Lake Side, dye from the ultramarine works at Backbarrow and whole tree trunks and larch pit props from Greenodd. There was also saltpetre and sulphur for two gunpowder works, one at Black Beck served by a horse-worked standard-gauge branch from Lady Syke, north of Greenodd (closed 1928), and the other at Low Wood which was linked to Haverthwaite station by a 3 ft 6 in gauge tramway (closed 1935).

Following closure, moves were made to reopen the line with the formation of the Lakeside Railway Estates Co Ltd in June 1967 and the Lakeside Railway Society a year later. The company established a locomotive depot at Carnforth, the genesis of Steamtown (see Chapter II), the original hope being that motive power for the branch would be based at this point. Unfortunately in 1969 the section south of Haverthwaite was sequestered for trunk-road improvements, the outcome being the formation of a new company with the object of restoring services on the remaining portion of the line. Steam locomotives and rolling stock were moved to Haverthwaite in 1970–1 prior to the severance of the rail link with the outside world, the next stage being the granting of a Light Railway Order on 13 October 1972. The Lakeside & Haverthwaite Railway was officially reopened on 2 May 1973 by Bishop Eric Treacy, public services commencing three days later.

Trains run in connection with the Windermere steamers, thus maintaining a tradition extending over more than a century. Railway involvement was first symbolised in the grand manner on 5 June 1869 when scenes of festivity and firing of cannon accompanied the launch at Lake Side by James Ramsden's wife of a new screw-driven steamer *Swan*. She joined the three existing paddle steamers, *Fire Fly*, *Dragon Fly* and *Rothay*, which were taken into direct railway ownership. In 1871 the Furness introduced *Raven*, a barge-like vessel which carried freight to and from the Lake Side railhead and provided a water-borne door-to-door delivery service to the many mansions scattered around Windermere. Two more passenger steamers, *Teal* and *Cygnet*, appeared in 1879, followed in 1891 by *Tern* and nine years later by *Swift*. The final Furness addition was the luxury steam yacht *Britannia*, originally built in 1879 for a colossal £12,000 and acquired for private charter at the bargain price of £360. By 1919 she was obsolete and was scrapped, the same fate having already befallen the three pioneer paddle steamers. In LMS days both *Cygnet* and *Raven* passed out of railway ownership and in 1936 and 1938 *Teal* and *Swan* were respectively replaced by new motor vessels of the same name. Finally, steam was completely ousted when *Swift* and *Tern* were converted to diesel propulsion in the post-war period.

'RATTY'

The Lake District's only narrow-gauge passenger line has a historical complexity out of all proportion to its size. Its origins go back to 1871 when Whitehaven Iron Mines Ltd found marketable quantities of haematite near Boot in Eskdale, exploitation being limited by the prohibitive cost of carting the ore to Drigg station. The upshot was incorporation on 26 May 1873 of the 7 mile Ravenglass & Eskdale Railway, the Act providing for a capital of £24,000 and a track gauge of 2 ft 9 in. On 14 March 1874 the Board of Trade sanctioned an increase in gauge to 3 ft and it was in this form that the line was opened to goods on 24 May 1875, the costs of ore transport promptly falling from 10s (50p) to 2s 2d (21p) per ton. Joseph Marshall, secretary of the mining company, later stated that the railway was built for £42,000 after a survey had indicated a figure of £80,000 for a standard-gauge branch. Passenger services did not commence until 20 November 1876, the delay being due to a most unfavourable report by a Board of Trade inspector who, after commenting on the incomplete stations, inadequate clearances, lack of signalling and shortage of motive power (there was only one engine!), added: 'I don't recollect having seen anywhere where the masonry was of such indifferent quality.'

'Ratty', as it has always been affectionately known, commenced alongside the Furness station at Ravenglass and then skirted the shady north side of Muncaster Fell before forsaking the valley of the River Mite in favour of that of the Esk which was followed to the terminus at Boot. There were intermediate stations at Irton Road, Eskdale Green and Beckfoot. An authorised ½ mile branch to Ravenglass harbour was not constructed but in 1880 a tramway was laid down from Dalegarth, between Beckfoot and Boot, to haematite mines on the south side of the river at Gill Force (these were closed in 1884 and the line removed about 1904).

From the beginning the railway was in trouble. It was unable to pay the contractor and in May 1877 became subject to an Order in Chancery, a manager and receiver being appointed two months later. In 1882 it lost its main source of traffic when the mining company failed, periodic attempts at revival being unsuccessful. The line was left to eek out a living by conveying tourists in its three coaches and assorted mineral wagons, endeavouring to attract custom by fancifully advertising itself as 'the route to the Alps'. By the turn of the century it was extremely run down, the atmosphere of the period being well captured by an article in *Wide World* in December 1903 in which Mary C. Fair described the 'comic-opera collection of relics' and the train's perilous progress up the valley on 'extremely crookedly-laid rails':

> It lurches, and groans, and rolls along in a manner that makes you wonder why you did not invest your spare coppers in insurance tickets. You also speculate whether the bottom will fall out of the carriage, the train pull up the rails, or the whole affair topple into the river.

Closure to all traffic took place on 30 November 1908, but the following year an Act of 16 August authorised the formation of a new Eskdale Railway Company with powers to rebuild the line and convert it to electric traction. Despite the issue of a glowing prospectus, funds were not forthcoming, although mining activities were resumed and a daily mineral and goods train was run from 24 June 1909. This soon became thrice-weekly prior to being suspended on 1 November 1910; it was reinstated on 20 April 1911 but from the following November trains ran only as required until 30 April 1913 when 3 ft gauge operations finally ceased.

Early in 1915 the derelict remains were inspected by R. Proctor-Mitchell, co-director with W. J. Bassett-Lowke of Narrow Gauge Railways Ltd which was looking for suitable sites for new miniature lines. Surprisingly, this company managed to lease the railway without the approval of outstanding creditors and prior to concluding any form of agreement commenced to convert it to 15 in gauge. Services as far as Muncaster began on 28 August 1915 (the station here was closed in November 1924) and were progressively extended up the valley to Irton Road on 10 October, Eskdale Green on 27 March 1916, Beckfoot on 20 April and Boot in April 1917. Some of the early miniature locomotives were winded by the steep gradients at the upper end of the line and as a result operations were cut back to Beckfoot in August 1918. The next move was for a new terminus known as Dalegarth to be opened on the initial part of the former Gill Force branch on 23 May 1920 (it was repositioned alongside the Eskdale road in 1926). Here many passengers would join a charabanc as part of a combined rail/road excursion which involved journeying to Wastwater and then rejoining the train at Irton Road. In 1922 a granite quarry at Beckfoot was reopened and two years later a crushing plant built at Murthwaite, a $2\frac{1}{2}$ mile standard-gauge branch being constructed to this point from Ravenglass in order to overcome transhipment problems. It was completed in July 1929, the 15 in gauge track being gauntletted between the full-size rails.

The quarrying activities led to the acquisition of Narrow Gauge Railways Ltd by the Keswick Granite Company in 1949. It in turn put the line up for sale in 1958 and it seemed likely the scrap merchants would move in, but salvation was again at hand when the Ravenglass & Eskdale Railway Preservation Society was formed and managed to make the successful bid at a public auction at Gosforth in September

1960. Over half the purchase price of £12,000 was put up by private individuals who in March 1961 formed an operating company, the Ravenglass & Eskdale Railway Co Ltd. Since then major changes have included large-scale rebuilding, the addition of several new locomotives and the reopening of Muncaster station as Muncaster Mill in March 1967. The water mill here has been restored to working order by the Eskdale (Cumbria) Trust, a separate non-profit-making organisation which has also established a railway museum at Ravenglass. The steam-hauled Cumbrian Coast Express (see Chapter V) is timed to allow a trip on 'Ratty' and has brought much extra traffic. On the operating side there has been a revolution with the railway pioneering the introduction in Great Britain of a system of centralised train control using radio instead of telephone or signals as a communications medium. Thus, of all the lines built into the Lake District it is strangely enough the one which was last in the field as well as being the most remote and impoverished which today is proving a pace-setter.

CHAPTER VIII

On – and off – the rails

MAIN-LINE SERVICES

Just as Roman chariots rushing north to Hadrian's Wall and juggernauts pounding Glasgow-bound along the M6 have had little direct influence on the way of life of the Lake Counties, so the area has formed merely a mountainous hiccup on the long journey of Anglo-Scottish expresses. In their heyday the crack trains on both the West Coast and Midland trunk routes paused but once in the region, at Carlisle.

Journey times at first altered but gradually. The fastest daytime schedule between Preston and Carlisle was 2 hr 40 min in 1853; it dropped to 2 hr 26 min in 1859 and almost thirty years later in 1887 was still 2 hr 7 min. The opening of the Settle–Carlisle line did not immediately stimulate major improvements, partly because the new route's initial service consisted of just one day and one night express from St Pancras, both of which divided at Skipton into Glasgow and Edinburgh portions covering the 86¾ miles to Carlisle in an even two hours.

Traffic on both routes steadily developed, services on the Midland line reaching a peak in the early years of the twentieth century. In the summer of 1904 Scottish departures from St Pancras began with an early morning train which divided at Skipton for Glasgow and Edinburgh. There were two other morning expresses, both running in separate Glasgow and Edinburgh portions throughout, and then an afternoon Glasgow service. Night trains began with the famous Highland Express conveying sleeping cars for Inverness via Edinburgh, followed by a Glasgow service with through coaches to Stranraer for the Larne boat. Next was another sleeper, which became separate Glasgow and

Edinburgh trains at Leeds, and finally the midnight departure to Glasgow alone. It added up to an impressive total of twelve expresses heading north every twenty-four hours, the best of them running from London to Carlisle in just 6¼ hours. The Midland however could not escape the fact that comparable services from Euston were both greater in volume and some twenty minutes faster.

Services were greatly augmented in the three or four days preceding the 'glorious twelfth' of August. Basil Bazley, writing in the *Railway Magazine* in 1953, gave fascinating details of the down sleeping-car expresses he saw at Carlisle in the 'grouse festival' of 1905. The arrivals during the 2½ hours from 12.50 am were remarkable not just for their frequency but also for the obscure destinations:

12.52	Midland	Edinburgh
12.59	Midland	Glasgow and Clyde Coast
1.28	LNWR	Perth, Aberdeen, Dava, Kyle of Lochalsh
1.45	LNWR	Inverness, Altnabreac
1.48	Midland	Inverness
1.55	LNWR	Aberdeen and Inverness
2.12	LNWR	Aberdeen
2.21	LNWR	Aberdeen, Alford and Ballater
2.24	Midland	Perth, Inverness and Redcastle
2.27	LNWR	Perth and stations to Aberdeen
2.37	LNWR	Inverness and Borrobol
2.43	Midland	Edinburgh, Fort William, Aberdeen, Alford and Cullen
2.47	LNWR	Oban and Creagan
2.53	LNWR	Stranraer
3.2	Midland	Stranraer
3.15	LNWR	Postal

The fastest journey time between Preston and Carlisle had by this time been cut dramatically to 1 hr 42 min, although over thirty years later in 1938 this figure had been improved by just one minute! Traffic density on the West Coast main line also remained relatively static for the next half-century; the table below contrasts the basic winter service of 1910 with that of 1961 and provides comparison with the Midland as well as the East Coast routes:

	West Coast		Midland		East Coast	
	1910	1961	1910	1961	1910	1961
Daytime restaurant-car expresses	6	8	4	3	5	7
Semi-fasts	5	2	1	—	4	2
Stopping services	4	2	4	2	2	2
Sleeping car expresses	3	10	4	2	3	7
	18	22	13	7	14	18

The sharp decline in traffic on the Settle–Carlisle was an inevitable consequence of the Grouping. By 1938 the basic summer service over the route from St Pancras had shrunk to morning and night-time trains running separately to Glasgow and Edinburgh, the daytime expresses by now somewhat prosaically being named the Thames-Clyde and Thames-Forth, and a lunch-time train dividing at Carlisle to serve both Scottish cities. There was also a morning Leeds to Glasgow and Edinburgh express which took on through carriages from Manchester at Hellifield. The run-down proved irreversible, closure of the 'Waverley Route' in 1969 bringing the end of Edinburgh services and leaving just a morning Leeds–Glasgow train, the Thames-Clyde Express and the Glasgow sleeper. Through London–Glasgow services over the line ceased in 1976, a pattern of three Nottingham–Glasgow trains each way continuing until 1982 when, as noted in Chapter III, their diversion by Preston was at the time seen as one of the final nails in the coffin of the former Midland route to Scotland.

The demise has gone hand-in-hand with quite staggering improvements in West Coast main-line schedules as a result of electrification. From 1974, several trains were scheduled to cover the 90 miles between Preston and Carlisle in a hitherto incredible sixty-five minutes at an average speed of 83.2 mph. The timing for the ill-fated Advanced Passenger Train over this same stretch was fixed at 56 minutes – and this included four minutes' recovery time!

AROUND THE COAST

Workings on the various lines making up the Carnforth–Barrow–Whitehaven–Carlisle chain were at first of purely a local nature, but gradually both the London & North Western and the Midland introduced significant through services. These began in earnest with the diversion of Midland steamers from Morecambe in 1867, through trains running between Leeds and Piel in connection with expresses from London which then still had King's Cross as their starting point. Typical times were those of 1875 when the Isle of Man boat train left Leeds at 10.30 am, connecting with the 5.15 am from St Pancras, and reached Piel Pier at 2.20 pm. Much faster schedules accompanied the transfer of sailings to Ramsden Dock, the equivalent service in 1887 leaving Leeds at 11 am and arriving at the dockside at 1.35 pm after avoiding Carnforth station, slipping a coach at Grange and calling only at Ulverston and Furness Abbey. By 1903 this train was carrying a through coach from Bradford, while the evening Belfast Boat Express had what the Midland timetable gloriously described as a 'Through Lavatory Carriage' from St Pancras. In the reverse direction the morning train in connection with the Belfast steamer at one stage covered the 28½ miles from Barrow to Carnforth in forty-five minutes, among the fastest runs ever operated over Furness metals. For some years boat trains were divided at Furness Abbey into portions for Barrow Central and Ramsden Dock, a practice that ceased when most of the sailings became Heysham based in 1904 and the surviving boats were then served by connecting services from Central. As some compensation for this relegation, from 15 July 1905 until September 1911 the North Eastern instituted through carriages between Newcastle and Ramsden Dock via Stainmore and the Hincaster Junction–Arnside line in connection with the Isle of Man steamer.

The slip carriage referred to on the Midland boat train was one of two in each direction serving Grange, the facility being introduced in 1887. Such workings were quite extensively developed from around the turn of the century until World War I, coaches also being slipped at Arnside, Ulverston, Dalton, Furness Abbey and Askam. Through coach workings were also at their peak during this period, with three departures from Whitehaven all conveying carriages for both St Pancras (until 1911) and Euston and two of them additional coaches for Liverpool Lime Street and Manchester Exchange. By 1910 the best Barrow–Euston time had come down to 6hr 5min. Other through coaches linked Whitehaven with Bradford and Cambridge, and on Fridays only Southampton via Leeds and Cheltenham, a working introduced to speed emigrating Cumbrians on their journey. It was conveyed over the Furness on the 'evening mail', a train which achieved the best Whitehaven–Barrow time of 1hr 25min.

Grouping brought few major changes, although most trains from Whitehaven were extended back to start at either Workington or Maryport. By the 1930s a journey could be made from Barrow to Euston in 5hr 40min by changing at Preston on to the Fylde Coast Express. The basic Whitehaven–Carnforth service survived into the 1960s with few alterations, apart from the introduction of a sleeping-car train to and from Euston, through carriages continuing to operate from Workington to London, Liverpool and Manchester. On the debit side the fastest 'express' from Barrow to London in 1961 took 6hr 36min, over half an hour slower than in 1910! Change came on 18 April 1966 when Whitehaven lost all its through trains to the south, services being taken over by diesel units which generally terminated at Barrow but in some cases ran right through from Carlisle to Lancaster, a journey taking almost four hours. Barrow has similarly suffered a progressive cut-back, although West Coast route electrification brought the town within 4hr 3min of Euston.

LAKELAND TOURIST TRAFFIC

With its fame resting on the minority attributes of scenic splendour and literary associations, the Lake District never assumed the same importance in traffic terms as the relatively nearby Lancashire coastal resorts of Morecambe and Blackpool. Yet both the feeder main-line companies made determined efforts to tempt visitors to the area and in their heyday developed a respectable pattern of services.

The London & North Western provided its gateway to Lakeland at Windermere with through carriages from Euston, Liverpool (Lime Street and Exchange) and Manchester Victoria. Neighbouring Exchange station was graced by the

Windermere Express, already referred to in Chapter VII and, in any event, a shade too plutocratic for the humble tourist. The company also operated through coaches from London to Keswick. The Midland regarded the Lake Side branch as its natural arm into Lakeland, and from 1897 until 1911 it was possible to reach the terminus from St Pancras without change of train. There were additional through workings from Leeds and Bradford, some direct over the Leven curve and others via Ulverston, one of which also conveyed a carriage that was taken forward to Coniston Lake. Especially popular was what the company's timetable billed as a 'Cheap Fast Train', leaving Leeds at 6.40 am and by a combination of rail, steamer and coach enabling, say, Grasmere to be reached at 11.50 am nicely in time for lunch. As mentioned in Chapter III, the Midland also had its eyes on Keswick, which in the 1910–14 period could be reached by through carriages from Leeds, detached at Penrith from its Lake District Express operating through to Glasgow via Ingleton. The North Eastern had similar designs; in 1906 it extended one of its Darlington–Penrith trains to Keswick and in 1911 added through carriages from Newcastle and York.

There was another way of reaching Lakeland which proved enormously popular in the golden age prior to World War I. Lancastrians and Blackpool holiday-makers took a train to Fleetwood and boarded a boat across Morecambe Bay to Ramsden Dock station at Barrow, from where another train took them to Lake Side or Coniston. One of Alfred Aslett's ventures to stimulate increased traffic, it was inaugurated in August 1900 by the paddle steamer *Lady Evelyn* which in the ensuing season carried 28,000 passengers, the service later being augmented by *Lady Margaret* (1902–8), *Philomel* (1908–13) and *Gwalia* – renamed *Lady Moyra* (1910–15) (Evelyn, Margaret and Moyra were daughters of the Cavendish family). By 1910 the three sailings daily in each direction were conveying 128,000 people per annum on the seventy-five-minute voyage across the Bay. For an all-in fare of 7s 6d (37½p) from Blackpool, holiday-makers could indulge in the 'Outer Circular' tour which from Lake Side involved a continuation of the journey by steamer along the length of Windermere and then a coach trip to Coniston before regaining Barrow by

train. The more modest – and perhaps slightly less fatiguing –
'Inner Circular' shortened the round trip by leaving the train
at Greenodd, taking a coach through the Crake Valley and
then a steamer along Coniston Water. By this time the Furness
was operating some twenty circular tours of the Lake District,
although the longer ones did not embrace the Morecambe Bay
crossing. One of the most popular was the 'Six Lakes' which
conveyed passengers from Furness Abbey to Lake Side by rail,
to Waterhead by steamer, over Kirkstone Pass by coach to
Glenridding, down Ullswater by steamer, on to Penrith by
coach, to Keswick by rail, past Derwentwater, Thirlmere,
Grasmere and Rydal Water by coach to Waterhead and so
back to the starting point.

Sadly, the cross-bay steamer services were not reintroduced
after the war. The Grouping also brought many changes, the
main casualty being the through workings from the West
Riding to Lake Side and Coniston. The pattern now was for
holiday trains from Leeds and Bradford to terminate instead
at Windermere; in order to avoid creating chaos by reversing
at Carnforth on a summer Saturday they were frequently
worked direct to Arnside and thence via the branch to
Hincaster Junction. This line was also used by through
Barrow coaches which were detached at Oxenholme from
some intriguing seasonal workings to Windermere from both
Willesden and Northampton. The LMS fostered traffic from the
Lancashire coast resorts to the Lake District, Blackpool being
linked direct with Windermere and also with Coniston by a
service that avoided Barrow and ran non-stop from Ulverston.
Morecambe had through trains to the same two termini and
also to Lake Side. Further north, a Sunday restaurant-car
return train from Glasgow to Keswick was introduced in the
late 1920s and gave Scots weary of Loch Lomond some five
hours to sample the delights of English Lakeland; it was
complemented by a similar buffet-car express from Newcastle
which proved equally popular.

Combined tours survived until the closure of the Lake Side
branch in 1965. In the 1950s a return fare of 10s 9d (54p)
would   convey   Morecambe   holiday-makers   on   the
'Windermere Circular' to the terminus, thence up the lake to
Waterhead and back to Bowness by steamer before returning

FURNESS RAILWAY.

Twenty Coach and Steam Yacht Tours
THROUGH THE ENGLISH LAKELAND
DAILY DURING JUNE, JULY, AUGUST, & SEPTEMBER.

No. 1.—**OUTER CIRCULAR TOUR**, embracing Windermere Lake, Furness Abbey, and Coniston. Fare from 5/3.

No. 2.—**INNER CIRCULAR TOUR**, embracing Furness Abbey, Coniston Lake (Gondola), and Crake Valley. Fare from 3/3.

No. 3.—**GRANGE and WINDERMERE CIRCULAR TOUR**, embracing Grange, Arnside, Kendal, and Windermere Lake. Fare from 2/9.

No. 4.—**MIDDLE CIRCULAR TOUR**, embracing Windermere Lake, the Crake Valley, and Coniston Lake. Fare from 5/9.

No. 5.—**RED BANK and GRASMERE TOUR**, via Ambleside and Skelwith Force, returning via Rydal Water. Fare from 2/9.

No. 6.—**THIRLMERE, GRASMERE, and WINDERMERE TOUR**, via Ambleside, Clappersgate, and Red Bank, and round Thirlmere Lake. Fare from 5/-.

No. 7.—**THE FOUR LAKES CIRCULAR TOUR**, viz., Coniston, Grasmere, Rydal, and Windermere. Fare from 5/9.

No. 8.—**CONISTON to CONISTON TOUR**, via Red Bank, Grasmere, and Ambleside, returning by coach to Coniston. Fare from 4/6.

No. 9.—**TARN HOWS TOUR**, via Ambleside and Coniston, returning by Tilberthwaite and Elterwater. Fare from 4/6.

No. 10.—**ROUND THE LANGDALES and DUNGEON GHYLL TOUR**, via Ambleside, Colwith Force, Grasmere, and Rydal. Fare from 5/-.

No. 11.—**ULLSWATER TOUR**, via Ambleside, Kirkstone Pass, and Brothers Water, returning via the Vale of Troutbeck and Lowwood. Fare from 5/6.

No. 12.—**DERWENTWATER (Keswick) TOUR**, via Ambleside, Grasmere, and Thirlmere. Fare from 6/-.

No. 13.—**THE FIVE LAKES CIRCULAR TOUR**, viz., Windermere, Rydal, Grasmere, Thirlmere, and Derwentwater. Fare from 11/6.

No. 14.—**WASTWATER TOUR**, via Seascale and Gosforth. Fare from 4/6.

No. 15.—**THE SIX LAKES CIRCULAR TOUR**, viz., Windermere, Rydal, Grasmere, Thirlmere, Derwentwater, and Ullswater. Fare from 12/-.

No. 16.—**THE DUDDON VALLEY TOUR**, via Broughton-in-Furness, Ulpha, and Seathwaite. Fare from 3/9.

No. 17.—**THE ROUND OF CONISTON LAKE** (New Tour). Fare from 3/10.

No. 18.—**ENNERDALE LAKE and CALDER ABBEY TOUR**, via Seascale, Gosforth, and Cold Fell. Fare from 4/6.

No. 19.—**ACROSS THE FERRY TOUR**, via Lake Side, Esthwaite Water, Hawkshead, and Storrs Hall. Fare from 3/6.

No. 20.—**CARTMEL PRIORY and NEWBY BRIDGE TOUR**, via Windermere (Lake Side), Backbarrow Falls, Holker Park, and Grange. Fare from 3/-.

For further particulars see "TOURS THROUGH LAKELAND" Pamphlets, to be had gratis at all Furness Railway Stations; of Mr. F. J. RAMSDEN, Superintendent of the Line, Barrow-in-Furness: at Messrs. THOS. COOK & SON'S Offices and the Polytechnic Institute, Regent Street, W.; or Messrs. W. H. SMITH & SON'S principal Bookstalls (price ½d.).

The **Palette Album**, illustrating the above Tours, in colours, can be obtained at the principal Railway Bookstalls, price 6d.

Picture Post Cards of the Lake District may be obtained at any Station on the Furness Railway, and on the Company's Steamers; also at Furness Abbey Hotel and the principal Bookstalls. Reduced price, 12 cards for 6d.

ALFRED ASLETT,
Secretary and General Manager.

BARROW-IN-FURNESS,
April 1904.

Furness Railway coach and yacht tours through Lakeland, 1904.

by train via Oxenholme. It was perhaps no coincidence that 1965 also saw the virtual end of through tourist services into the area with the withdrawal of the Lakes Express, a name bestowed in 1927 on an existing working from London Euston. It had blossomed into a full restaurant-car train, dividing at Oxenholme into separate portions for Windermere and Workington via Keswick.

INDUSTRIAL LINES

Far removed from the genteel world of Lakeland tourism were the industrial lines which performed their humdrum and unglamorous tasks virtually unnoticed. As is only to be expected in an area of such contrasts, they came in all shapes and sizes, performed an amazing variety of functions and often eeked out their existence in the most unlikely locations. Some have already been mentioned in the preceding chapters by virtue of their overall historical importance (the West Cumberland colliery wagonways) or special traffics (the gunpowder tramways on the Lake Side branch and at Milnthorpe, and the roadside tramway linking paper mills near Burneside with the Windermere branch).

In their heyday a dominant group were the colliery systems around Whitehaven, Workington and Maryport, although these did not have the same fascination as Lord Carlisle's railways serving the isolated Naworth coalfield, on the fells above Hallbankgate in the north-east corner of Cumberland. Commencing in 1799 with a gravity- and horse-worked wooden wagonway to a staith at Brampton, this line soon proved to be in the forefront of development by making the first commercially successful use of wrought-iron rails in 1808. The network greatly expanded from 1819 with the appointment as colliery agent of twenty-five year old James Thompson, a disciple of George Stephenson who as early as 1825–9 extended the line in a form suitable for locomotive haulage. In 1836 most of the original alignment was replaced by a new route which included an inclined plane from Hallbankgate to Kirkhouse and connected with the embryo Newcastle & Carlisle Railway at Brampton Junction. On 15 July 1836, four days before the opening of that company's

Greenhead–Carlisle section, Thompson stole a march on it by hiring a pair of locomotives and operating the Lake Counties' first steam-hauled passenger service between Kirkhouse and Brampton. Another place in the history books was secured in October of the same year when Robert Stephenson's famous *Rocket* was purchased from the Liverpool & Manchester Railway. It entered service in May 1837 but soon proved too light and was laid aside in 1840, becoming derelict before being sent to Stephenson's works at Newcastle in 1851 and subsequently presented to the Patent Museum (now the Science Museum). By 1838 Thompson was building his own locomotives in the workshops at Kirkhouse, but the pioneering days were now almost over and in the second half of the nineteenth century the system slipped into gradual decline. The Brampton Junction–Brampton section was leased to the North Eastern Railway in 1912 and closed in 1923, other parts of the network surviving under the aegis of the National Coal Board until 1953.

Rivalling the colliery lines in extent and exceeding them in terms of locomotive fleets were those serving the ironworks and haematite mines. The greatest concentration was at Workington, closely followed by Barrow where the steel works still had some ex Furness Railway engines in service in the 1950s. Their grey world was enlivened by occasional moments of excitement when a saddle tank propelling ladles of molten material on to one of the slag banks hard by the sea shore would get out of control and make a spectacular dive on to the beach below. In recent years the most interesting of the mine sites was Hodbarrow, which at closure in 1968 retained several veterans including an 1890 Neilson crane tank now preserved at Lytham St Annes. Prior to the decline of haematite extraction there were numerous other smaller systems, often worked by native Lowca-built engines and including an extensive 3 ft 3 in gauge network to the north of Dalton-in-Furness.

In the same part of the world is Burlington slate quarry, the largest in England, which from its commencement in 1843 concurrent with the formation of the Furness Railway developed a complex of 3 ft 2¼ in gauge lines worked by horse, gravity and self-acting inclines. Animal power survived for

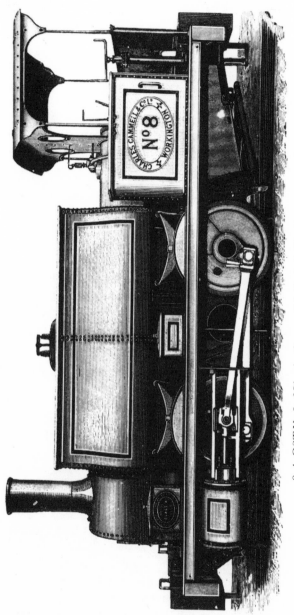

0–4–0ST No 8 of Charles Cammell & Co Ltd, Workington, built at the Lowca Engineering Works, Parton, in 1885.

over a century until superseded by a battery locomotive in 1946, although down the years there were problems of a time-and-motion nature. In his remarkable book *Burlington Blue-Grey*, R. Stanley Geddes relates how horses were left to proceed on their own in certain parts of the quarry and, realising they got a bag of oats irrespective of their speed, ambled along in such a dilatory fashion that it was necessary to put a dog on the payroll in order to speed up operations! The outstanding feature was the Long Incline, almost a mile in extent and descending from an altitude of 460 ft at the quarry floor almost to sea-level at the Kirkby exchange sidings. The brakesman at the top was thoughtfully provided with a powerful telescope to check the availability of empty wagons at the bottom, the position of the bypass loop points and the proximity of any stray sheep. On more than one occasion some of the local Herdwicks met a grisly fate and there was also a narrow miss with three black pigs! In the peak period the incline pulleys could get so hot that copious amounts of water had to be poured on them, but World War I brought an irreversible decline and ultimately road transport triumphed with the last run down to Kirkby being made in 1952 and use of the internal quarry lines ceasing in 1971. Smaller in area but infinitely more spectacular in location are the slate quarries on top of Honister Pass where a 2 ft gauge system was established in 1878. At its maximum extent it comprised 6 miles of track, mainly underground but including three self-acting inclines clinging precariously to the face of Honister Crag with at the top an almost sheer drop of 600 ft to the road below. Diesel and petrol locomotives were introduced in 1927, although virtually all the surface lines were lifted for scrap by prisoners of war in 1941.

Less than 30 miles away but in an environment that could scarcely be more different was a modest 3 ft gauge system on the southern tip of Walney Island. It was originally built about 1880 to serve Barrow salt works, but by World War I it had proved impossible to compete with Cheshire interests and operations were taken over by the Piel & Walney Sand & Gravel Co. Extending from gravel pits to a wooden pier, the line enjoyed long periods of moderate activity interspersed with periodic phrenetic bursts when a boat would come in and every available engine would be pressed into service in an endeavour to load within the eight or nine hours the tide would allow. The stud included two extraordinary vertical-boilered locomotives with corrugated-iron cabs built about 1876 by Balmforth Bros of Rodley. When the original boilers finally expired in 1956, two replacements were bought second-hand, one from a Robey traction engine and the other from a Burrell showman's engine, and were duly fitted complete with their existing chimneys and cylinder castings on top of the barrel! The railway closed in 1963, leaving Europe's largest mixed colony of herring and lesser black-backed gulls to enjoy the area in peace.

Several 2 ft gauge lines, all petrol- or diesel-worked, still survive close to sea-level on the Solway plain where they remain a more practical proposition than road transport for extraction of peat from the mosses. In the same area are fragments of a once vast network laid down during World War I to serve the Ministry of Munitions complex centred on Gretna. Standard-gauge lines with their own stations extended from west of Dornock on the Glasgow & South Western Railway right through to Longtown, via a connection with the Caledonian Railway at Mossband where there was an interchange platform. The internal narrow-gauge system was on an even larger scale than that of another major military presence in Cumberland, the Royal Naval Armament Depot at Broughton Moor on the Cleator & Workington Junction's northern extension, with its maze of 2 ft 6 in gauge tracks carefully concealed from prying eyes.

Among other industrial lines in the Lake Counties were several in the Eden Valley for extraction of gypsum, including one serving the Thistle Plaster Works at Kirkby Thore. Here may still rest the rusty remains of a pair of 2 ft gauge steam locomotives, a Fowler and a Bagnall tank, which during the 1920s were unceremoniously dumped in a pool and then subsequently covered with waste material. There were also a number of gunpowder lines in addition to those already mentioned; for example, the Elterwater Gunpowder Mill in Great Langdale had a tramway linking the various buildings which were deliberately scattered in order to minimise destruction in the event of an explosion. This was standard practice, as was the rejection of steam locomotives in favour of horses specially fitted with non-ferrous copper shoes, although despite such precautions serious accidents were quite frequent in the early years.

Finally, it is not fully appreciated that the first railways in Britain were in the Lake Counties. These were to be found underground in copper mines established in 1566–8 at Grasmere, Goldscope in the Newlands Valley and Caldbeck to the north of Skiddaw. The 'tracks' consisted of parallel planks set close together, the resulting slot being used to accommodate an iron guide-pin fitted to small wagons. This method of transport, already in use in Germany and Austria, was imported here along with miners from these two countries by the Company of Mines Royal, an enterprise with a familiar ring in that it represented a Tudor attempt to bolster Britain's flagging position against its more technologically advanced European competitors.

ACCIDENTS

Lines in the Lake Counties have with one exception remained remarkably free of serious accidents. That exception is the Settle & Carlisle, a setting peculiarly appropriate for death and disaster, where within the space of three years two tragic collisions occurred on typically dark and stormy nights. The first of these happened in the early hours of Christmas Eve 1910 as a result of the Hawes Junction signalman overlooking the presence of two light engines standing on the down main line. They moved away when he pulled off the signals for a down express, which soon afterwards came pounding north at over 60 mph and ran into the engines near Shotlock Hill tunnel. In the resulting derailment and fire, caused by gas-lit coaching stock, twelve passengers died and nine were injured. The outcry against the Midland was eclipsed by that following the second accident on 2 September 1913 which had several contributory factors. The night sleeper from Glasgow and Stranraer was not only overloaded but had such poor quality coal that it came to a stand through lack of steam just ½ mile short of Ais Gill summit. The following train from Inverness and Edinburgh was also having serious steaming problems, which preoccupied the driver and fireman to such an extent that they ran through all the Mallerstang signals. The subsequent rear-end collision again brought with it the terrors of fire, and in all sixteen passengers died and thirty-eight were injured. There have been other fatal accidents on the route: on 19 January 1918, when a down Glasgow express ran into a landslip in Long Meg cutting; and on 21 January 1960 at Settle as a result of a Britannia Pacific fracturing its piston rod and spreading the opposite track just in front of a passing freight train. In addition, the up Thames-Clyde express was spectacularly derailed on facing points at Blea Moor on 18 April 1952, causing injuries to twenty-six passengers.

The West Coast route has been more fortunate, although a serious collision occurred on the bitterly cold night of 4 March 1890 when a Scotch express swept through Carlisle Citadel totally out of control and hit a stationary Caledonian engine. Four passengers were killed. The accident had its origins way back at Shap summit, where the driver had stopped to detach the pilot engine and had erroneously confused the controls on his dual braking system so that vacuum was lost. Twenty years earlier on the night of 9–10 July 1870 there had been an equally disturbing incident at Carlisle on the old St Nicholas crossing, where the Canal branch intersected the West Coast main line on the level. A goods train, returning from Canal in the charge of the fireman owing to the intoxicated state of the driver, failed to observe signals and sliced through an up Anglo-Scottish express killing six passengers and injuring a further thirty. There have also been occasional troubles with banking on Shap, the background to one such fatal accident on 28 January 1876 being graphically described by G. P. Neale, the London & North Western Superintendent, in his book *Railway Reminiscences*:

At Tebay there was always stationed a pilot or bank engine in readiness to pursue, and to back up at speed, the passenger trains travelling up Shap bank, and it was one of the points of interest on the journey, so soon as the train has cleared Tebay, for passengers to watch the bank engine putting on steam and hurrying up to catch the running train. The impact upon the buffers was generally very perceptible. The plan was in force for many years without any untoward event, until on one occasion, through the failure at the critical moment of the train engine, a severe crush was experienced at the rear end of the train, and this led to the abandonment of the practice.

The coast lines have had an excellent safety record. Both the Furness and Maryport & Carlisle companies could at the Grouping proudly boast that no serious accident involving passenger fatalities had ever occurred on their system. However, the Furness had a lucky escape on 27 February 1903 when a 100 mph gale blowing up the Leven estuary brought down the telegraph wires on the viaduct. These became entangled with the 4.25 am Carnforth–Barrow mail train which was forced to stop, a violent gust of wind then overturning all ten vehicles. Fortunately the couplings held and the coaches stayed on the viaduct but even so each of the thirty-four passengers was injured in some way. Had a fully loaded train travelling in the opposite direction been involved, the result would have been a catastrophe of Tay Bridge proportions for it would inevitably have been blown straight into the turbulent waters of the estuary. As a result of the accident, a wind gauge was installed on the viaduct so that, when gusts reach 70 mph, alarm bells sound in Cark and Plumpton Junction signal-boxes.

An accident which achieved even greater infamy happened at Lindal ore sidings on 22 September 1892. An 0–6–0 goods engine was shunting some wagons when the crew had the unnerving sensation of suddenly feeling the ground give way beneath the engine. They leapt from the footplate just in time to see their steed fall chimney first into a gaping hole! The tender was retrieved, but it was later estimated that the engine had sunk some 200 ft below ground level into old iron workings which had caused the subsidence. There it still remains as the ultimate challenge to preservationists.

This was not the only accident in the Lake Counties where disaster was interlaced with comedy. The strange happenings spread over a 6 mile single-line stretch of the Cockermouth, Keswick & Penrith Railway on 14 April 1882 had all the elements of a knock-about farce. They began when a 'double-load' westbound mineral train with two North Eastern engines at the front and two brake vans at the rear shut off steam to pass through Bassenthwaite Lake station. At this moment the rear van became detached, leaving the two guards who were travelling in it together to contemplate the superb lakeside scenery. They managed to stop the following mineral train, which proceeded to propel the stranded van towards the station. The drivers of the first train had reached Embleton before they realised their loss but then detached the leading engine and sent it back to search for the missing vehicle and men. Unfortunately it was allowed to proceed beyond Bassenthwaite Lake station which had not yet been reached by the following train. When the drivers saw one another it was too late to stop and a head-on collision ensued, the crew of the light engine jumping off the footplate after they had put it in reverse in a vain attempt to stop. After impaling the brake van on the buffer beam of the propelling locomotive, the engine thus promptly set off westbound on its own accord, passing once more through Embleton where there must have been great confusion and consternation. Luckily it was possible to telegraph a warning to Cockermouth where the 1.25 pm Maryport & Carlisle departure was quietly standing at the platform. The staff managed to bundle the passengers out of the coaches with less than a minute to spare before the runaway crashed into them at an estimated 30 mph and caused severe damage. Even this was not quite the end of the story for the impact uncoupled the engine of the passenger train which also set off with no one on board. Fortunately it was stopped by a porter just as it was about to gain speed on the 1 in 70 gradient west of the station, thus bringing this quite extraordinary sequence of incidents to a close.

Such high jinks provide a tempting finale for this volume, but there is perhaps something even more maliciously satisfying about a runaway at Harrington that certainly equalled the best efforts of movie producers. It happened on a mineral line descending at a precipitous 1 in 15 from Rosehill to Harrington harbour which was contiguous with the almost equally perilous 1 in 17 incline down from Copperas Hill on what became the Harrington & Lowca Light Railway. The calamity was described in the *Barrow Pilot* of 3 May 1873 in the best traditions of Victorian reportage:

As a train consisting of an engine, tender and one passenger carriage was travelling along the line conveying a number of workmen to Harrington, the engine got beyond the control of the driver ... and dashed along with fearful velocity. The engine driver shouted to the passengers to warn them of their danger and advised them to leap for their lives ... The train rushed down the incline till it reached a sharp curve near the harbour, where it left the metals, dashed through some coal wagons, knocked over a crane, and finally both engine and passenger carriage fell into the harbour upon a steam tug, which was greatly damaged.

The punch line appeared in the following week's issue of the paper in the form of a touchingly brief and laconic announcement:

Notice to Ship Captains. In consequence of an accident to the Harrington Steam Tug, there is now none available for towing vessels in or out of that port.

Postscript: 1990

In the eight years that have elapsed since publication of the first edition of this book, the remarkable feature is not how much has changed but how little. The railways of the Lake Counties have settled down to a period of consolidating what is left, giving an outward impression of an era of stability unknown since the days before Beeching. The one exception is the Midland's Settle–Carlisle route, although even here someone who had been off this planet during the 1980s would not notice too many obvious changes on his return.

Withdrawal of through Nottingham–Glasgow services in 1982 proved to be but the first stage in a planned run-down of the Settle & Carlisle. The line was closed to through freight traffic on 16 May 1983, leaving its signalmen plenty of time to enjoy the scenery as they handled just two passenger trains each way daily. For many years it had been the practice on Sundays for West Coast main line services to be routed over the Midland route in the morning and early afternoon so that essential engineering work could take place, but this came to an end with the winter 1984/85 timetable. Virtually the whole of Cumbria now became devoid of Sunday morning trains, passengers southbound from Carlisle having to face a 2½ hour bus journey to Preston or wait until as late as 3.45pm for the first train of the day to Euston. Northbound, the morning Liverpool–Glasgow service made a massive detour via York and Newcastle.

The inevitable closure announcement came in August 1983, British Rail arguing that withdrawal of passenger services would enable the tracks to be lifted north of Ribblehead quarry and south of Appleby, bringing a net annual saving of £1.5 million and a total saving in capital expenditure of £6.7 million, mainly on Ribblehead viaduct. Had the approach smacked less of what was described as 'closure by stealth', then opposition might not have been quite so determined. As it was, existing groups combined to form the highly professional Settle–Carlisle Railway Joint Action Committee which broke new ground by becoming a limited company with full-time staff. By the end of the statutory period, the number of objectors to closure totalled a quite unprecedented 22,265.

A curious twist in the saga was the determined attempt by British Rail to maximise revenue in the period leading up to abandonment. Successful marketing brought such an upsurge in passengers that the two regular trains soon extended from four to as many as eleven coaches. A bold move on 29 September 1986 was the re-opening on a daily basis of the intermediate stations previously used only by weekend 'Dales Rail' trains. This paved the way for a much improved 1987 service of five trains each way.

While these positive developments were taking place, British Rail and its opponents remained locked in conflict with report following report and rumour being heaped upon rumour. The end appeared nigh when in May 1988 the then Transport Minister, David Mitchell, announced to a hostile House of Commons that he was 'minded to consent' to the closure proposals, although a final decision would be delayed to allow time for a private bidder to come forward with proposals to run a preserved railway. This attempt to use the line as a test-bed for privatisation foundered, but even so objectors were taken off guard by the sudden announcement in April 1989 by Paul Channon, the Transport Secretary, that he was refusing the closure proposals. British Rail put on a brave face, proclaiming it welcomed the decision because it removed uncertainty, and began a major programme of repairs. These had as their first priority Ribblehead viaduct, the structure that nine years earlier had triggered off this extraordinary sequence of events.

Events on the West Coast main line have by comparison been unexciting, the 1980s seeing a general decline in speed of passenger services. By 1988 the Royal Scot was the only remaining 110mph train, coming north from Euston to Carlisle in 3hr 29 min, over a quarter-of-an-hour faster than the best time between the two cities in 1982. With other trains there has been a policy to insert more stops, one result being that Oxenholme is now much better served. With greatly improved facilities, it is actively promoted as a park-and-ride station and serves a wide rail-head, as indicated by its new if rather clumsy name of 'Oxenholme Lake District'. There has also been an increase in the number of through services on the West Coast main line, so that it is now possible to travel without changing from Carlisle to Brighton, Poole, Penzance and even London Paddington.

At Carlisle itself one of the main changes of the decade came without warning. In the early hours of 1 May 1984 the rear part of a down Freightliner train became detached on the descent from Penrith. Initially left behind by the front portion, the breakaway vehicles then began to pick up speed, a massive pile-up in Citadel station only being avoided by a quick-thinking signalman in Carlisle power-box who switched the runaways on to the goods lines. They passed Rome Street Junction at an estimated 60–70mph but failed to take the following curve and demolished the bridge over the River Caldew. The damage was so extensive that rebuilding could not be justified and the goods lines from Rome Street Junction to Caldew Junction were officially closed on 15 December 1985. Since the accident all freight traffic has had to travel through Citadel station, creating considerable congestion in the peak period at night, especially following the diversion of all Anglo-Scottish sleeping-car services to the West Coast main line. A lesser but controversial change at Carlisle was the 1988 closure of Kingmoor Traction Maintenance Depot and consequent transfer of diesel unit servicing to Heaton, Newcastle.

Away from the main lines, the Cumbrian Coast route from Carnforth to Carlisle via Barrow and Whitehaven continues in its own quiet way. In May 1985, locomotive-hauled trains from Barrow to such destinations as Manchester, Liverpool, Crewe and Nottingham were almost entirely replaced by diesel units venturing only as far as Lancaster or Preston. Improvement came in May 1988 with introduction of a 'Sprinter'-operated Barrow to Manchester Victoria service. At Barrow the glory has continued to depart and it is difficult to visualise this was once the headquarters of a proud and ambitious railway company. There is now virtually no originating freight traffic, just a pathetic single line threading its way through the once vast Barrow yard to serve the Trident complex. The branch from Salthouse Junction to Roosecote power station was dismantled in April 1989, its former traffic from Maryport opencast depot having been lost to road during the 1984/5 miners' strike.

Nuclear flasks for reprocessing continue to be transferred from ship to rail on the south side of Ramsden Dock and taken north to new unloading facilities at BNFL Sellafield. Rail is also used to transport 'low-level waste' from Sellafield to the former Royal Ordnance Factory at Drigg where new sidings and colour-light signalling have been installed. Other freight traffic on the coast line remains sparse but varied and includes chemicals, scrap steel, coal, timber and rails.

The one surviving branch line, from Oxenholme to Windermere, has clung to life and now has its own Lakes Line Action Group. A through Sunday return working from Manchester Victoria was introduced in 1985, and Sunday services were extended throughout the year from 1986. Rumours of electrification and reinstatement of run-round facilities at the terminus surface periodically, leading to hopes that locomotive-hauled trains and through coaches to Euston may one day reappear. They would fulfil a real need, now that the Lake District is the most popular tourist area in the country after London. Its roads are becoming increasingly choked with traffic, and as this reaches unacceptable levels there may be real cause for regret that Britain's prime National Park was turned into a railway desert. The Keswick line and the Lake Side branch would have been perfect destinations for today's generation of long-distance leisure travellers.

Acknowledgements and Further Reading

My first thanks must be to Peter W. Robinson, who relieved me of the awesome task of preparing the maps for this book and also read the manuscript in draft. He was one of the founders of the Cumbrian Railways Association, now a flourishing society with a quarterly magazine which is essential reading for anyone with an interest in this region. Details of the Association can be obtained from the author at Hole Bottom, Hebden, Skipton, North Yorkshire.

The manuscript was also read in whole or part by Michael Andrews, C. R. Clinker, George Taylor and David Tee; their comments and help have been much appreciated. Assistance in preparing the text has been given by British Rail, Preston; Harold D. Bowtell; R. A. Cook; John Hammond; Daniel Hay; Brian Hilton; J. D. Marshall; Alan Pearsall; and John Thomas. I apologise for any names I may accidentally have omitted.

Research facilities have been provided by the Public Record Office, Kew; the Scottish Record Office; the House of Lords Record Office; the National Railway Museum; the Barrow and Carlisle record offices of Cumbria County Council; the University of Lancaster library; and the public libraries at Barrow, Carlisle, Kendal and Whitehaven.

Finally, a debt of gratitude to David St John Thomas and Professor Allan Patmore, co-editors of this series. Their tact and patience over an inexcusably long period has been remarkable. So too has that of my wife, Judith, and my sons and daughter, to whom I extend my deepest thanks for encouraging this project to completion.

Further Reading

The literature of the Lake Counties' railways is tantalising in that it is extremely scattered and in considerable measure comprises items that are out of print and scarce. Relatively few adequately researched works have in fact appeared. The bibliography below is a selected—and at times critical—guide to relevant published material.

Abbreviations

CR	*Cumbrian Railways* (journal of the Cumbrian Railways Association)
CW2	*Transactions* of Cumberland & Westmorland Antiquarian & Archaeological Society: New Series
HSLC	*Transactions* of Historic Society of Lancashire & Cheshire
NH	*Northern History*
RCHS	*Journal* of the Railway & Canal Historical Society
RM	*Railway Magazine*
RW	*Railway World*
SLS	*Journal* of the Stephenson Locomotive Society
TH	*Journal of Transport History*

GENERAL WORKS

An excellent and detailed introduction to the social and economic history of the area is provided by *The Lake Counties from 1830 to the mid-twentieth century*, J. D. Marshall & John K. Walton (Manchester, 1981). More general in scope is *A History of Cumberland and Westmorland*, William Rollinson (Chichester, 1978).

Roy Millward & Adrian Robinson have written two informative physical and human geographies, *The Lake District* (1970) and *Cumbria* (1972). There is also a great deal of relevant material in *The Industrial Archaeology of the Lake Counties*, J. D. Marshall & M. Davies-Shiel (Newton Abbot, 1969) and *Road Transport in Cumbria in the*

Nineteenth Century, L. A. Williams (1975), especially Chapter 4 'Competition for Traffic'.

Primarily pictorial works on the railways of the area as a whole have been *Railways of the Lake Counties*. David Joy (Clapham, 1973), *Railways of Cumbria*, Peter W. Robinson (Clapham, 1980) and *British Railways Past and Present: Cumbria*, John Broughton & Nigel Harris (Carnforth, 1985). *Forgotten Railways: North-West England*, John Marshall (Newton Abbot, 1981) contains two chapters on Cumbria, whilst *Cumbrian Coast Railways*, David Joy (Clapham, 1968) and *Rails round the Cumbrian Coast*, Richard Kirkman & Peter van Zeller (Clapham, 1988) cover all lines to the west of the West Coast route. A valuable survey of the public-transport situation in the area at the beginning of the 1960s is provided by *Lake District Transport Report*, David St John Thomas (Dawlish, 1961).

On the Right Track (1985) is a useful list of Cumberland railway records deposited in the Cumbria Record Office at Carlisle.

CHAPTER II

The basic history is well summarised in *Crewe to Carlisle*, Brian Reed (1969), which concentrates on nineteenth century development, the story being continued in *Over Shap to Carlisle: The Lancaster & Carlisle Railway in the 20th century*, Harold D. Bowtell (1983). The transformation of recent years is described in *Electric Euston to Glasgow*, O. S. Nock (1974). It is also worth consulting Chapter 8 'Shap' of *Joseph Locke: Railway Revolutionary*, N. W. Webster (1970) and 'The Lancaster & Carlisle Railway', G. O. Holt (RM 97, 1951, 505–10). *The Stainmore Railway*, K. Hoole (Clapham, 1973) gives details of the North Eastern connecting lines at Tebay and Penrith.

CHAPTER III

It is hardly surprising that the Settle & Carlisle—alone among the lines covered in this volume—should have a surfeit of literature. The most meaty work is *North of Leeds: The Leeds–Settle–Carlisle Line and its Branches*, Peter E. Baughan (1966), a veritable quarry of information. There is much stimulating content—especially visual—in *Rails in the Fells*, David Jenkinson (Seaton, 1973), primarily a geographical study which also looks closely at buildings. These receive detailed attention in *Stations and Structures of the Settle & Carlisle Railway*, V. R. Anderson & G. K. Fox (Poole, 1986). *The Story of the Settle–Carlisle Line*, Frederick W. Houghton & W. Hubert Foster (Bradford, 1948) is the pioneer modern work. The tumultuous events of the 1980s are covered in *To*

Kill a Railway, Stan Abbott (Hawes, 1986) and the most recent edition of *Settle to Carlisle: A Railway over the Pennines*, W. R. Mitchell & David Joy (Clapham, 1989). For a contemporary account of construction see *The Midland Railway: Its Rise and Progress*, Frederick S. Williams (1876); a newer study in this field is *Shanty Life on the Settle–Carlisle Railway*, W. R. Mitchell (Settle, 1988).

For the Clapham–Ingleton–Low Gill line consult *The Lowgill Branch: A Lost Route to Scotland*, R. G. Western (Lingfield, 1971) and *The 'Little' North Western Railway*, Donald Binns (Skipton, 1982). There are also two valedictory articles: 'Westmorland loses a Traffic Link', G. O. Holt (*Cumbria* 3, 1953–4, 418–22) and 'The Ingleton Branch', A. W. H. Pearsall (RM 100, 1954, 388–94).

CHAPTER IV

The complex history and operating practises of railways in the 'Border City' are ably covered in *Rail Centres: Carlisle*, Peter W. Robinson (1986). Two other useful sources are the Cumbrian Railways Association publication *Carlisle: 150 Years of Railways* (1986) and chapter 13 'Merrie Carlisle' in *Crewe to Carlisle* (see above). 'The Battle of Carlisle Crown Street', G. O. Holt (RM 109, 1963, 575–9) is an excellent account of the turbulent events of the 1840s.

A painstaking study of private lines in the Brampton area is *Lord Carlisle's Railways*, Brian Webb & David A. Gordon (1978).

CHAPTER V

It is most unfortunate that the Furness Railway does not have a reliable and detailed company history. Both *The Furness Railway: its rise and development 1846–1923*, W. McGowan Gradon (Altrincham, 1946) and *The Furness Railway 1843–1923*, R. W. Rush (Lingfield, 1973) need to be used with considerable care. The formative years are however well covered by 'Early Railway History in Furness', J. Melville & J. L. Hobbs (Kendal, 1951) and 'The Origins of the Furness Railway', Michael Andrews (RCHS 11, 1965, No 4, 7–11; 12, 1966, No 1, 1–7). The latter author has also written in more local vein of 'The Railways of Barrow' (RM 105, 1959, 149–57) and 'The Railway System of Barrow-in-Furness' (CR 1, 1976, No 2, 4–8). The influence of the FR on urban development in this town is covered by S. Pollard & J. D. Marshall in 'The Furness Railway and the Growth of Barrow' (TH 1, 1953, 109–26). 'Recollections of the Furness Railway', R. R. Mester (RW, 1982, 174–80; 408–11) contains material not readily available elsewhere, while two good pictorial studies are *The*

Furness Railway: A Photographic Recollection, Raymond Sankey & K. J. Norman (Clapham, 1977) and *Reflections of the Furness Railway*, C. R. Davey (Barrow, 1984).

The life and activities of the creator of Barrow's iron and steel industry are examined in *H. W. Schneider of Barrow and Bowness*, A. G. Banks (Kendal, 1984). Another local personality comes under the microscope in *The Patent Narrow Gauge Railways of John Barraclough Fell*, E. A. Wade (Huddersfield, 1986), which looks at his experimental lines at Parkhouse. Valuable detail on the Ulverstone & Lancaster Railway is provided by 'Railway Construction in Mid-Nineteenth Century North Lancashire: A Study based on the diary of James Stelfox 1855–70', P. J. Gooderson (HSLC 122, 1970, 137–51).

Many works on the economic and social history of the region inevitably contain railway material, in particular the substantial *Furness and the Industrial Revolution*, J. D. Marshall (Barrow, 1958) and also *Barrow and District*, F. Barnes (Barrow, 2nd ed, 1968). So too do the writings of Alan Harris on the area's iron industry and its associated settlements: 'Carnforth, 1849–1900: the rise of a North Lancashire town' (HSLC 112, 1960, 106–19); 'Askam Iron: The Development of Askam-in-Furness 1852–1920' (CW2 65, 1965, 381–407); 'Millom: a Victorian New Town' (CW2 66, 1966, 449–67); and *Cumberland Iron: the Story of Hodbarrow Mine 1855–1968* (Truro, 1970). The same author has also examined a more genteel form of railway-inspired development in 'The Seaside Resorts of Westmorland and Lancashire North of the Sands in the 19th Century' (HSLC 115, 1963, 147–62); two specific and contrasting examples are discussed by J. D. Marshall in *Old Lakeland* (Newton Abbot, 1971), Chapter 12 'Two railway resorts: Grange and Seascale'.

CHAPTER VI

As with Furness, the difficulty is the lack of published company material. Two pioneer works in book form are *The Maryport & Carlisle Railway*, Jack Simmons (Chislehurst, 1947) and *The Track of the Ironmasters: A History of the Cleator & Workington Junction Railway*, W. McGowan Gradon (Altrincham, 1952), both compiled in an era when little primary source material was available. Useful coverage of the latter line is also given by 'The Cleator & Workington Junction Railway' (CR 2, 1982, No 11, 3–7; No 12, 10–14) and by David R. Webb in 'Cumbrian Demise' (RM 127, 1981, 84–8). The same author has also outlined the history of the area in 'Between the Solway and Sellafield' (RM 110, 1964, 674–9, 786–92). Another general account is 'Railways of West Cumberland', C. A. Knight (RM 100, 1954, 757–

65). 'North-West Coast Railway Politics in the Eighteen-Sixties', Sidney Pollard (cw2 52, 1953, 160–77) attempts to unravel the complex period of inter-company amalgamation. At a more local level, the Rowrah & Kelton Fell Railway has a chapter to itself in *The Kelton & Knockmurton Iron Mines 1852–1923*, R. E. Hewer (Sheffield, 1988). Additional coverage is provided by 'Bairds' Lines in Cumberland', J. F. McEwan & Harold D. Bowtell (cr 2, 1983, No 15, 3–9) and W. McGowan Gradon's article 'The Rowrah & Kelton Fell Mineral Railway' (rm 98, 1952, 202–5).

The Scottish lines in West Cumberland have attracted more attention – for example, G. Thomlinson's splendid series of articles 'Rails on the Solway' (cr 2, 1983, No 14, 10–13; 3, 1985, 74–8 and 162–6). *Solway Junction Railway*, Stuart Edgar & John Sinton (1986) is an outline history in duplicated pamphlet form, while there are also articles on this line by G. J. Aston & D. S. Barrie (rm 70, 1932, 27–34) and J. F. McEwan (sls 48, 1972, 39–50). For the North British lines see *Solway Steam: the story of the Silloth and Port Carlisle railways 1854–1964*, Stephen White (Carlisle, 1984) and also chapter 11 of *The North British Railway*, Vol 1, John Thomas (Newton Abbot, 1969). 'Horse-power to Port Carlisle', Charles E. Lee (rm 89, 1943, 6–9) and 'The Port Carlisle Branch', David R. Webb (cr 2, 1982, No 12, 3–5) are both informative. For the later Silloth branch, there is 'From Carlisle to Silloth', M. F. Barbey (rm 101, 1955, 92–6) and 'Railways and Resort Development in Victorian England: the Case of Silloth', J. K. Walton (nh 15, 1979, 191–209).

The horse-worked colliery lines are covered in 'Early Waggonways in Cumberland', Bertram Baxter (rchs 7, Sept. 1961) and Chapter 8 of *Early Wooden Railways*, M. J. T. Lewis (1970). *Steam from Lowca: A History of the Rise and Fall of Locomotive Building at Lowca Foundry 1840–1921*, Ian Kyle (Moresby, 1974) is a brief but informative study of a later form of motive power.

Outstanding among local studies is the 3rd edition of Daniel Hay's *Whitehaven: An Illustrated History* (Beckermet, 1979). It includes a chapter on the area's railways, as does *The Iron & Steel Industry of West Cumberland: An Historical Survey*, J. Y. Lancaster & D. R. Wattleworth (Workington, 1977). There is also relevant background material in the weighty *West Cumberland Coal 1600–1982/3*, Oliver Wood (Kendal, 1988).

CHAPTER VII

Material on opposition to railways in Lakeland is fragmented but there are useful references in *The Lake District: A Century of*

Conservation, Geoffrey Berry & Geoffrey Beard (Edinburgh, 1980) and 'The Tourist Trade in Victorian Lakeland', J. K. Walton & P. R. McGloin (NH 17, 1981, 153–82). Chapter 9 'The defence of Lakeland' in Marshall & Walton's *The Lake Counties* sets the matter in context.

The Windermere branch receives attention in both *Crewe to Carlisle* and *Main Line Over Shap* (see under Chapter II), and also has its own study, *Kendal and Windermere Railway*, Julian Mellentin (Clapham, 1980), a work which makes extensive use of oral history. 'By Rail to Ambleside', E. H. Fowkes (*Cumbria* 25, 1975–6, 467–9) describes the attempted extension of 1887. 'The Windermere Tourist Trade in the Age of the Railway, 1847–1912', an invaluable paper by J. K. Walton, is included in *Windermere in the Nineteenth Century*, ed Oliver M. Westall (Lancaster, 1976). One should also consult *The Great Age of Steam on Windermere*, George H. Pattinson (Windermere, 1981).

The Cumbrian Railways Association publication *The Coniston Railway* (1985) places particular emphasis on track plans. Its neighbouring branch is covered by *Lakeside and Haverthwaite Railway*, H. I. Quayle & S. C. Jenkins (Clapham, 1977) and also features in 'The Midland Railway and the Lake District', V. R. Webster (RW 39, 1978, 606–9). Moving north, an in-depth 200–page treatment is now provided by *Rails through Lakeland: An Illustrated History of the Workington–Cockermouth–Keswick–Penrith Railway 1847–1972*, Harold D. Bowtell (St Michael's on Wyre, 1989).

Finally, one of the shortest lines in the Lake Counties has an almost equally detailed history in *The Ravenglass & Eskdale Railway*, W. J. K. Davies (Newton Abbot, 2nd ed, 1981). There is also *The Eskdale Railway: A Pictorial Study of 'La'al Ratty'*, Peter van Zeller (Clapham, 1985).

Appendices

The following verbatim extracts from reports and letters by three famous personalities give a fascinating insight into contemporary attitudes on some widely differing aspects of the railways of the Lake Counties. In the first George Stephenson forthrightly comments on the impracticability of taking an Anglo-Scottish main line over Shap and expresses his preference for a roundabout route across Morecambe Bay and along the Cumbrian coast. The second appendix is plucked from the verbose and disjointed protestations which Wordsworth sent to the Press when at the age of seventy-four he championed the case for excluding railways from the core of the Lake District. Finally, there is a fascinating report from an unexpected quarter on the small, independent railways of the area which had as one of its joint authors Thomas Bouch, born at Thursby, near Wigton, in 1822 and at the age of twenty-two one of the engineers on the Lancaster & Carlisle Railway.

APPENDIX I

Report by George Stephenson to the Whitehaven Committee of the Grand Caledonian Junction Railway, August 16th, 1837

In compliance with my instructions from the Caledonian Railway Committee of the 1st of September, 1836, that I should make an Ocular Survey of the Country between Lancaster and Carlisle, by Ulverston and Whitehaven; and also between Lancaster and Carlisle, by Kirkby Lonsdale and Penrith, and that I should report to you my opinion as to the practicability of the two routes, and which I would recommend should be adopted as the best line for the promoters and the public...

As an act has been obtained for a Railway between Maryport and Carlisle, and plans are deposited in the Parliamentary offices for a Railway between Whitehaven and Maryport, I may suppose that these Lines will be made independently of any Railway from the

South to Scotland, and that the local traffic is sufficient to make them pay. I therefore find that by the Coast Line the number of miles of Railway to make for the purposes of a communication from Lancaster to Carlisle is, as nearly as I can measure from the map, about forty-nine miles and a half...

From Lancaster to Carlisle, by Kirkby Lonsdale and Penrith, would require from the same measurement, sixty-six miles and a half of Railway, giving a distance of fifteen miles in favour of the West Coast Line.

The distance between Lancaster and Carlisle by the West Coast Line is eighty miles and three quarters; and by the Kirkby Lonsdale and Shap Line sixty-six miles and a half, leaving in favour of the Shap Line twenty-two miles and a quarter.

If the line by Shap Fells be about five hundred feet above the Coast Line, the merits of the two Lines would be nearly equal in point of time in travelling between Lancaster and Carlisle, providing the inclinations are such that the engines can travel up them with facility.

There is a very serious consideration which has not heretofore been sufficiently regarded by companies projecting Railways over high countries, namely, the great length of the winters, the quantity of snow falling in high lands, and the length of time it remains upon the ground. These considerations, coupled with the effect produced by the ice upon the rails, in retarding the engines, will, in my opinion, be an insurmountable difficulty to the passing of the Shap ridge, especially as the inclinations at the summit must be steep. The snow posts erected on this ridge, to point out to travellers the course of the road when covered with snow, are a sufficient indication of the great severity of the winters. And as this Line would form the Western thoroughfare between England and Scotland, it would be of the greatest importance that there should be no impediment which could prevent the engines travelling on it at all times. My opinion is, that a Line across these hills would be interrupted by the severity of the winters for weeks together.

The Coast Line would be entirely free from this objection, owing to the lowness of its levels, and its proximity to the sea breeze, where neither frost nor snow are ever severe, and where snow almost immediately disappears from the ground.

It may be objected that the sea would occasionally break into the sands enclosed across the Bay, and wash away the Railway; this could not, however, take place if the structure were properly executed.

The Coast Line being almost a dead level, would form the most certain thoroughfare that could possibly be constructed, and might be travelled upon at all times, at almost any velocity, as it would be entirely free from sharp curves, which must be very frequent on the Shap Line.

As regards the local population the Coast Line has also greatly the advantage, as it affords an immediate communication between the Towns of Ulverston, Whitehaven, Workington, and Maryport to the South, and very convenient branches may be made to Kendal, Milnthorp, and Cockermouth; whereas I think the Shap Line only accommodates Kirkby Lonsdale and Penrith.

I am inclined to favour the Coast Line from the following considerations. First — It will be very much cheaper to make, considering the land gained at Morecambe equal in value to the cost of gaining it; secondly, it does not interfere with ornamental property of any description; it accommodates a much larger population; it runs through country almost perfectly level; and affords communication to many harbours along the coast, which must be of great importance to the country; it is free from objections in winter from the snow and ice; affords easy communications to several towns by branches; and it gives the MOST EXPEDITIOUS, CERTAIN, AND SAFE CONVEYANCE which can be obtained through this country.

It is true that the Shap Line has the advantage in point of distance, but when I take into consideration the difficulty of the country through which it would pass, the expense of construction, and the great height of the summit to be attained, it would be found to take more time travelling upon it than the Coast Line, and with the other disadvantages it possesses, and feeling NOT THE SLIGHTEST DOUBT of the easy practicability of carrying the Line across Morecambe Bay, I have no hesitation in expressing my decided conviction of the superiority of the Coast Line.

Letters from William Wordsworth to the Morning Post *on the projected Kendal & Windermere Railway, December 1844*

Some little time ago you did me the favour of inserting a sonnet expressive of the regret and indignation which, in common with others all over these Islands, I felt at the proposal of a railway to extend from Kendal to Low Wood, near the head of Windermere. The project was so offensive to a large majority of the proprietors through whose lands the line, after it came in view of the Lake, was to pass, that, for this reason, and the avowed one of the heavy expense without which the difficulties in the way could not be overcome, it has been partially abandoned, and the terminus is now announced to be at a spot within a mile of Bowness. But as no guarantee can be given that the project will not hereafter be revived, and an attempt made to carry the line forward through the vales of Ambleside and Grasmere, and as in one main particular the case remains essentially the same, allow me to address you upon certain points which merit more consideration than the favourers of the scheme have yet given them . . .

The projectors have induced many to favour their schemes by declaring that one of their main objects is to place the beauties of the Lake district within easier reach of those who cannot afford to pay for ordinary conveyances. Look at the facts. Railways are completed, which, joined with others in rapid progress, will bring travellers who prefer approaching by Ullswater to within four miles of that lake. The Lancaster and Carlisle Railway will approach the town of Kendal, about eight or nine miles from eminences that command the whole vale of Windermere. The Lakes are therefore at present of very easy access for all persons . . .

The wide-spread waters of these regions are in their nature peaceful; so are the steep mountains and the rocky glens; nor can they be profitably enjoyed but by a mind disposed to peace. Go to a pantomime, a farce, or a puppet-show, if you want noisy pleasure— the crowd of spectators who partake your enjoyment will, by their presence and acclamations, enhance it; but may those who have given proof that they prefer other gratifications continue to be safe from the molestation of cheap trains pouring out their hundreds at a time along the margin of Windermere . . .

The directors of railway companies are always ready to devise or encourage entertainments for tempting the humbler classes to leave their homes. Accordingly, for the profit of the shareholders and that of the lower class of innkeepers, we should have wrestling matches, horse and boat races without number, and pot-houses and beer-shops would keep pace with these excitements and recreations, most of which might too easily be had elsewhere. The injury which would thus be done to morals, both among this influx of strangers and the lower class of inhabitants, is obvious; and, supposing such extraordinary temptations not to be held out, there cannot be a doubt that the Sabbath day in the towns of Bowness and Ambleside, and other parts of the district, would be subject to much additional desecration...

Consider also the state of the lake district; and look, in the first place, at the little town of Bowness, in the event of such railway inundations. What would become of it in this, not the Retreat, but the Advance, of the Ten Thousand? Leeds, I am told, has sent as many at once to Scarborough. We should have the whole of Lancashire, and no small part of Yorkshire, pouring in upon us to meet the men of Durham, and the borderers from Cumberland and Northumberland. Alas, alas, if the lakes are to pay this penalty for their own attractions!...

With the town of Bowness I have no minute acquaintance; but of Ambleside, Grasmere, and the neighbourhood, I can testify from long experience, that they have been favoured by the residence of a gentry whose love of retirement has been a blessing to these vales; for their families have ministered, and still minister, to the temporal and spiritual necessities of the poor... Many of these friends of our poor would quit this country if the apprehended change were realised, and would be succeeded by strangers not linked to the neighbourhood, but flitting to and fro between their fancy-villas and the homes where their wealth was accumulated and accumulating by trade and manufactures...

Almost every reach of the winding vales in this district might once have presented itself to a man of imagination and feeling under that aspect, or, as the Vale of Grasmere appeared to the Poet Gray more than seventy years ago... Were the Poet now living, how he would have lamented the probable intrusion of a railway with its scarifications, its intersections, its noisy machinery, its smoke, and swarms of pleasure-hunters, most of them thinking that they do not fly fast enough through the country which they have come to see...

A railroad is already planned along the sea coast, and another from Lancaster to Carlisle is in great forwardness: an intermediate one is therefore, to say the least of it, superfluous. Once for all let me declare that it is not against Railways but against the abuse of them that I am contending.

Report by Messrs Thomas Bouch, Engineer, and John Bathgate, Secretary, to the Directors of the Peebles Railway Company, July 22nd, 1854

The North British Railway Company having proposed to work the Peebles Railway at 1/3d per mile for passenger trains and 1/6d for goods trains, and you having in consequence remitted to your Engineer and Secretary to make enquiry as to the working arrangements of some other Lines similarly circumstanced to the Peebles Line, they immediately proceeded to make the necessary investigation. The principal object of enquiry to which your Reporters, in terms of your instructions directed their attention, was, whether it was practicable for a small Railway such as the Peebles Line to be wrought independently with greater advantage to its proprietors than would accrue if wrought by Contract or Lease of the working, upon such terms as have been proposed by the North British.

This question could best be answered by an investigation of the manner of working of a cluster of small independent Railways in the North-west of England, whose length, works and traffic shewed the nearest analogy to your own Railway. These Lines are the Maryport and Carlisle, 28 miles; Whitehaven Junction, 12 miles; Whitehaven and Furness, 36 miles; Cockermouth and Workington, 9 miles; Kendal and Windermere, 10¼ miles. The most of these were single Lines and were incorporated in 1845, with the exception of the Maryport, which was incorporated in 1837. Every information was willingly afforded by the Officers of these Companies, and, after a minute investigation, your Reporters are forced by the results presented to them, to the conclusion, that beyond all question a small Company is able to work their own Line more economically and to greater advantage themselves, than when under such a Lease or Contract as has been proposed.

On examination of the Accounts of several larger Companies it will be found that sixpence a mile is an average cost of Locomotive power, including wages, coke, &c; and if 2d a mile be added which is the average for repairs, the average be increased to eight pence. If two pence per mile be added to that sum as Coach and Waggon repairs, the working expenses will average ten pence a mile.

On the Maryport and Carlisle Railway the average of eleven Engines used by them was for cost of working and repairs only five pence and one farthing per mile, and the whole expenses of Locomotive power, Carriages and Trucks, was less than 7d a mile, being a difference of upwards of 30 per cent as compared with the larger Lines. One of their Engines which, from being new, had required little repair, had ran a full mileage for two half years at an average cost of three pence halfpenny per mile for the first half year and only three pence per mile for the second.

On the Kendal and Windermere Railway the average cost of Locomotive power and rolling stock was, for the half year ending December last, only sixpence halfpenny per mile, being still less than the Maryport; and, for the half year just ended, only a small fraction above five pence, shewing actually that this Line is wrought, as compared with the larger Companies, at one half the cost, or 50 per cent cheaper. This Line is a favourable instance for guiding you in coming to a decision, as it was originally wrought by the London and North Western at fifteen pence a mile, and afterwards by Messrs Wilson, of Leeds, at a Shilling. So long as they were under the Contract mileage system no dividend was paid. A saving was attempted by economising the mileage, which produced injurious results to the traffic. Now the traffic is developed by increased facilities being given to the public with the happiest results, and their working Expenses are one half cheaper altho' the mileage run has increased 50 per cent...

Gentlemen acquainted only with the working of great Companies cannot form a proper estimate of economical working by a smaller Company. They are accustomed to see everything done on a great scale and without an attempt at economy. Their undertakings are too large for the supervision of any one man, and the oversight is broken down into a variety of departments without any unity in the control. From some correspondence lately published it was seen, that from a little more care being exercised by the Enginemen on part of the London and North Western Railway, owing to their receiving a percentage of their savings, a general saving would accrue to the Company on coke alone of £40,000 a year. In a small Company, owing to everything being under proper control there can be no extravagant expenditure on stores.

The result indicated as to the greater economy in small Lines is shewn also by the average cost of working and maintenance. The average of the great Lines may be stated at forty-five per cent of the Receipts. The Caledonian is 43; the North British about 53; the Edinburgh, Perth and Dundee about 60. The Kendal and Windermere is only 33; the Cockermouth and Workington about the same, and the Manager there is hopeful when he has got his plant into thorough repair it will be as low as 30.

In every point of view the smaller Lines are proved to be wrought more economically than the larger undertakings. It is found that two or three Mechanics, with a Bench at the side of the Engine Shed and a foot lathe, are amply sufficient for all the ordinary repairs of Locomotives and Carriages. All outlay for expensive Workshops is thus avoided. When wheels require to be re-tired, or new axles are wanted, the wants are supplied at the nearest Foundry, at a far less cost to the Company than maintaining separate and extensive Workshops for the manufacture and repair of every article needed.

To apply this system to the Peebles Railway ... one Engineman and Fireman are quite sufficient for our traffic; but the Mechanic and chief Carpenter would also be qualified to act as Engineman and Fireman on special occasions. This is adopted on the Kendal Line. The traffic on the Peebles Line would not exceed at first, three passenger Trains each way daily. With these might be mixed Merchandise Waggons, as is done on the Cumberland Lines... Two Engines appear to be quite sufficient for one year at least. The Whitehaven and Furness, which is double the length of the Peebles Line, had only two for a twelvemonth after starting. At this moment some of their engines run 190 miles per diem.

Index

Bold type is used to indicate principal references; illustrations are shown in italics.